THE SACRED COMPLEX
IN HINDU GAYA

MAP OF GAYA

THE SACRED SEGMENTS AND ZONE

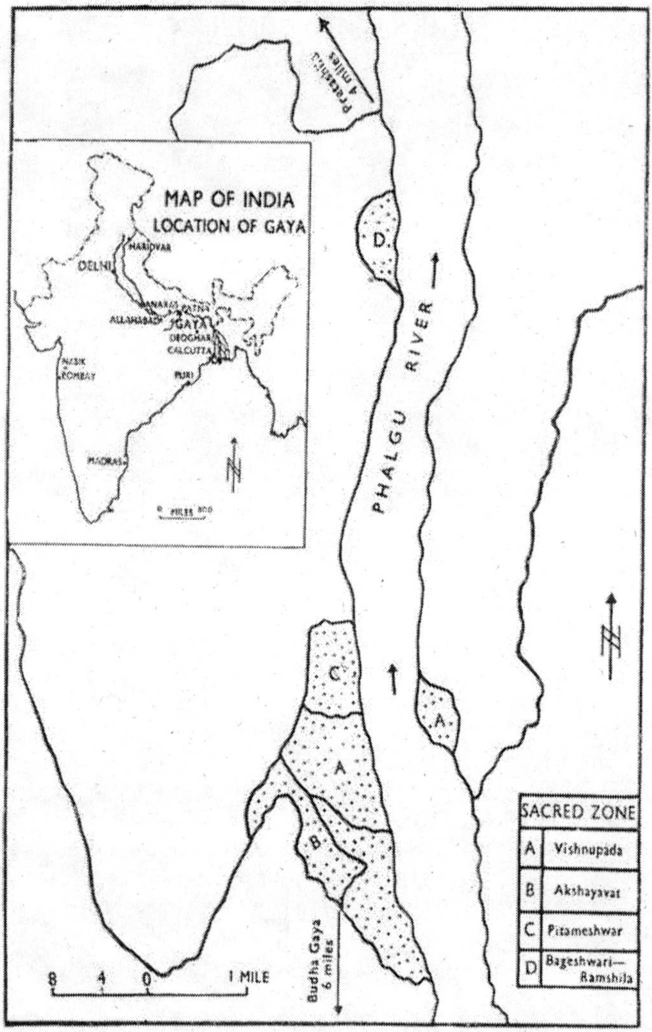

THE SACRED COMPLEX IN HINDU GAYA

L. P. VIDYARTHI

Second Edition
with
New Introdution

CONCEPT PUBLISHING COMPANY PVT. LTD.
NEW DELHI-110059

ISBN : 978-93-5125-166-8

Edition 2021

Published and Printed by

Concept
Since 1974

Concept Publishing Company Pvt. Ltd.
A/15-16, Commercial Block, Mohan Garden,
New Delhi-110059 (INDIA)
T : +91-11-41101460
E : publishing@conceptpub.com, *W* : www.conceptpub.com

CONTENTS

LIST OF TABLES

PLATES

FOREWORD

DR. VIDYARTHI has done me a great honour by asking me to write a foreword to his book *The Sacred Complex in Hindu Gaya*—a study of the Gayawal of Bihar. Good wine does not need any brush and neither does Dr. Vidyarthi want me to give him a testimonial. As a distinguished pupil, and a loyal one, he has roped me in to show his courtesy, and I am indeed happy to be associated with his useful work, on a levitical sect which has had a spectacular past but today faces an anxious future. I had some acquaintance with an earlier manuscript of his, on his field assignment, for his M.A. Degree at Lucknow where Dr. Vidyarthi recorded the Culture of the dying Gayawal Community. In the present volume Dr. Vidyarthi has given an analytical study of the sacred complex that had motivated the survival of the Community in the past. The changing values and attitudes in popular Hinduism have made significant dents into the Cultural life of the Gayawal, their ritual status has declined, and the structural facades are showing signs of fissures which are widening into schisms likely to destroy the structure itself. In the present volume, Dr. Vidyarthi comes to grips with theoretical problems and has selected the part of Gaya, which incidentally shapes into the study of a traditional city, and of a traditional community and brings out the importance of Gaya as a pilgrim city with its sacred specialists, the Gayawal. The methodological orientation is the unique feature of Dr. Vidyarthi's contribution. The theoretical stand and the rich material on which Dr. Vidyarthi elaborates provide an excellent analytical study of a levitical sect that faces evil days.

In the context of the growing tourist traffic, the question of a professional order, alive to the needs of the tourist public with adequate education and training associated with our larger temples and sacred cities, has assumed significance. One feels unhappy, if not bitter, when one meets the temple priests and guides who sell our religion and mythology to the inquisitive tourists and pilgrims, for they are indeed a miserable lot, both physically and mentally. These render a dubious service to the visitors and pilgrims, and they are more pitied than liked, for most of them have been reduced to penury and social incompetence, and parade the temples and their precincts with the beggar's bowl. The proposed institution of a cadre of temple guides, for more informed service to the public and international tourists is so far so good and will certainly raise the effectiveness of our foreign exchange approach, but it would be pertinent to ask how far our temple and religious lore will be safe in the hands of the new initiates, and how far the values of our society will remain in tact when secularization is pushed to its logical end. The rehabilitation of the levitical communities, particularly of those that cater to our religious education in the centres of sacred contacts, requires a planned approach, and it would be a halfway measure to replace the traditional caterers of religion by a new order whose interests and orientation may be entirely secular.

Our temples and centres of religious pilgrimage are our heritage and give the configuration of India's personality. The folk beliefs, rituals and learning that are associated with them are difficult to separate, or even indentify. The story is not merely in the scriptures and temple art and architecture, but in the folkways and the mores which are inextricably woven into the "sacred complex" of the cities and temples. The levitical community which still survives, possesses this knowlledge, and even the illiterate among it have a deep interest and knowledge of the oral literature that provides the benchmark data on the religious life of our people. It is necessary to recover this knowledge ; to rediscover them from the memory of these people and from the palimpsest manuscripts that some families do still preserve. What is needed is not a sudden divorce from traditional practice, but a *modus vivendi,* which will secure the sacred lore and ritual practices on the one hand, and provide an orientation for the levitical community on the other, both of which will help in the rehabilitation of the latter, particularly those that already manifest signs of exhaustion and maladaptation. The Gayawal, or for that matter any priestly community who live on temple traffic and the benefits of pilgrimage (and there are many such communities in India), need to develop initiative, which they had and have lost, and the Government of the country owes it to them to find out solutions for their miseries and maladaptation.

To millions of Hindus in India, Gaya is holy and very important. Volumes have been written about the sacred character of the place, its architecture, its traditional history and its place in orthodox Hindu society. Gaya is the passport for the future life of the pious Hindu and his happiness beyond. Prof. Kane has discussed the "sacred complex" of Gaya in his inimitable erudite style, and has opened up the hidden recesses that have stored up the knowledge and wisdom of our saints and prophets, of bygone days, (*History of Dharmashastra*, Vol. IV, Poona, 1953). Prof. Kane writes of Gaya as follows, 'Gaya appears to have passed through several vicissitudes. Some centuries before the Christian era it was in existence and was a flourishing town. By A.D. 400 it had been reduced to desolation.' But in the Seventh Century the Chinese traveller Hiouen Th Sang, notes that Hindu Gaya was a town with a thousand Brahmin families. Later on when Buddhism waned and vanished, Gaya came to comprehend even Buddhist remnants since the *Vayu Purana* speaks of Gaya as extending from Pretasila to the Mahabodhi Tree (a distance of about thirteen miles according to R. L. Mitra).

It is no use entering into an academic discussion about the antiquity of Gaya. Our problem is that of the Gayawal. Prof. Kane writes, 'The Gayawals are notorious and ignorant and they are a dying race.' According to O'Malley 'the families of Gayawals were 1484.' In Buchaman Hamilton's time they numbered about a thousand. In 1893, Gayawal families in the Census of 1901, there existed 168 males (as pure Gayawal) and 153 families (*Ibid*, p. 644).

Writing about the literature on Gaya, Prof. Kane says "the most important work on Gaya relied upon such works as the *Tristhali Setu* and in modern times is the *Gaya-Mahatmya* that occurs at the end of the *Vayu Purana* (Chapters 105-112 of the Amandasrma Edition)". Scholars differ about the antiquity of the chapters. Rajendra Lal Mitra assigned the *Gaya Mahatmya* to the Third or Fourth Centuries A.D. O'Malley was inclined to hold that the legend of Gayasura was invented in the Fourteenth or Fifteenth Centuries, principally on the ground that the Gayawal profess the Vaishnava faith established by Madhavacharya and acknowledge as their spiritual head the Mahant of Hari Nara Singhapura (Vide J.A.S.B., Vol. LXXII, 1903, No. 4, p. 644, *History of Dharamsastra*, Vol. IV, Poona, 1953). Dr. Vidyarthi has given an account of the legend of Gayasura.

The Gayawal claim to have been especially created by Lord Brahma. They minister to the needs of ceremonial service to the Hindus, at the time of the *Shraddha*, and they are supposed to be the sole ministers at the latter ceremonies. Dr. Vidyarthi has collected a lot of first hand data on the Gayawal community and the analytical study he has presented, will be of immense value in the field of 'current' anthropology, which reduces, and eliminates in some cases, the distance between urban and rural, tribal and caste societies. The methodology that Dr. Vidyarthi has projected into this analytical study, probably would be open to challenge for the concepts, like 'great' and 'little' traditions, cultural specialists, cultural performances and cultural media have not been standardized and we do not always speak with the same voice. Dr. Vidyarthi knows the strength and weakness of the concepts, like 'great' and 'little' traditions, which now have come into fashion. Again the concept of continuity of folk and urban traditions, has its zealous champions in our country, but Dr. Vidyarthi has a critcial and yet appreciative mind. He has for example, shown the process of conflict and compromise between Hindu and Buddhist ways of life and thought, and incidentally, similar conflict between urban and rural living. This is in keeping with the background of our culture-history. Our sacred literature depicts the succession of cultural traditions. Imposition of one culture on another, and the mixture and assimilation of culture by culture. Neither is there ample or convincing proof of the cultural continuity in India as Prof. Milton Singer, has figured out. There has not been any systematic study of urban and rural life in India, there has not been much meticulous analysis of Indian Culture, as such, and our concepts of Indian Culture, particularly those that are now being imported are based on meagre and often superficial acquaintance with Indian life and institutions. Indian Culture if it admits of reconstruction, is characterised by diversity rather than unity, and a superficial acquaintance with it has underlined similarity and strangeness.

In a paper on Japanese folk-beliefs Prof. Ichiro Hori (*Am. Anth.* Vol. 61, No. 3, pp. 405, 436 ; 1959) has referred to the Japanese folk-beliefs, the essence of which he writes "lies in the interaction of two belief syystems, a little tradition which is based on blood or close community ties, and a great tradition, introduced from without which is adopted by individual or group choice." By 'little' tradition Prof. Hori means the native or folk religions including the advanced Shinto which came out of the ancient Japanese geographic and cultural circumstances ; by the 'great' tradition, he means, Confucianism, Taoism and Buddhism—highly developed religious and philosophical importations. Apparently Prof. Hori could not give more specific configuration to 'little' and 'great' tradition, and he coined another phrase 'the more advanced little traditions'. This is inevitable, when one delves into the belief systems in countries which have a continuity of civilization for thousands of years, and had to receive and accept beliefs, practices and values, imparted from outside, producing a complex web of life and culture. There are little traditions, big traditions and great traditions, even greater, and it is hardly possible to isolate them, to be of use as diagnostic recipes.

Dr. Vidyarthi has formulated and used terms like, sacred centres, sacred segments, sacred cluster, sacred zone, sacred ground, sacred geography, to describe the social organization of the temples. He describes the sacred complex of a place of pilgrimage, and thinks that such a concept is applicable even to tribal religions in India, with their sacred groves, sacred performances, and sacred rituals. Dr. Vidyarthi, however, does not use 'sacred' in the sense in which E. Durkheim had used it, i.e., 'sacred' as distinguished from profane. He has used 'sacred' as distinct from 'secular' and has shown the possibility of a reorganization of the sacred complex, which might show the way to rehabilitate the sacred community of the Gayawal.

Dr. L. P. Vidyarthi has done a good piece of original work, he has not followed the traditional path that anthropologists in India have so long preferred to follow ; which has been uptil now the 'great tradition' of Indian Anthropology, viz., the study of tribal cultures or rural life. He has pointed to the new foci of anthropological interest, the study of cities and centres of culture, and I am sure others will follow in the study of problems of urban complexes and the process of 'secondary urbanization', as he prefers to categorize it.

I am happy that I could add a few words to highlight the rich fare, the book has provided, both for the professional anthropologists and also for the anthropologically oriented laymen.

D. N. MAJUMDAR

INTRODUCTION TO THE SECOND EDITION

It gives me an immense pleasure to ackowledge the courtesy shown to my researches on Gaya by the academic world as, now, it enters the second edition. Though the book was of specialized nature, dealing with a Hindu place of pilgrimages, it attracted the attention of scholars of civilization and complex societies. They found this study useful in understanding the cultural roles of a traditional town in context with the complexity of Indian civilization. The descriptive terms and concepts used in this study were found rather useful by other researchers in this little explored field and their researches have further established the wider applicability of the terms and concepts proposed in this book. Personally, it gives me a spiritual satisfaction that this work of mine inspired several researchers to take up contextual studies of our places of pilgrimages (*tirtha*). I hope that this effort will continue till the other centres of civilization in India and elsewhere are properly studied by social scientists, particularly cultural anthropologists so that their traditional roles as centres of integration and development may be faithfully recorded, before they fade away under the influence of modernism.

The Sacred Complex of Gaya, as described in this book on the basis of my field researches in 1951-56 remains rather unchanged. It has persisted through ages and will perhaps continue to survive in the future as a great symbol of cultural unity and continuity in India. There are, however, some evidences of change, if one carefully scrutinizes the contemporary (1974), sacred geography, the sacred performances and style of life of the sacred specialists of Gaya.

During the last 20 years, the sacred zone of Gaya i.e. Andar Gaya, religiously termed as Gayaji, has put on a somewhat modern look. It was not possible to enter the main arena of the Vishnupad temple and the locality of the religious complex by an automobile. The three-wheel rickshaws could go to some distance towards the temple. But now (1969) a fairly wide metalled road connects the secular Gaya (Chandchaura) with the gate of the main temple of Vishnupad. Near the temple a wide area for car parking has been laid out and thus the temple is easily accessible by the modern means of transportation. A modern park was also laid out in the same year near the Vishnupad temple. The extension of the road along with the park cost Rs. 1.50 lakhs which were met by the fund of the Lodging House Committee, chaired by the District Magistrate of Gaya.

Facing the temple compound and next to the parking area, the Rotary Club of Gaya has put up an impressive shed for the sojourn of the pilgrims who visit the temples. In addition to providing shelter to pilgrims during the winter and rainy seasons, the shed also provides lodging to poor pilgrims. Such a traditional role of constructing *Dharmshala* by a secular international service organisation provides an example of traditionalisation of modern institutions and symbols. The Rotary Club of Gaya has also financed the construction of a shed in the cremation Ghat on the sacred river Phalgu, a little removed from the main Vishnupad temple.

Opposite the Vishnupad temple on the other side of the river Phalgu, a new temple of Panchakosi Mahadeva has recently (1968) been constructed by an industrialist, Shri Dalmia of Calcutta. As a mark of fulfilment of a vow the temple costing Rs. 10,000 has been set up adjacent to the Sita Kund. It is said that when Shri Dalmia came to Gaya for his ancestor worship, he was pained to remember that in the absence of his son, he would not attain salvation. He went to Sita Kund and took a vow to construct a temple, if he was blessed with a son.

At a level of short range history, it is an example to establish that, as in the past, the fulfilment of vows and patronage of rich men help in the development of sacred geography in places of pilgrimage.

Along with the rich men, the saints and seers as well as the religious persons continue to raise donations for construction and renovation of temples. While a researcher of mine visited Sita Kund in 1970, he found a Brahmachari of the Kund on indefinite fast to collect fund to renovate the old Sita Kund temple. In a few weeks the saint succeeded in collecting adequate fund, by the grace of God, to fulfil his mission.

In the sacred segment of Manglagauri-Akshayavat a similar plan for the renovation of the ancient temple of Janardan was undertaken. The fund was collected by religious-minded local people and the ancient temple located adjacent to popular shrine of Manglagauri has been salvaged.

While traditional sacred zone of Gaya has been elaborated, renovated and modernised during the last 20 years, the sacred performances there have changed very little. Interviews with the priests and pilgrims lead me to infer that neither any sacred centre has been abandoned nor neglected during the last two decades. The local devotees and pilgrims continue to visit the same sacred centres that they used to do in the mid-'fifties. The influx of pilgrims to Gaya has evidently accelerated owing to transportation and credit facilities in the rural part of India. Though accurate figures are not available, a rough estimate indicates 30% estimated increase in *suphal* gifts in comparison with that in mid-'fifties. This reflects enhancement in the religiosity of the average Hindu. However, in view of the rise in price index such increase has not improved the lot of the priests.

The style of life of the sacred specialists (the *pandas*), however, was marked with certain significant changes during the last two decades. The feudalistic pastimes of wrestling, music and dance-watching and bird-keeping, which were on the decline during my last field work, have completely died out during the last 20 years. There have also been changes in their attitude towards education and acceptance of non-traditional occupations.

While there was not a single graduate in Gayawal community in 1956, our recent field survey throws out 15 graduates, four post-graduates with master's degree in arts and two in law. Some of these persons are employed as teacher in Military school (1), Lecturer in Philosophy in a college (1), advocate (1) and Government servants (2). In addition, a few of the Gayawal youths have gainfully taken up private business : transport (1), of maintaining a hotel (1), a cosmetic shop (1), and building contract (1). Though an indication for undertaking non-traditional jobs was evident during my field work in the mid-'fifties, these cases of adoption of new jobs have occurred after the 'sixties.

One of the biographies collected then indicates how he was badly condemned by his other castemen for starting a coal depot but now, such deviations, it seems, receive implicit approval of the community.

With the economic depression and further decline in the profession of priestcraft, the social structure and traditions of the Gayawal have also undergone considerable transformation. According to knowledgeable informants, (as door to door census was not possible), the population of the Gayawal continues to decline though the number of families since mid-'fifties has increased from 120 to 137. Such an increase was explained, in terms of the break down of joint families during the last 20 years. Owing to increasing individualism and the disintegration of old values, after marriage and specially when they have an issue, Gayawals usually separate from their parents or elder brothers' family. They live in the same house and under the same roof of the traditional home, but they have their separate hearth and count themselves as separate families.

The important initiation ceremony 'sacred thread' continues to be observed but owing to financial stringency it is postponed for a later date and in many cases instead of the age of 8, it is now observed at the age of 12 to14. The pomp and grandeurs and the lavish expenditure on food and clotbes have been reduced to the minimum.

In spite of decline in population, the Gayawal continue to maintain the tradition of local caste endogamy, though of late some proposals for marriage among similar Maharashtrian Brahmins have been under consideration. Their interesting marriage rituals persist but the lavish expenditure on this occasion has been drastically cut. The marriage age of both the boys and girls has gone up and a girl may be married at the age of 20-22 years, while the boys may be married still later. The Gayawal women continue to remain indoors and also perhaps unaffected with the development outside, though they do face silently the brunt of economic crisis in the family.

At the community level, the Gayawal society has witnessed a complete collapse of all the professional, recreational, social and religious organizations. During the mid-'fifties, a Gayawal leader made his last effort to maintain the Gayawal's monopoly on the pilgrims but his efforts evidently did not succeed and, in disgust, he left the locality of the Gayawal to live elsewhere in the city. Owing to this, there has been an increase in unauthorized pilgrim solicitors and several types of secular intermediaries, and the exclusive monopoly of the Gayawal in dealing with the pilgrims has completely broken. In view of this, the *suphal* and other gifts ordinarily received by them, are now being shared by other unauthorized *pandas* or secular intermediaries.

With the breakdown of this organization the cut-throat competition among the Gayawal themselves, has also increased and respect for any type of leadership as well as pride for their own community and traditional profession have completely gone. Most of the informants were of the opinion that economic depression has caused the extinction of all the community based institutions. The last to disappear was Gayawal Sankirtan Samaj, which was kept alive by one Gayawal who breathed his last recently.

Taken on the whole then, the Sanskritic as well as feudalistic traits of Gayawal culture which co-existed in the mid-'fifties are in the process of extinction. The proletarian phase has been further strengthened and the Gayawal are passing through a Cultural crisis.

While they have realized the need for higher education and diversification of profession, they have no means and resources left to achieve such objectives. Each individual, boys, girls, young and old Gayawals except the women are after pilgrim-eliciting to earn some money to meet their daily needs. Unless they are assisted by the State Government in matters of education and undertaking non-traditional occupations, their struggle for survival is likely to be seveer and more precarious.

Except these minor changes, however, the sacred complex of Gaya continues to remain unchanged, and the description presented in the book, on the basis of earlier field researches, holds good.

The researches on other such places of Hindu pilgrimage of varied regional and all-India spread confirm, more or less, similar phenomena to that observed at Gaya, with but certain regional variations in the sacred performances and the organisation of the sacred specialists. However, these researches and further thinking on this little explored field of the study in sacred complex, bring to light certain facts which need to be examined in depth in Gaya as well as elsewhere

The institution of pilgrimage itself, for example, deserves to be studied carefully from different angles, (NARAYAN, S.[1] 1974, CHAKRAVARTI[2], 1974) in all its ramification. The various types of holy circuits[3] (SARASWATI, 1965), the social composition of the pilgrims who wander from one part of India to other or undertake local holy circuit, their spiritual preparedness inspiration and objective, their sacred and secular experiences during the journey as well as the varied involvement with the sacred complex and centres of pilgrimage and then their status, role and spiritual activity after their return to their village, etc., deserve to be carefully studied. It is my belief that a careful analysis of these sacred institutions will be of immense help in understanding the complexities of the Indian civilization in general and sacred complex in particular.

Currently researches have also brought to light varied types of 'secular incentives' (SARASWATI, 1974 : 13) linked with the sacred complex.[4] The use of the places pilgrimage as trade and manufacturing centres and the use of the network of pilgrimage organisation and *mathas* by the Gosains[5] for promoting trade

[1] Refer to Dr. Narayan's Paper on "Pilgrimage to Kashi", published in symposium on the Sacred Complex in India, edited by Prof. Vidyarthi and Dr. M. Jha, 1974.

[2] Refer to Shri Prafulla Chakravarti's paper on "Some observations of the Pilgrims and their Pilgrimage : A Case study at Tarakeshwar", published in Symposium on the Sacred Complex in India, edited by Prof. Vidyarthi and Dr. M. Jha, 1974.

[3] Refer to Dr. B.N Sareswati's paper on "The holy Circuit of Nimsar" published in the Journal of Social Research, Vol. VIII, No.2, 1965.

[4] Refer to Dr. B.N. Saraswati's paper on "Studying Sacred Complex in Kashi", published in Symposium on the Sacred Complex in India, edited by Prof. Vidyarthi and Dr. M. Jha, 1974.

[5] Refer to Professor Bernard S. Cohn's paper on "The role of the Gossain in the Economy of Eighteenth and Nineteenth century Upper India", published in Symposium on the Sacred Complex in India, edited by Prof. Vidyarthi and Dr. M. Jha, 1974.

(COHN, 1974) evidently open up new area of research to explore the sacred-secular continuum in context with centres of civilization as well as regional and all India network of institution of pilgrimage.

In addition, several new facts about the sacred geography, sacred performances, and sacred specialists and their interactions have been brought to light by several researchers in the study of Janakpur[6] (JHA, M.,1971) DEOGHAR[7] (NARAYAN, S., 1972), Tirupati[8] and Rameshwaram[9] (SAHAY, K.N., 1972), Dwarka and Ayodhya[10] (UPADHYAYA, V.S., 1972 and .973) and Bhubaneshwar[11] (MAHAPATRA, M., 1971) which confirm cross-regional applicability of the terms and concepts used in the study of Gaya.

In order to attempt a broader frame for describing a centre of Indian civilization and to make up the shortcoming of wider coverage in the study of Gaya undertaken by one investigator, I took up a group research of the great 'traditional city' of Kashi which is described as 'microcosm of Indian civilization and symbolizes the totality of Indian Cultural traditions. If the study of Gaya provides the basic structure for such studies, the study of Kashi, I hope, will provide the complete superstruc-

[6] Refer to Dr. Makhan Jha's book on "The Sacred Complex in Janakpur" (in Nepal) published by the United Publishers, Allahabad, 1971.

[7] Refer to Dr. Narayan's Ph.D. Thesis on "The Sacred Complex in Deoghar" submitted to Ranchi University, Ranchi in 1972.

[8] & [9] Refer to Dr. K.N. Sahay's preliminary paper on "The Sacred Geography of Rameshwaram and Tirupati" published in Symposium on the Sacred Complex in India, edited by Prof. Vidyarthi and Dr. M. Jha, 1974, which is based on his field work along with the Post-graduate students of the Department of Anthropology, Ranchi University, Ranchi in 1972.

[10] Refer to Dr. V.S. Upadhyay's paper on "The Sacred Geographay of Dwarka", published in Symposium on the "Sacred Complex of India", edited by Prof. Vidyarthi and Dr. M. Jha, 1974 which is based on Dr. Upadhyay's field work at Dwarka along with a batch of Postgraduate students of the Department of Anthropology, Ranchi University, Ranchi in 1972. He also carried out field work at Ayodhya along with the Post-graduate students in 1973.

[11] Refer to Dr. Manmohan Mahapatra's Ph.D. Thesis on "The Lingaraj Temple", submitted to the Utkal University, Bhubaneshwar in 1971.

ture in all its details. Perhaps the various questions raised in the mind of the reader of this book, about the manifold dimensions of Indian civilization will find adequate answer in the book on Kashi.

In the end, it is my privilege to express my gratefulness to all my readers who found my book on Gaya so stimulating as their interest in it made it possible to give it the second edition. I am also grateful to several of our colleagues who found in it certain new source materials. I am specially grateful to Dr. B.N. Saraswati, Dr. Makhan Jha, Dr. Sachindra Narain, Dr. K.N. Sahay, Dr. V.S. Upadhyaya and Dr. N. Mishra who have been helpful to me in persuing this area of research.

L.P. VIDYARTHI

INTRODUCTION TO THE FIRST EDITION

ANTHROPOLOGY is a comparative newcomer to the study of contemporary complex societies and civilisations. Until recently, wedded as it was to the study of isolated primitive communities, the complexity of a civilisation *e.g.* historic structure and continental expansion, could easily escape its attention. But as the scope of anthropology extended to the study of peasant societies and cultures, the need for revising the traditional methodological tools was realised. Field investigations by several anthropologists brought into light the interactions of peasant villages with larger societies or civilisations of which they were parts. Concepts like "rural cosmopolitanism" (Lewis, 1955), "processes of universalization and parochialization" (Marriott, 1955 a), and "extensions of a village" (Opler, 1956) emerged with the study of village India by American anthropologists, and ways and means to develop an anthropological approach to the study of a civilisation were keenly studied.

In recent writings, Redfield (1955 a, 1955 b, 1956) and, with him, Singer (1955; Redfield and Singer, 1956) have been deeply concerned with the theoretical and methodological problems of studying a civilisation. As the present study has freely used their concepts and propositions and has been deeply influenced by their thinking, it would not be out of place here to make a brief reference to some of their contributions relevant to the present context. However, it will be also evident from a critical reading of this book that I have attempted to modify some of these concepts in the light of my empirical data.

Redfield develops his propositions about a civilisation on the concepts of "great and little traditions", "cultural specialists", "style of life", "cultural performances" and "cultural media".[1] With the village as a point of reference, the higher and intellec-

[1] The last two concepts have been explicitly developed by Professor Milton Singer in his methodological study in India. See his paper *The Cultural Pattern of Indian Civilization* (1955).

tual influences that come from the outside are termed the "great tradition" and those that come from within the village are termed the "little tradition" (Redfield, 1955 b). He introduces the term "cultural specialist" (which includes literati) for such organised groups of people who mediate between the great and little traditions. He suggests Max Weber's phrase "style of life" to indicate that which is most fundamental and enduring about the way of such a group persisting in history. He further introduces Singer's concept of "cultural media"—singing, dancing, acting, sanskritic knowledge, technique of dramatic recitation, etc.—through which cultural specialists communicate to the masses and thus establish continuity between the two traditions.

Having formulated these terms and concepts, he puts forward his explicit definitions of a civilisation in three ways. First, he defines civilisation as a complex structure of great and little traditions (Redfield, 1955 b). This definition in terms of traditions emphasizes culture content together with its historical sources and levels of development. Second, with the emphasis on the social structure of traditions but in terms of the same concepts used above, he defines civilisation as an organisation of a special kind of role-occupiers in characteristic relation to one another, and to lay people performing characteristic functions concerned with the transmission of tradition (Redfield, 1955 b: 20). Third, with Singer, he proposes another definition of civilisation in terms of self-axis, that is, in terms of a characteristic world-view, ethos, temperament, value system, cultural personality, etc. (Redfield, 1955 a: 79). This definition represents the shift of description from products of culture to its psychological characterisation. These three definitions of civilisation can be interpreted and conceived in terms of the above-mentioned conceptions, and, although distinct in emphasis, the three kinds of definitions may be complementary ways of conceiving a civilisation.

In his methodological field study in India, Singer (1955) applies some of Redfield's views, stated above, to the study of Indian civilisation. He examines Redfield's concept of "cultural specialists" in Indian situations and formulates some other concepts "cultural media", "cultural performances", and "cultural stages",[2] as referred to in the preceding paragraphs. He makes a distinction between the unit of cogitation and the unit of observation. He calls such units of observation as prayers, rituals, readings, recitations, rites and ceremonies, "cultural performances". He terms "cultural stages" the places where the cultural performances occur. They may occur in the home or in the temple or in any other sacred or secular place under a separate priesthood. He further suggests that concepts like "great and little traditions" or "social organization of traditions" can be formulated on more abstract levels.[3]

On the basis of this methodological approach Singer suggests four hypotheses regarding the civilisation of India, which may be stated as follows:

(1) That the great tradition is culturally continuous with the little tradition to be found in diverse regions, villages, and castes;
(2) That this cultural continuity was the product and cause of a common cultural consciousness shared by most Indians and expressed in essential similarities of mental outlook and ethos;
(3) That this common cultural consciousness has been formed in India with the help of certain processes and factors which also play an important role in other primary civilisations, *i.e.*, sacred books and sacred objects as fixed points of worship, a special class of literati (Brahmans) who have the authority to recite and interpret the sacred scriptures, professional story-tellers, a geography of sacred centres (temples, pilgrimage places, shrines, etc.), and leading personalities who, by their identification with the great tradition and with the masses, mediate the one to the other;
(4) That the cultural continuity is so great that even the acceptance of modernising and "progress" ideologies result in the "traditionalizing" of apparently modern innovations.

[2] In a personal communication Professor Milton Singer suggests the use of "cultural centre" instead of his original term "cultural stage" to avoid the evolutionary connotation.

[3] Personal communication.

II

The present study of the sacred city in all its complexities as a place of Hindu pilgrimage provides an appropriate area of research for the application and testing of some of the above-mentioned concepts and hypotheses put forward by Redfield and Singer. But these concepts are so broad-based, and the hypotheses regarding Indian civilisation so comprehensive that, in view of the present problem chosen and the availability of the data at hand, I use them only under certain specifications.

First, since my interest is confined to the study of some aspects of Hinduism, I would like to limit my frame of reference to Hindu civilisation instead of Indian civilisation, thereby keeping out of my focus the factors of such other religions as Islam and Christianity but including countries like Pakistan, Ceylon, Nepal, and Burma insofar as they fall within the Hindu universe.

Second, in conformity with the same argument and need for further limitation, I will continue to use the word "sacred" in place of "cultural" which will enable me to discover such analytic concepts as "sacred centres", "sacred performances", and "sacred specialists".

Third, I will introduce the term '"sacred complex" to indicate the pattern which emerges in a sacred city with the combination of these sacred elements.

Having made these specifications about the concepts of civilisation suggested by Redfield and Singer, the following would be the precise formulation of my present hypotheses expressed in terms of abstraction and generality:

(1) That the sacred complex—the sacred centres, the sacred performances, and the sacred specialists—of a Hindu place of pilgrimage reflects a level of continuity, compromise and combination between great and little traditions;

(2) That the sacred specialists of a place of pilgrimage maintain a distinct style of life and transmit certain elements of the great tradition to the rural population of India by popularising certain texts, by organising pilgrimages and by officiating as the ritual and temple priests;

(3) That the sacred complex in general and the sacred specialists in particular have been in the process of modification and transformation as a result of general developments in the larger universe of Hindu civilisation of which they are a part.

III

In the formulation and testing of these hypotheses I have depended mainly on my field work at the sacred city of Gaya and among the caste of sacred specialists, the Gayawal. Though, being a resident of Gaya I have had a chance to observe the Gayawal from my boyhood, my active interest in them dates back to 1948 when I studied the city of Gaya as a graduate student of geography. When I became interested in anthropology my choice fell on the Gayawal for intensive field work. For a number of years (1951-54) I carried on field work and wrote about the Gayawal under the theoretical and methodological influence of the functional school.

In the latter period of my field investigation (March, 1954-April, 1956) I had the opportunity of discussing my data and forms of thought with Professors Redfield and Singer. Their discussions and writings induced me to look at the Gayawal in the larger framework of the Indian scene. Additional field work in the light of their suggestions was made possible by a grant from the Ford Foundation executed by them. All these processes of field work enabled me to apply all possible techniques for collecting data of various nature for writing the present dissertation.

In addition to my intensive field work at Gaya, I made short trips to other sacred places like Banaras, Bhubaneshvar, Deoghar, Puri, and visited many rural temples and bathing centres.

In order to get some idea about the time perspective as well as to relate the great traditional elements to texts, I also consulted literary sources—the scriptures, gazetteers, survey reports and handbooks—which were available. Such materials, however, were very inadequate. I also looked for some systematic sociological or historical account of other priestly communities or places of pilgrimage, but unfortunately not a single study of this type has yet been done in India.

IV

The materials thus collected through field work and literary sources have been organised and analyzed to test the above-mentioned three hypotheses about Hindu civilisation. While I have found the analytic concepts of Redfield and Singer useful in describing the sacred complex of Gaya in context with the Hindu universe, I also felt the need for introducing certain descriptive terms, such as, "sacred cluster", "sacred segment", and "sacred zone" to describe the sacred centres constituting the sacred geography of Gaya ; "local", "regional", and "universal" to indicate the scope of some of the elements of the sacred complex and folk", "sanskritic", "feudalistic", and "proletarian" to describe the nature of the priesthood. Such terms, perhaps, provide a typology for describing the pattern of a sacred complex ; and might be applied with certain modifications in cross-regional and cross-cultural situations. Ultimately, such terms should also be of assistance in any comparative work in this little-explored field of anthropology.

In general, my approach has been largely synchronic, but wherever possible I have drawn relevant diachronic evidence from religious texts, historical literature, mythology and folk beliefs to bear upon my ethnographic data. While it has been my practice to refer to any available diachronic evidence relevant to the problems discussed, I have been primarily concerned with a manageable unit of about 150 years (1810-1955) for assessing the direction of some of the changes in the sacred complex of Gaya.

With these theoretical and methodological considerations the material has been organised into six chapters, which in turn are divided into several sections.

The first chapter outlines the sacred geography of the city of Gaya as it is reflected in numerous types of sacred centres of varying spatial and temporal significance. In discussing the spatial significance, the different levels of elaboration and expansion of the sacred centres—local, regional, and universal—have been brought out. Next, the processes of continuity, compromise and combination between the great and little traditions of India as reflected in the sacred geography are discussed.

The second chapter focuses on the same processes of continuity, compromise and combination of great and little traditions in so far as they are expressed through the sacred performances at Gaya. In its first section, by way of introduction, the different types of sacred performances observed at Gaya, as well as at other sacred places, have been briefly indicated with a view to suggesting their diverse elements which exist side by side and, in many cases, as parts of the same unit of sacred performances. In the second section a description of the Gaya shraddha as an example of an elaborate sacred performance has been presented, and its continuity with similar rites observed by the folk and peasants of India has been indicated.

The following chapters—three, four and five—are mainly devoted to the study of the Gayawal as an example of sacred specialists. These chapters are supplementary to each other and have been broken down for the convenient understanding of the ways of life of an Indian priestly caste in a place of pilgrimage in relation to the different roles within the caste group with other local sacred specialists, and then with the whole framework of Hindu civilisation.

In the first section of the third chapter, the different types of priestly specialists—local, regional, and universal—have been recognised and their roles have been briefly described. In the second section, the traditional style of life of the Gayawal priestly caste has been described. As a matter of method, the data have been organised around a set of descriptive terms which eventually provide a model for the style of life of a Brahmanical priestly caste. This model also provides the basis for understanding the direction of change among the Gayawal.

The fourth chapter examines the Gayawal in all their extensions. It brings out the network of structural relationship of the Gayawal with the sacred intelligentsia on the one hand, and with the lesser people of the Hindu universe on the other. It also examines their priestly relationship with other sacred specialists recruited from different castes as well as with the folk priests. Here, again, the traditional and persisting elements, more or less, have been described.

Chapter five is essentially a study in the dynamics of the social organisation of the Gayawal in context with their caste organisation as well as their relationship with the Hindu universe. Taking the data described in chapter four, two phases of change—from sanskritic (puritanic) to feudalistic, then to the proletarian—have been distinguished among the Gayawal during the last 150 years. Factors of change have been mainly suggested under two major heads: (1) impact of the patrons on the Gayawal; (2) westernization and modernization of the Indian universe. Evidences of change have been systematically brought out under the set of terms indicated in chapter four for describing the priestly way of orthodox life. On the diachronic level, the heterogeneity of the Gayawal has been hypothesized, and it has been further suspected that the sacred complex of Gaya has entered the phase of secondary urbanisation—a phase of reorganisation which can perhaps be best understood in context with the changes that are going on in and around India.

Chapter six briefly summarizes the findings of the preceding five chapters and relates them at the various levels of abstraction and generality to verify the hypotheses set forth for testing.

V

The present study, though dealing with a substantial body of data, does not provide answers to all the questions that come to my mind in the course of analysis. I feel I could have more materials to bear upon the problems of the Dhami as the folk priests, of the pilgrim hunters as the city proletariat, and of the thousands of pilgrims coming from all parts of the Hindu universe. In addition, several related areas for further investigation and consequent vindication of the theories and methods herein set forth have been brought to my light and interest. I feel stimulated to investigate into the historical phases of the primary and secondary urbinisation of Gaya in all its social, political, and economic spheres, bearing upon the problem of the orthogenetic and heterogenetic cultural roles of a city (Redfield and Singer 1956). The present study also inspires me to make a promise to investigate some other sacred complex chosen from another region of India, with a view to examining the significance of the conclusions arrived at by this study regarding the problems and methods for the understanding of a sacred complex as a part of the larger civilisational framework.

Though I alone am responsible for the conclusions arrived at by the present study, I am indebted to a number of teachers, friends, informants, and institutions without whose help and cooperation the present work would have remained a dream for me. While it is not possible to express my gratitude to each individually, I have most happily to acknowledge my indebtedness to a few of them who have been actively associated with my work.

First of all I take this opportunity to thank my respected teacher Professor D. N. Majumdar to whom I owe a lot for my initial stimulation to study the Gayawal. Moreover, I am extremely indebted to him for my earlier training in anthropology, for his constant guidance and for his keen professional interest in moulding my career.

It is my unique privilege to express my profound indebtedness to my respected teacher Professor Robert Redfield for his initial stimulus and scholastic guidance during the present study. His criticism of my papers presented in several seminars has proved a guidepost to me on my way. I am equally very grateful to Professor Milton Singer for his valuable comments and suggestions when I was formulating my problems and was writing some of the preliminary papers on the Gayawal. In the course of preparing the manuscript, Dr. McKim Marriott unreservedly placed his scholarship and time at my disposal. I am deeply indebted to him for his critical reading of my preliminary manuscript and for providing me with his valuable comments.

I wish to express my gratitude to Professor Fred Eggan for reading part of the manuscript and giving me general advice regarding the form of organisation of my data. I have also to record my thanks to Professors N. K. Bose and M. N. Srinivas ; Dr. Bernard Cohn, and Dr. Julian Pitt-Rivers for their suggestions, and to Professor Sol Tax for his general guidance, encouragement and stimulation.

I am also very thankful to Dr. K. K. Dutta, Dr. Narmadeshwar Prasad and Dr. S. C. Chatterjee of Patna University ; to Dr. Nand

Lal Chatterjee and Dr. Raj Narain of Lucknow University; to Sri Baldeo Prasad, General Secretary of the Society of Indian Culture, Gaya, to Sri Ambika Kant Singh, M.A. and my Pupils Sri K. N. Sahay, M.A. and Sri S. B. Sahay, M.A. and to many other teachers, friends and acquaintances who have been helpful to me at the various stages of field work writing of the material on Gaya and preparing the index. I have also to record my deep sense of respect for my brother, Sri Nageshwar Dayal who not only inspired me by his kind words to undertake this research assignment, but also made certain official data easily available to me for this purpose.

Those whose works have been useful to me, have been mentioned whenever I have used their materials. But I am specially obliged to Professor A. C. Kashyapa of Gaya College, now Principal at S. S. College, Aurangabad, who most generously gave me materials about the history of Gaya and also accompanied me to the field in course of my investigation and collection of data.

I cannot forget to thank my Gayawal friends and informants including Sri Mohan Lal Mahto Viyoga, Sri Govinda Lal Gurda, Sri Narayayn Lal Katariar, Sri Bachu Lal Budhia, Sri Shankar Lal Parwatia, Sri Bhole Nath Dhokari, Sri Panna Lal Barik, Sri Munni Lal Guput, Sri Chhotelal Bhaia, Sri Panna Lal Mahto Hiradya without whose co-operation and good will my attempt to write this book would have remained unsuccessful. I have to record my profound indebtedness to Sri Viyogi Jee, who unreservedly placed his store of knowledge and time at my disposal for several months and provided me with all types of data and insight regarding Gaya and the Gayawal.

I have to acknowledge with thanks the support of Fulbright and Smith-Mundt aid for making it possible for me to study and work in the United States, and the Ford Foundation for first aiding my field work and then financing my stay for writing it—the latter support being made available to me through the kindness of Professors Redfield and Singer. I have also to express my appreciation to Bihar University which granted me a leave of absence and thus enabled me to work in the States.

CHAPTER I

THE SACRED CENTRES OF GAYA

THE CITY OF GAYA[1] is located in the state of Bihar in the eastern part of India. Physiographically, it is situated in the transitional zone between the Gangetic plain in the north and the Chota Nagpur plateau in the south. It also marks a place of cultural transition: to its north and east is the ancient kingdom of Magadha, the stronghold of Hinduism and Buddhism; and to its south and southwest, only ten miles from the city, starts the tribal belt of Chota Nagpur.[2]

According to the records of the city municipality consulted in the year 1950, Gaya covers an area of eleven and three-fourths square miles. The municipal records also show the expansion of the city from six square miles in 1931 to eight and one-half square miles, and then to about twelve square miles in 1950. The census report (*India 1953*: 18) also gives an idea of the increase in its population—from 88,005 in 1931 to 105,223 in 1941, and then to 133,700 in 1951. In general, the increase in the area and population of Gaya during the last several decades is due to the expansion in industry and commerce, railway and administration, and influx of refugees from Bengal and the Punjab after the partition of India in August 1947.

In point of functional and cultural importance, broadly speaking, the city of Gaya can be easily distinguished into two zones: the sacred[3] and the secular. The sacred zone extends

[1] For most of the Indian terms in the text, exact transliterations of Hindi and Sanskrit are given in the Glossary.

[2] G. A. Grierson, writing in the late nineteenth century (*Notes on the District of Gaya*: 1891), makes an interesting comparison between the predominantly Aryan civilization of the northern part of Gaya district and the aboriginal culture of the southern part of this district. Also quoted by O'Malley (1906: 17).

[3] In the use of the term "sacred", I have found Redfield's definition (1941: 351-55) very useful for my present study. While Durkheim (1915: 37) makes a profitable enumeration of sacred objects and their features which have been considered here, his dichotomy between the sacred and profane does not appear useful for my purpose. I have tried to maintain the distinction between sacred and secular as far as possible.

over three square miles in the southern part of the city and is characterized by a large number of shrines, old markets, and old buildings of the Gayawal priests, Brahman ritualists, and such other functionaries who are related to the religious performances. This zone is known by different names to distinguish it from the secular zones. The residents of the city call it Andar Gaya (Inner Gaya) or Purana Gaya (Old Gaya). Perhaps these names reflect the antiquity of this zone which finds expression in the narrow lanes and roads, old and gorgeous architecture of the temple and the residential buildings of the priests, the concentration of old shrines at one place, and, above all, the general old settlement pattern of the zone. The pilgrims coming from the outside call it Gaya Ji (Respected Gaya) as a mark of reverence for the place. Perhaps, in the past, it was the exclusive name for the sacred zone and through this name it was known to the whole of India. But now, the same name is used for the whole municipal expansion of Gaya.

The secular zone that has developed through the Muslim and British rules was known by different names until recently. It was perhaps known as Allahabad[4] by the Muslim as recorded by Buchanan in 1811 (Buchanan: 1811-12) but presently we come across a predominantly Muslim locality known as Alamgirbad. In addition to Alamgirbad, of course, many other Muslim localities scattered here and there have grown under different names. During the British rule, this zone underwent further expansion and was formally named Saheb Ganj[5] (the locality of the administrators), by Mr. Law, a district officer at Gaya during the late eighteenth century. In his survey of Gaya, Buchanan (1811-12)

4 "Allaha" is the term used to denote God and "bad" is usually the word for settlement. It appears quite likely that the Muslims living around the mosque named their settlement after "Allaha". However the present investigator could not trace any locality of this name. At Gaya, there is a fairly large area inhabited by the Muslim which is collectively known as Alamgirbad after the Mughal king who established this township.

5 The English officers and residents were known as "Saheb" in India; "Ganj" is usually used in Hindi to denote a colony. So literally "Saheb Ganj" means the colony of the British or English people. This name was given to the whole of the commercial and administrative areas of the secular zone of Gaya to contrast it with sacred Gaya, which is inhabited by priests and highlighted by religious activities.

considers Saheb Ganj and Gaya as two towns separated by an extensive open place called Rumna. The open place now has been occupied by residential buildings and some sacred shrines but it is still known by its original name. Rumna, located on the margin of the Old Gaya, now connects the two zones of the sacred (Old Gaya) and the secular (Saheb Ganj) in the present single municipal Gaya. During the last several centuries the secular zone of Gaya has witnessed extensions and elaborations in terms of administrative, educational, commercial, industrial and transportational sectors and for all practical purposes constitutes a zone of cultural heterogeneity.

In addition to these two zones which are now continuous in the territorial expansion and form parts of the same municipal administration, there is another sacred zone six miles from the city which is called Buddha Gaya to distinguish it from (Hindu) Gaya proper. This place is noted for being the birthplace of Buddhism since the fifth century B.C., and has been a place of pilgrimage for both Indian and foreign Buddhists both in the past and the present (Fa-hsien A.D. 399-414: 53 ; Hiuen Tsiang A.D. 629: 113-19 ; Mitra 1878). In the course of its long history, Buddha Gaya has witnessed a series of ups and downs and has been in closer interaction with the Hindu priesthood in the past than in the present time. As the situation exists today, in addition to the ancient temples, stupas, monasteries, the Bodhi tree, the celebrated tanks, etc., several new foreign monasteries, run by the Chinese, Tibetan, and Ceylonese Buddhist monks, constitute the sacred landscape of the Buddha Gaya sacred zone. Though it is a predominantly Buddhist sacred place, the Hindu pilgrims also visit the Bodhi tree to make *pinda* offerings and to pay respect to Lord Buddha. Recently the place has become the centre for the religious and cultural fair observed on the full-moon day of Baisakh (mid-April to mid-May), which commemorates the day of Buddha's Enlightenment under the Bodhi tree. The festival is largely attended by people of all religious followings.

With this simple picture of the cultural or functional zones of Gaya, I now turn to examine some of the complexities and significance of the sacred zone as well as other scattered sacred centres of the Hindus in Gaya. In such an approach, my method is to describe and categorize the sacred centres on various levels of observation and complexity, and my purpose is to show the extent to which the different traditions of Hindu civilization are reflected in the sacred geography of Gaya.

On the concrete level of observation, we note thousands of gods and goddesses, deities and divinities that find symbolic expression through images, idols, rivers, tanks, trees, stones, engravings, and paintings on the walls. A large number of vedic, pauranic, and epic deities like the sun god, the various incarnations of Vishnu, Ram, Krishna, Hanuman (monkey god), and Ganesh are symbolized in images indicating their mythological physiognomy and personal equipment. Such a representation of deities through images is a common characteristic of the Hindu world and several collections of the pictures and images of these Hindu deities have been published by missionary authors (Moor 1861; Thomas n.d.). Certain deities, again, are symbolized through mystical idolatrous forms. The Shiva, for example, finds universal representation through a black stone of "phallic significance". Except at one place where Shiva is represented by an image, everywhere at Gaya, he is expressed through this mystical form. The goddesses, Manglagauri and Sitla, are represented by lumps of stone symbols. The Manglagauri shrine is symbolized by two rounded stones which are believed by the local priests to be emblems of the two breasts of the mythological Sati, the first wife of Lord Shiva.[6] Spiritually, the goddess is worshipped as the protector of the universe. At Sitla shrine, there are seven such rounded stones which are said to represent the seven sisters of the goddess Sitla. The famous shrine of Lord Vishnu, known as Vishnupada (Vishnu's foot), is represented through an engraving of his right foot in the basalt. Usually such images and idols are housed in temples which are constructed with all the sacred considerations as prescribed in the sacred texts (Kramrisch 1946: Vol. I). However, as in the villages, several images and idols are noticed at Gaya under the trees, or on the corners of some religious buildings or on the wall shelves.

[6] Mythologically, Manglagauri derives its sanctity from the Shaiva tradition of fifty-one centres in India resulting from the fall to earth of the dismembered body of the dead Sati.

Some of the sacred centres at Gaya, as in other parts of India, are represented by rivers and tanks. The Phalgu river, especially where it flows through Gaya, is said to be saturated with the essence of Lord Vishnu and it is universally known as a sacred place for ancestor worship. Also, tanks like Baitarani, Brahma Kunda, Uttarmanas are said to represent legendary celestial objects of worship, and they are visited especially by the shraddha sacrificers.

Some of the sacred places are marked with trees which are worshipped. At Gaya, two types of trees, the banyan (bat vriksha) and pipal, are considered especially sacred. Among many sacred places marked with trees, Akshayavat (the undying banyan tree) and Bodhi Drum (the tree of knowledge) are of special veneration, and detailed reference will be made to them in appropriate places. The worship of the small plant, tulsi (botanically, *ocymum sanctum*), which is said to be pervaded by the essence of Vishnu and his wife Lakshmi, is a very common domestic rite. Hills and hillocks are also abodes of gods and spirits. All the hills that are in or around Gaya—Ramshila, Brahmyoni, Murali, Pretashila—are named after some deities and are crowned with temples.

Locational Significance

If I look at these shrines and other symbols of worship closely, I note a certain locational significance which also can be related to certain sectarian and ritualistic considerations. I note the need for formulating terms like "sacred centre", "sacred cluster", "sacred segment", "sacred zone", and "sacred ground" to indicate, firstly, the location of one shrine in relation to another, and secondly, to help me in the precise analysis of some of the complexities of the sacredness of Gaya (see Table 1).

In the course of such a geographical survey of the various shrines and other symbols of worship, I feel the need of calling the smallest unit of worship, represented by an image, river, tank, or tree, the sacred centre. A sacred centre represents a single spot where a sacred performance takes place. Such a sacred centre may be variously located. It may be isolated, as I observe is the case in a number of Shiva temples (Shivalaya), the houses of epic deities (thakurbadi), or other types of sacred

TABLE 1

LOCATIONAL AND FUNCTIONAL ELABORATION OF SACRED CENTRES IN GAYA

Sacred Centres	*Sacred Clusters*	*Sacred Segments*	*Sacred Zone*
Vishnupada, Narsinha, Mahabir, Sorah Vedi, Gajadhara, Lakshmi, pipal trees, Sakshi Mahadeo	Vishnupada		
Five ghats on the Phalgu, Ram Gaya, Sita Kund	Phalgu	Vishnupada-Phalgu-Surya Mandir-Gayeshvari Gaya Sir	
Surya Mandir, Surya Kund, the banyan tree, other temples	The Surya temple		
The Durga or the female deity of Gaya, other minor deities, Ahilya-bai temple	Gayeshvari		
Gaya Sir, Gaya-Kup	Gaya Sir		
Manglagauri, Shivalaya, Janardan, Go Prachar, Bhim Gaya, the son-giving tree, Homalaya, Bali vedi (sacrificial altar)	Manglagauri		
Akshayavat, Parpitamaheshvar, Gadalol	Akshayavat	Mangalgauri-Akshayavat	*Gaya Kshetra.*
Adi Gaya, Brahmyoni, Giddhkut	Scattered, Abandoned		
Pitamaheshvar, Mahavir, Parvati, the sacred pipal tree	Pita-maheshvar	Pita-maheshvar-Uttarmanas-Sitla	
Uttarmanas, Sitla, Shivalaya, maths, the Phalgu ghat	Uttarmanas-Sitla		
Bageshvari, the sacrificial altar, the sacred banyan and pipal trees, Kali Devi	Bageshvari		
Ram temple, Shiva temple, Yama sacred centre, the famous tree (spirit)	Ramshila (hilltop)	Bageshvari-Ramshila	
Shiva, Ganesh, Brahma Kunda, the Phalgu	Ramshila (foothill)		
Pretashila, Pretabhavani, Vishnu, Ram Kund, Kak Bali	Pretashila		
Scattered sacred centres of minor local importance	Scattered, abandoned		

centres scattered in the city. Then, a sacred centre may be in a cluster of many other sacred centres in its adjacent neighbourhood. For example, I discover Manglagauri is in a cluster of sacred centres devoted to Shiva, Krishna, and Vishnu; Ramshila is in a cluster of sacred centres dedicated to Shiva, Ram, and Yama; and Pretashila combines in itself several centres—Pretashila, Pretabhavani, and Vishnu. Similarly, in Old Gaya, several clusters of sacred centres surrounding such dominant sacred centres as Vishnupada, the Phalgu, the Surya temple, Gayeshvari, and Gaya Sir may be distinguished. In the northern margin of Old Gaya there are the two sacred clusters of Pitamaheshvar and Sitla. To denote such a combination of sacred centres around a dominant sacred centre, the term "sacred cluster" has been used. Usually such sacred clusters are under a single set of priests. They also might be characterized by a single set of sectarian deities. There are notable exceptions, however, to this rule. At Manglagauri, we notice sacred centres devoted to Vishnu and Shiva; at Ramshila, we find non-Brahmanical deities of ghosts in addition to Shaiva and Vaishnava deities. In a cluster of sacred centres, however, the form of worship is usually modified according to the dominant sacred centre. For example, in the Manglagauri and Bageshvari clusters, where the goddess mother forms the dominant sacred centre, the rites of animal sacrifice continue in spite of the fact that the sacred centres dedicated to Shiva and Vishnu happen to be there in close proximity. Similarly, the goddesses Sitla and Gayeshvari, located in the neighbourhood of the vegetarian-dominant sacred centres Pitamaheshvar and Vishnupada, respectively, are never worshipped with any type of animal sacrifice.

On another locational and organizational level, two or more clusters forming a continuous segment may be termed a "sacred segment". At this level, the Vishnupada-Phalgu-Surya Mandir-Gayeshvari-Gaya Sir group would form one sacred segment; Pitamaheshvar-Uttarmanas-Sitla would form another; Manglagauri-Akshayavat would form a third; and far to the north, Bageshvari-Ramshila would be still a fourth sacred segment. On the segmental level, the combination and compromise of different types of symbolic representation, the various types of sectarian deities, and several orders of priesthood find full expression.

Let me illustrate this point by referring to the Vishnupada-Phalgu-Surya Mandir-Gayeshvari-Gaya Sir segment which is the most celebrated and typically elaborated segment under our study.

In this segment all types of symbols or emblems of divinities and deities are represented. There are magnificent images of the sun god, various manifestations of Vishnu, as well as mystical idols represented by the Shiva shrine (Shivalaya) and the Vishnupada. The Phalgu is the celebrated river and the Surya Kund is the important tank for the worship of the sun. There are two extremely large pipal trees in this sacred segment that receive occasional worship from the worshippers and sacrificers. In addition to all these sacred centres, there are almost countless deities represented by stones, images, engravings, and paintings which are enshrined here and there on the wall shelves, under the trees, or near the larger temples. All of these add up to make the sacred segment the crowded city of deities.

Considered from the viewpoint of representation of the sectarian deities, all the five principal sects of the Hindus—Vaishnava, Shaiva, Shakta, Saura, Ganpatyas—are represented. Though the segment is particularly sacred for the cult of Vishnu, the other sectarian deities are not neglected. The sacred centres devoted to the remaining sects are located in close proximity to the Vishnu sacred centres and are worshipped by the Hindus without much sectarian discrimination. The temple of the sun, in front of which is a tank called Surya Kund (sun tank), especially attracts a large crowd of devotees on the occasion of the Chhatha Vrata (sun vow). The Gayeshvari is also an important sacred centre devoted to the goddess of power (Shakti), but as it is officiated by Dasnami priests and falls in the segment of Vaishnava dominance, there is no animal sacrifice. The Shiva sacred centre and the Ganesh sacred centre, which are each represented in this segment by one temple, are not so celebrated but receive offerings from the worshippers.

The coming together of priestly orders for maintaining and receiving gifts at different sacred centres of this segment is another interesting feature. The Gayawal priests are the custodians of the Vishnupada sacred centre, several families of the Sakadvip Brahman are the officiating priests of the sun temple, while mahants of the three orders of the Dasnami Sannyasi—Giri, Puri, and Bharati (Buchanan 1811-12: 111; Ghurye 1953: 92-4)—who reside there in a math share the gifts offered at the Gayeshvari sacred centre. All of these are priests belonging to the Brahman varna but of different sectarian denominations. Two other sacred clusters, however, are officiated by the non-Brahman priesthood, about which mention will be made at the appropriate places.

Considered from the ritualistic point of view, the major sacred centres of this sacred segment are visited by the devotees from different motives. In the case of the Vishnupada temple when 200 worshippers were interviewed on three specific days, thirty-five per cent made vague replies which, in essence, signified their intentions to worship for general reasons of health and prosperity. Forty per cent of the worshippers were more or less specific about their intentions—they came either to make offerings after the fulfilment of some vows or to make fresh vows. Their visits were related to the resolution of certain problems that confronted them or their families. Some of the specific problems were to secure jobs, to win suits, to pass in the school or college examinations, to succeed in business or in other new undertakings, or to get a child. Twenty-three per cent of them replied that they wanted to earn merit for happiness in the next life, while two per cent of them were there to celebrate some initiation rites.

Though any sacred centre, or the combination of two or three, may be visited by worshippers with the above-mentioned or other purposes, sacred centres of this segment, as in the case of other sacred centres of other segments, have become especially efficacious for the fulfilment of certain specific desires. For example, the Vishnupada and the Phalgu are especially celebrated for the shraddha sacrifice, while the Gayeshvari is particularly efficacious for securing a suitable husband or for a childbirth. Visits to the sun temple and baths in the sun tank are especially undertaken to get rid of sickness like leprosy and other serious skin diseases.

The other sacred segments of Gaya—the Manglagauri-Akshayavat, the Pitamaheshvar-Uttarmanas-Sitla, and the Bageshvari-Ramshila—bring out, more or less, the same characteristics as described for the Vishnupada-Phalgu-Surya Mandir-Gayeshvari sacred segment. But a sacred segment need not be considered as a complete organization. Segments are related to each other in the sense that a worshipper or sacrificer goes from one segment to another to make offerings to the deities. From the locational point of view, again, the sacred segments—Vishnupada-Phalgu-Surya Mandir-Gayeshvari-Gaya Sir, the Manglagauri-Akshayavat, and the Pitamasheshvar-Uttarmanas-Sitla—can be categorized together to make one sacred zone (see TABLE 1) so as to contrast it with the heterogeneous zone of secular Gaya. In the sacred zone, then, there are three sacred segments which are more or less connected through the residence of priests and other sacred specialists. It is a zone of specialization for sacred activities and ritual performances. To summarize, then, in Gaya, I have been able to define a sacred zone of Old Gaya, one sacred segment of Ramshila-Bageshvari, one sacred cluster of Pretashila, and several isolated sacred centres—all of which fall within the sacred ground of Gaya.

The sacred ground of Gaya also can be understood in terms of the mythology which is celebrated in the Vayu Purana (n.d.: chaps. 105-106).[7] According to this mythology, which found wide recognition in the Hindu universe, Gaya is named after the holy demon Gaya Asur, who was killed by Vishnu and all the other gods and goddesses. He was so holy that all the gods and goddesses promised to reside on his body. His head covered two miles and his body extended over six miles. This mythology (Vayu Purana n.d.: chap. 105, vs. 112; chap. 106, vs. 65) sanctions the location of all the sacred centres within the area of ten miles, with the area of two miles being the most sacred. If we compare the contemporary sacred geography with the mythological text, we note that the Old Gaya which is said to be located on the head of the holy demon Gaya still constitutes the sacred zone of Gaya. The other sacred centres and clusters that are believed to be located on the body of the Gaya Asur are comparatively less sacred and also little specialized.

The mythology of the Gaya Asur thus sanctions the growth of all types of sacred centres on the extensive area of ten miles.

[7] A summary of the mythology is given in Appendix I.

It also integrates all the sacred centres to the single mythology that is so widely celebrated in the Vayu Purana. Moreover, it recognizes that a demon could also be so holy that he could endanger the status of gods and goddesses who would like to live on his body in recognition of his holiness.

With these observations about the locational significance of the sacred centres of Gaya, I now turn to examine the spatial and temporal characteristics of these sacred centres. By spatial characteristic, I refer to the extent and scope of a sacred centre in terms of the worshippers it attracts from the local, regional, and universal boundaries of Hinduism. Under this scheme, the influence of a sacred centre might vary from a Hindu household to the entire universe of Hinduism. Between these units of domestic sacred centres and the universal sacred centres, several minor and major local sacred centres as well as regional sacred centres may be distinguished.

The sacred group of Gaya provides all units of sacred centres. First, all the Gayawal families and perhaps many of the Hindu families of high castes maintain domestic sacred centres. Such a domestic sacred centre is usually located in one of the rooms of the house and is represented by the ancestor and other family deities. It is exclusively a sacred centre for the joint family, and the form of worship is regulated by the family customs and traditions. Some householders, in addition, maintain a sacred centre of epic deities known as thakurbadi.[8] Though this is mainly a domestic shrine, it is open for worship to friends and other relations.

The second smallest unit of sacred centres that may attract worshippers, but only from surrounding locality, might be termed a minor local sacred centre to distinguish it from those sacred centres that attract worshippers from every part of the city. The minor sacred centres that are numerous in Gaya are mainly represented by the temples of Shiva and Mahavir, the thakurbadi of Ram and Krishna, and the trees of banyan and pipal which

[8] Thakurbadi literally means the house of deities. The deities usually enshrined are the families of epic gods like Ram and Krishna. Either a room in the household or a separate house may be used. Architecturally, the house devoted to such deities is not in any way distinguishable from other houses.

are accompanied by several idols on the platform encircling the sacred trees. Such sacred centres are usually established in the fulfilment of a vow or as an act to earn merit by some rich persons living in the locality. These minor sacred centres are maintained with the income arising out of the property dedicated in the name of the sacred centres by the particular person or his family. Such minor sacred centres are named after the family designation of the owner (e.g., Sen's thakurbadi) or after the name of the locality (e.g., Murarpur's shivalaya).

The major sacred centres are those which have undergone elaboration and are mostly located in clusters. Such sacred centres are well-known to the entire Hindu population of the city and they attract devotees from every part of the city. Such sacred centres are attended by hundreds of worshippers on special weekdays; and on the occasion of certain religious fairs, the crowd reaches to thousands. On these latter occasions, the crowd is largely local but some people from the neighbouring villages usually add to the bulk.

At Gaya, such sacred clusters as Bageshvari, Pitamaheshvar, and Manglagauri may be classified as major centres. In addition to the daily worship performed by the officiating priests, a few worshippers, from forty to seventy-five in number, come to these places to make offerings. On the special weekdays, as Monday for Pitamaheshvar and Tuesday for Bageshvari and Manglagauri, the number of devotees usually increases by two to three times. Some of these worshippers, in addition to the usual offerings of worship to the deities, sit in the adjoining veranda facing the deities and read or recite the particular sacred books that are prescribed for the deity to whom they are offering worship. Such inexpensive sacred books as the Vishnu Chalisa,[9] Shiva Chalisa,[10] and Durga Astuti[11] are usually recited by these worshippers. Special forms of worship—consisting of elaborate

[9] Vishnu Chalisa literally means forty couplets for Vishnu. Such hymns in the praise of a particular god are taken, adapted, and translated from Vishnu Purana.

[10] Shiva Chalisa literally means forty couplets for Shiva. They are usually adapted from Shiva Purana.

[11] These are Sanskrit hymns in praise of the goddess Durga. I did not come across the Hindi version; perhaps they are always recited in Sanskrit.

TABLE 2

SACRED FAIRS ASSOCIATED WITH SACRED CENTRES

Sacred Fairs	*Sacred Centres*	*Month*	*Fortnight and Days*	*Translation or Implication*	*Spatial Scope*
Shraddha	Phalgu, Vishnupada, and Akshayavat	Chait	1:1-15	Ancestor worship	Universal
Ram Naumi	Vishnupada	Chait	2:9	Ram's ninth	Local and adjoining villages
Bishua (Mekh Sankranti)	Phalgu river	varies	varies	Twentieth	Regional
Rath Yatra	Deities of thakurbadi collected at one place	Asar	2:2	Chariot	Local and adjoining villages
Jhulan	All the thakurbadi	Shravan	2:11-15	Swinging of gods	Local and adjoining villages
Saloni Mangala	Bageshvari	Shravan	On every Tuesday	Pleasant Tuesday	Local and adjoining villages
Pitri Paksha (Mahalaya)	Phalgu, Vishnupada, Akshayavat, and others	Asin	1:1-15	Ancestors' fortnight	Universal
Navratra	Manglagauri and Bageshvari	Asin	2:1-9	Nine nights	Local
Kartik Purnima	Phalgu and Vishnupada	Kartik	2:15	Kartik full moon	Regional
Chhatha Vrata	Surya Kund and Phalgu	Kartik	2:4-6	Vow of Six (sun worship)	Local
Ram Vivah	Vishnupada	Aghan	2:5	Ram's Marriage	Local
Shraddha	Phalgu, Vishnupada and Akshayavat	Pus	1:1-15	Ancestor worship	Universal
Shiva Ratri	Ramshila and Pitamaheshvar	Phalgun	1:14	Shiva's night	Local and adjoining villages
Grahana	Phalgu	varies	varies	Capture (eclipse's bath)	Regional

rituals and offerings accompanied by bands, distribution of alms to the beggars and rich gifts to the priests—are observed by some worshippers on occasions of fulfilment of vows, cure from serious illness, or on some success in life.

In addition to such special worship and weekly visits, certain sacred fairs are also associated with these major sacred centres (see TABLE 2). At Bageshvari, on the four Tuesdays of the month of Shravan (mid-July to mid-August), local citizens assemble in the courtyard as well as in the vicinity of the temple. Several shops are temporarily established to sell sacred objects like flowers, garlands, incense, earthen lamps, sweets, and fruits. Shops selling toys, pet birds, and many other types of things for children, as well as utensils, toilets, ready-made clothes, etc., for the women are also set up. People from the neighbouring villages find it convenient to come there after completing their sowing season. It provides them with an unique opportunity for making vows for a rich harvest and also for doing a little shopping.

The other religious fair is held at Ramshila hill and Pitamaheshvar on the occasion of Shiva Ratri, a day devoted to the worship of Lord Shiva and his consort Parvati. Shiva Ratri (Shiva's night) is held on the fourteenth of the dark half of Phalgun (mid-February to mid-March) and is believed in Gaya, as in the whole of Bihar, to be the night of Shiva's marriage with Parvati. On this occasion crowds of thousands are seen on the hill-shrines during the afternoon of Shiva Ratri festival. From evening until very late in the night the worshippers collect at the other major sacred centre for Shiva, Pitamaheshvar. In addition to the local citizens, some villagers from the neighbouring areas also come to join in the worship at these two places.

On the occasion of the last day of the Navratri, i.e. on the ninth day of the light half of Asin (mid-September to mid-October), a small crowd of devotees assembles at Manglagauri and Bageshvari, and sacrifices of goats continue for the whole day at both places.

There are some other sacred centres at Gaya that need to be considered in still larger spatial connections. Among them the river Phalgu and the temple of Vishnupada need special attention. The river provides a series of sacred ghats for baths on the days and months prescribed by the Hindu ritual calendar. It also provides a place for the observance of sun worship to thousands of citizens on the days of Chhatha Vrata. But in addition to this strictly local significance, baths in the Phalgu are especially efficacious for earning spiritual merit on certain sacred days of the Hindu ritual calendar.

It is regionally known as a place for special bath on Kartik Purnima, the full-moon day of the month of Kartik, and on Bishua, which occurs on the day of Mekh Sankranti which falls in Chait or Baisakh according to the Hindu calendar. These two occasions also mark the organization of cattle fairs on a regional scale. Farmers within a radius of about 100 miles come to earn merit as well as to trade in all types of cattle. The cattle fair and the Phalgu bath on the occasion of Kartik Purnima appear to be an imitation of the famous cattle fair held on the same occasion at the river Gandak at Sonpur in north Bihar. The Baisakh Bishua, as far as my information goes, is only regionally observed in Bihar. It includes a bath in the sacred river followed by eating of powder of gram and barley (sattu) which is made from the new grain.

Again, on the occasion of an eclipse a large crowd on the regional scale assembles to dip in the sacred waters of the Phalgu. The eclipse known as grahana, the capturing of the moon or the sun by the evil planet Rahu, is believed to put the Hindu in a state of pollution. On this occasion large crowds assemble on the bank of the Phalgu to take the sacred bath.

Moreover, the Phalgu is universally known as a place for offering tarpans (libation of water) for the emancipation of the ancestors. On the occasion of Pitri Paksha, the fortnight of ancestor worship, large crowds of more than 1,00,000 gather on the bank of the Phalgu to offer water to their ancestors. The tarpan in its elaboration has come to be called Gaya shraddha, a ritual of universal significance which is the subject of detailed treatment in the following chapter.

The other universally famous sacred centre, the Vishnupada, located on the right bank of the Phalgu, serves the local population in the ways the other major local sacred centres do. Elaborate daily and special weekly worship is offered both by the officiating priests and hundreds of other worshippers. On every Sunday and on the eleventh day of each fortnight (ekadashi), the number of worshippers increases by more than three times the usual daily crowd. Then on the days prescribed for sacred baths when people come to dip in the Phalgu, the Vishnupada sacred centre becomes especially crowded by devotees from the regional areas. And when the sacred period for the fortnight of the ancestors commences, the overcrowding of worshippers and sacrificers from all over India needs to be regulated by both the local and state administrations.

In addition to the above two sacred centres of universal importance, there are several other sacred centres like Akshayavat, Pretashila, Bodhi Drum, and Baitarani where shraddha sacrificers are conducted by priests for pinda offerings. Traditionally, there are forty-five such sacred centres which are mainly dedicated to shraddha sacrifice and are expected to be visited by the shraddha sacrificers coming from different parts of India. In this sense, they are universal sacred centres; their names are also mentioned in the Vayu Purana. Today, however, their significance is fast decreasing. Some of them have been completely abandoned and forgotten, and, to the general pilgrims, Gaya pilgrimage essentially consists of their worship at the Phalgu, Vishnupada, Akshayavat, and a few other places.

Thus far, I have attempted to examine the sacred geography of Gaya strictly on a synchronic level. In doing so, however, I have arranged the data in a way that can help us in understanding the process of growth and elaboration of sacred centres in a place of pilgrimage. The above material brings out two interesting processes for the understanding of the development of the sacred geography in a sacred city of indigenous civilization. It shows how a single sacred centre in the course of time develops into a cluster, a segment, and ultimately into a sacred zone and sacred ground. It also brings out the expansion of the scope of a sacred centre, ranging from the domestic and local area in the wide region and, ultimately, to the entire Hindu universe. In such a process of integration, we note the factors of combination and compromise between various symbols, sects, traditions, and priesthood. With these broad results arrived at in respect to the sacred centres of Gaya studied on a synchronic level, let us turn at this point to look at them from a diachronic point of view.

Such an approach—to examine the historical setting as well as the factors and processes governing the evolution of the sacred centres—attempted in all its details would perhaps prove exceedingly profitable. But in view of the multiplicity of sacred centres and because their spread in time of more than 2,000 years constitutes a stupendous task for the social historian, it is not proposed here to enter into all the historical implications. It is also unfortunate that the few historical works (Cunningham 1871, 1882; Cunningham and Garrick 1883; Buchanan 1811-12; Mitra 1878; O'Malley 1901, 1906) that are available do not provide materials that can be adequately helpful in understanding the historical processes. Recently, Professor Kashyapa[12] collected some historical materials on Gaya, and, in the light of all these sporadic writings and evidences, I attempted to reconstruct the antiquity of the Gayawal priests and the sacred centres with which they are associated [13] (Vidyarthi 1954). With such diachronic awareness, I will use the historical materials along with the ethnographic data to point out some of the processes that are reflected through some of the sacred centres during the last two centuries that are relevant to the present study.

Abandonment and Transformation of Sacred Centres

The first process of change which impresses an investigator is the reduction at the present time in the number of sacred centres that were visited by the pilgrims in the past. Buchanan (1811-12: 108) gives a list of forty-five shrines that were usually visited by the Maratha and other rich sacrificers[14] (see Table 3).

[12] Professor A. C. Kashyapa of the local Gaya College kindly allowed me to read some of his notes and manuscripts relating to the history of Gaya.

[13] Some of the data collected by me about the history of Gaya and the Gayawal priests have been incorporated in Gaya District Gazetteer prepared by Sri P. C. Roy Chaudhary (Roy Chaudhary 1958: 89-94).

[14] Sri Baldeo Prasad, in collaboration with some of the Sanskrit scholars of Gaya, has prepared a comprehensive list of the sacred centres (Vedi) of Gaya. His list includes names of 381 sacred centres which have been traced on the basis of sacred literary sources specially Vayu Purana, Agni Purana, and Garur Purana. However, a majority of them have been

In the eight chapters of the Vayu Purana (105-112), the names of a few sacred centres which are not mentioned in Buchanan's list are given. They are Gadadhar, located in the Vishnupada-Phalgu-Surya segment, and Janardan, Prapitamaheshvar, and Giddhkut—all located in the Manglagauri-Akshayavat sacred segment. Among those who appear on Buchanan's list for which licences were granted by the local administrative authorities in his time (Buchanan 1811-12: 103-4, 108), several have completely fallen into the background or have been forgotten even by the priests, owing to their constant neglect during the last several decades.

Of the forty-five sacred centres noted for shraddha sacrifices, eleven have been almost abandoned but their location can be identified, while eight sacred centres, for which licences were granted to the shraddha sacrificers, have almost been completely abandoned and forgotten—so much so that even our priest-informants could not trace their location accurately.

The sacred centres that have been abandoned or forgotten are perhaps some of the earliest sacred centres, and most of them fall in the Manglagauri-Akshayavat sacred segment. This may indicate a shift of the sacred activities from one segment to another—both segments continuing to be sacred and connected, but with one segment, through elaboration of its sacred centres, gradually assuming more importance while the other, through neglect, eventually undergoes abandonment.

The exceptional rise of the present Vishnupada-Phalgu-Surya segment over the Manglagauri-Akshayavat segment can be explained in terms of three historical incidents. The first is the construction of the highest (100 feet) and most gorgeous temple at Gaya over the shrine of Vishnupada by Ahilya Bai Holkar, a Maratha widow queen who visited Gaya in the late eighteenth century. Connected to this temple were the magnificent ghats along the Phalgu. The temple, which is said to have cost Rs. 3,00,000 and required constant labour for ten to twelve years, was constructed by a large group of temple architects brought from Jainagar in Rajasthan. It seems that with its construction not only other sacred centres but also that of the Gadadhar

forgotten, and their locations are not traceable. The list is given in Appendix 2.

TABLE 3

SACRED CENTRES FOR SHRADDHA SACRIFICE IN THE PAST AND THE PRESENT

	Sacred Centres at Various Time Levels			
	Vishnu Sutra ca. A.D. 100 (*Jolly*)	*Vayu Purana* ca. A.D. 500 (*Dikshitar*)	*Buchanan's Report 1811-12*	*Field Work 1952-1956*
Vishnupada-	Phalgu	Phalgu	Phalgu	Phalgu
Phalgu-Surya-	Vishnupada	Vishnupada	Vishnupada	Vishnupada
Segment	Kanakhala	Kanakhala	Kankhal	—
	(also in the	Gadadhar	—	Kankhal*
	Himalayas)	Udichi	Udichi	Udichi*
		Dakhinmanas	Dakhinmanas	Dakhinmanas*
		Ram Tirtha	Ram Gaya	Ram Gaya*
			Sita Kund	Sita Kund
			Jihwalol	Jihwalol*
			Sorah Vedis[a]	Sorah Vedis[b]
Manglagauri-	Gaya Sirsa	Gaya Sirsa	Gaya Sir	Gaya Sir*
Akshayavat	Vata	Akshayavat	Akshayavat	Akshayavat
Segment	(Akashyavat)	Gadalol	Gadalol*	—
	(One in	Parpita-	—	—
	Prayag)	maheshvar	—	—
		Janardan	—	—
		Bhasmakut	—	—
		Brahmyoni	Bhim Gaya*	Bhim Gaya*
		Bhim Gaya	—	—
		Giddhkut	Go Prachar	Go Prachar*
		Go Prachar	Munda	—
			Pristha*	Gaya Kup*
			Gaya Kup*	—
			Adi Gaya*	
Pitamaheshvar-	Uttarmanas	Uttarmanas	Uttarmanas	Uttarmanas*
Uttarmanas-	(One in			
Sita Segment	Kedar Mts.)			
Ramshila		Pretaparvat	Ramshila	Ramshila
Cluster		Brahma Kunda	Brahma	Brahma
			Kunda*	Kunda*
Pretashila		Pretashila	Pretashila	Pretashila
Cluster		Kak Bali	Kak Bali	Kak Bali*
				Ram Kund*
Buddha Gaya	Matangavapi	Bodhi Drum	Buddha Gaya	Bodhi Tree
Zone			Matangavapi	
			Dharmaranya	

* Indicates partial neglect.
– Indicates complete neglect.

[a] 16 other centres ; actually 22 names.
[b] Separate names forgotten.

sacred centre, which is so highly celebrated in the Vayu Purana (n.d. chap. 106, vs. 76) as a shraddha shrine, were thrown into the background. In the early nineteenth century, Gadadhar was known as a witness-deity,[15] but at the present time even that little association with the shraddha is lost. On the other hand, the sacred centre of Vishnupada which finds casual mention in the Vayu Purana (n.d. chap. 111, vs. 45) and Vishnu Sutra (n.d. chap. LXXXV, vs. 40) has become much celebrated and well known perhaps owing to its architectural association and royal patronage.

The second factor that led to Vishnupada-Phalgu-Surya segment to greater prominence over the Manglagauri-Akshayavat sacred segment in the last two hundred years was the organized movement of the Gayawal priests from the Manglagauri-Akshayavat sacred segment and other scattered areas to the neighbourhood of the Vishnupada temple and the new ghats on the Phalgu. This collective resettlement of the Gayawal priests was made possible with the grant of 400 bighas of free-lease land (Jagir) made to Gayawal for this purpose by one of the Mugal rulers (Lal 1953: 21-22; Vidyarthi 1954: 15-16). The Gayawal constructed their buildings around the Vishnupada temple and along the river bank and became mostly concerned with the two sacred centres, the Phalgu and the Vishnupada.

The third factor that led to the neglect of the sacred centres was the gradation of sacred centres and the imposition of licence fees based on the number of sacred centres a pilgrim wanted to visit. In one class, a pilgrim visited one sacred centre, the Phalgu, and paid a licence fee of Rs. 2 As. 1$\frac{3}{4}$. In the second class, he visited two sacred centres, the Phalgu and Vishnupada, and paid Rs. 3 As. 5$\frac{3}{4}$, while in the third category of licence (which is actually the second class in terms of importance) the pilgrim visited thirty-eight places and paid Rs. 8 As. 4$\frac{3}{4}$. Those intending to visit all the forty-five sacred centres (first class in order of importance) paid Rs. 14 As. 2$\frac{1}{2}$. Such gradation as well as imposition of fees (between 1770 and 1920) further restricted the

[15] At the completion of the shraddha ritual a few deities, including Gadadhar, are invoked to stand as witnesses for the performances at Gaya. This part of the ritual is known as sakshi shravana, which literally means utterances for witness. Also see Chapter II.

choice of the poor pilgrims to visiting only the two places. However, the rich and the orthodox pilgrims continued to visit as many shrines as was possible for them. When the licence fee was repealed under the Pilgrims' Act of 1920, the pilgrims had their option to go to other sacred centres as well, though under the changing economic conditions and the secularizing attitude they found it convenient to restrict the ritual to a few places.

Another interesting feature that can be examined at the level of some of the sacred clusters is the later addition or adaptation of Brahmanical deities to the original sacred centres noted for spirit or ghost worship. On the whole it is true that, in the course of long and continued Brahmanical influence, most of the folk deities have been transformed to Sanskritic names and have been integrated into the general Hindu fold. There are some indications which tell us about the process of such integration and I will refer briefly to four examples to bring out this point.

First, the Uttarmanas tank, located originally at the northern end of Old Gaya, was perhaps at one time regarded as an abode of ghosts. That isolated tanks are the abodes of ghosts and spirits, is even today not an uncommon belief in folk and rural India (Roy 1928: 90, 99-100; Whitehead 1916: 43-44). Later, it appears, this sacred centre was included in the Brahmanical ritual of ancestor worship (shraddha) as mentioned in the Vayu Purana (n.d.: chap. 110, vss. 2-4) and was given a Sanskritic name after the famous sacred tank located on the Kedar mountain in the Himalayas (Vishnu Sutra n.d.: chap. LXXXV, vss. 5, 36). The Uttarmanas continued to be an important sacred centre for shraddha sacrifice at least up to the beginning of the nineteenth century (Buchanan 1811-12: 108, 122) but in recent years one finds it turned into a filthy and weedy tank devoid of any devotees. Similar neglect of other tanks which were once famous as shraddha sacred centres and celebrated in the Vayu Purana—Gadalol, Ram Kund, and Brahma Kunda—also is to be observed. But, interestingly enough, around Uttarmanas there has developed the sacred clusters of Sitla and Pitamaheshvar which have been described earlier and which constitute one of the sacred segments of Gaya holy ground (kshetra).

Second, the Ramshila cluster tells us a somewhat similar story. Originally it was called Pretaparvat, or mountain of the ghosts, and was believed by the people to be haunted by ghosts and spirits. Such a belief that the hills and mountains are haunted by spirits is still another belief common with the contemporary folk and peasant people in India (Roy 1928: 57 ; Majumdar 1950: 262-63 ; Dube 1955: 129) and offerings are made to the spirits for their appeasement. Thus, it is quite likely that this folk sacred centre might have been included in the series of Brahmanical sacred centres devoted to shraddha sacrifice as its old name, Pretaparvat, is celebrated in the Vayu Purana (n.d.: chap. 110, vss. 8, 9). Little is known about the change in its name, but it can be assumed with a considerable amount of certainty that when the temple of Ram was built, the mountain ghosts (Pretaparvat) might have been renamed the mountain of Ram (Ramshila). Such a change seems to have occurred only in the immediate past as Buchanan (1811-12: 128) found the people remembering both names. However, the previous connection in name is now completely forgotten by the local people, but the function of both the original worship of spirits and those of Shiva and Ram continues side by side. And. strangely enough, the ancient non-Brahmanical priests also officiate over the Brahmanical and non-Brahmanical sacred centres and sacred performances.

Third, another hill shrine, Pretashila (the rock of ghosts), also mentioned in the Vayu Purana (chap. 108, vs. 67), perhaps indicates a similar process of transformation from a folk sacred centre for spirit worship to a sacred cluster for ancestor worship (shraddha) on the universal scale. But its old name probably remains unchanged as the old sacred centre is represented by a perpendicular rock 8 feet 5 inches high. However, two other important sacred centres, Pretabhavani (the goddess of ghosts) and Vishnu, have been added. Though all these sacred centres are worshipped by the shraddha sacrificers, the first preference in order of worship is given to the indigenous "rock" sacred centre. The name of the first deity, added to this cluster, provides an interesting example of how half of the indigenous name can be combined with the second half of a Sanskritic name (Bhavani is the usual Sanskritic name for the goddess of power, Kali). The other Sanskritic deity, Vishnu, is a pure addition of Sanskritic name and god. Iconographically, it is just the imitation of the engraving of the foot of Vishnu as we have noticed in the Vishnupada temple. All these sacred centres, again, continue to remain under the non-Brahmanical priests, the Dhami, who work in compromise with the Gayawal priests in dealing with the shraddha sacrificers who come there for pinda offerings. I will examine this feature of compromise between the Brahmanical and non-Brahmanical priesthood in Chapter IV.

Fourth, the Bageshvari sacred cluster (not associated with shraddha sacrifice) provides another example of recent transformation from the folk shrine to the Brahmanical shrine. The growth of this sacred cluster dates back about 100 years, and its transformation from a lesser and simpler folk shrine to the major and elaborate sacred cluster as it is today, is still alive in the memory of the local old men and the officiating priests. Originally it was marked a "rock" sacred centre of some Dhamis who lived in its neighbourhood. When they sold their forested land to the Brahman monk known as Buddhauli Mahant, the shrine also came to him. The Brahman monk in the interest of his religious profession further enshrined the image of Bageshvari, the goddess of power in tigress manifestation on the original rock shrine.[16] It is very interesting to record that the neglected and forested area of Gaya began to attract devotees every day especially on Tuesday. Moreover, on every Tuesday of the month of Srawan, Bageshwari attracts a large religious fair, and for all purposes it has become one of the important local sacred centres of the Hindu.

Buddhist and Hindu Sacred Centres

Another important feature at some of the sacred clusters is reflected in the appropriation of Buddhistic images and emblems as Hindu deities. Mitra (1878: 124-6) considers with all confidence that the mark of Vishnu's foot enshrined in the Vishnupada temple was originally a Buddhist emblem which

[16] Gital P. Steed also reports about the goddess Bageshvari from Gujrat in her paper "Personality Formation in a Hindu Village in Gujrat" (1955: 141-2).

was appropriated by the Hindu priests at the time of the conversion of Gaya to Hinduism. General Cunningham (1871: 9-10) lends further support to this view. However, to the thousands of pilgrims who come every year from different parts of India, it symbolizes the legendary foot of Lord Vishnu. They in no way have the slightest association with Buddha at the time of worshipping it and they never identify it with Buddhism. It is a commonplace sight to see Buddhistic images in many of the verandas or wall shelves of the temples, or under the trees, or near the sacred ghats. These images, however, are not identified with Buddha and are worshipped by the important and devoted Hindus as their own gods and goddesses.

With regard to the Bodhi tree under which Buddha is said to have got Enlightenment, the process of absorption by Hinduism is neither complete nor free from conflict. The Bodhi tree has a definite association with Buddhism as it is located right at the back of the temple of Buddha in the sacred zone of Buddha Gaya. It is also one of the sacred centres which the shraddha sacrificers visit on the fourth day of their rounds. The latter appears to be a case of appropriation as an object of adoration by the Hindus. When it was so appropriated we have no means of knowing; but it seems certain that it was an object of worship by the Hindus as early as the seventh century A.D., for about A.D. 600 Sasanka, a devoted adherent of Brahmanism, dug it up and burnt it with fire "desiring," as Hiuen Tsiang says, "to destroy it utterly and not leave trace of it behind" (Hiuen Tsiang A.D. 629: Bk. VIII, 117-8). It appears probable that the Brahman priests might have adopted the tree as a suitable object for veneration on the decline of Buddhism and in this way made profitable use of the worship it received from the Buddhists. In Vayu Purana[17] (chap. 111, vss. 24-27, 80) its worship is highly celebrated and special invocations are given for it. Buchanan also mentions worship being offered to it in 1811, though he goes on to say that some zealous

[17] The special mantra partly runs as follows: "I salute, repeatedly salute, thee, Asvattha-tree, the tremulous-leaved, the yajna [sacrifice personified], the Bodhisattva, the eternal source of permanence . . . . O noble pipal tree, since Narayana always reside within thee, therefore are thou the most beneficent among the trees . . ."

person had lately built a stairway on the side of the terrace "so that the orthodox may pass without entering the porch and thus seeing the hateful image of Buddha".[18]

The conflicts between the Brahmanical priesthood and the Buddhists are reflected through the judicial actions that the Mahabodhi Society of Ceylon and India[19] took in the nineteenth and early twentieth centuries to secure the possession of the Buddha Gaya temple from the Hindu Mahant of the Giri ascetic order (O'Malley, 1906: 47-58).

A compromise has recently been attained through the active interference of the state government on the judgement of the Patna high court when, in 1952, the possession of the temple was transferred from the Hindu mahant to a committee consisting of members of both the religious groups as well as of the government.[20] Now, as the activities of the last five years indicate, both the Hindus and the Buddhists very enthusiastically participate in the newly started religious festival on the occasion of the anniversary of Buddha's Enlightenment (Baisakhi Prava).

Local and All-India Patronage

Another interesting feature relevant to the present study is the patronage of rich devotees of the different parts of India which is reflected in the financing of the development of the sacred landscape of Gaya. In the discussion on the spatial factor of the secred centres, it has been clearly brought out that the

[18] Quoted by L. S. S. O'Malley (1906: 49) in the *Gaya Gazetteer*. I could not trace this passage in Buchanan's Report (1811-12). However I noted that for the Shraddha Sacrifices it was not considered ritualistically efficacious to go to the temple of Buddha, when they go to the Bodhi tree for offering pindas.

[19] I am thankful to the Mahabodhi Society of Gaya for furnishing me with relevant documents for checking my information.

[20] The management of the Buddha Gaya temple is in the hands of a Committee, Bodh Gaya Temple Management Committee, which consists of eight members—four Buddhists and four Hindus—who are nominated by the Government of Bihar. The District Magistrate is its Ex-Officio President. In case he is not a Hindu, the Additional Collector becomes the President. In addition to this Committee, there is an Advisory Committee of twenty members in which all the Buddhist countries find representation.

sacred centres of minor local importance have been built by the local rich devotees. It has also been shown how the local monk of the district financed the construction of the Bageshvari temples. Several ghats and the construction of other sacred centres have been financed by the landlords of the district of Gaya. Evidences also have been marshalled by Mitra (1878) and Cunningham (1871) to show that many temples and the railing around the main temple at the Buddha Gaya sacred zone had been constructed by the great emperor Ashoka, whose capital, Pataliputra, was only about sixty miles from Gaya. On these evidences, it can be conjectured with some certainty that the earliest phase in the construction of local sacred centres—temples, tanks, stairs, ghats, dharmashalas, maths, etc.—was primarily financed by the local and regional landlords and other rich devotees. But as religious interests in Gaya received wide acceptance, it seems a large number of constructions, added to the original sacred centres, were financed by persons from different parts of India. Such Pan-Hindu interests in financing the construction of sacred buildings can be established on the basis of inscriptions and other records that dated from A.D. 1000 to A.D. 1900.

In an inscription reported by O'Malley (1906: 61) Vajrapani of Nayapala (A.D. 1060) boasts of raising Gaya from a small place into Amravati (city of Indra which is noted for its magnificent buildings and gorgeous decoration). Another inscription of later date (A.D. 1242) records the pilgrimage and religious construction of some Rajput minister from northwest India.[21]

The sun temple with a fine statue of the sun god is one of the oldest temples in Gaya. Buchanan (1811-12: 109, 123) on the basis of an inscription dates its construction to the thirteenth century by one Pratap Rudra of Warangal in Mysore. The adjoining sun tank (Surya Kund), though old, is reported to have been lined with bricks and plaster by Mitrajit of Kashmir in the eighteenth century.[22]

[21] Quoted by O'Malley (1906: 62) from the Report of the Archaeological Survey, Bengal circle, for 1901-02. Unfortunately, I could not find out the original source and have depended for this information on O'Malley.

[22] Sir Ramkrishna G. Bhandarkar in his paper "Vaisnavism, Saivaism,

Mention has already been made of the patronage of Ahilya Bai Holkar, a Maratha queen who financed the construction of several temples, ghats, and dharmashalas at Gaya. In addition to the construction of the famous temple of Vishnu and the magnificent ghat on the Phalgu river, Ahilya Bai is said to have replaced the old temple at Pretashila with the present one. Ahilya Bai, incidentally, also constructed a large number of temples at Banaras. These constructions of sacred buildings have made her well known to the Hindu population of India. At Gaya, she has been deified in a separate temple, and offerings and reverence are also given to her by the worshippers.

Another person, Madan Mohan Dutta of Calcutta in Bengal, who was a manager for the Board of Trade in the early nineteenth century, financed the construction of stairs leading to the hills, Ramshila and Pretashila ; he also repaired the old temples and built new temples on these two hills. His name, title, and date are inscribed in several places at the Pretashila sacred cluster. He is also said to have metalled the road joining the Pretashila sacred cluster with the town of Gaya.

In addition to these major constructions, some smaller constructions, repairs, and donations to the temples have also been reported. A gateway that lies between the Vishnupada temple and Surya temple was made by Krishna Deva and his wife Tirumala Devi in A.D. 1521. They were the great king and queen of Vijayanagar in south India (Buchanan 1811-12: 109). A dharmashala located on the right corner of the main ghat of the Phalgu is evidenced to be built by Ray Ballava, son of Raja Ray Ballava, the company's devan (manager) during the government of Hastings. The main bronze bell that hangs in the Vishnupada temple was presented by Sri Ranjit Pandey,

and Minor Religious Systems" (1913: 153) reports about an inscription dating to A.D. 1137-38 found at Govindpur in Gaya district. It makes mention of the Magian or Persian priests who are said to have constructed sun temples in many parts of India. He also infers that such priests were absorbed in the Brahmanical varna under the name of the Sakadvip caste. At Gaya we find presence of the sun temple, the sun cult, and the Sakadvip Brahman, and it is quite likely that some beliefs of the Magian priests and cults might have been absorbed into the general system of Hindu belief and practice. It provides a good problem for further research. Also see Buchanan (1811-12: 315-8).

the minister of the Rana of Nepal. Another bell that hangs at the entrance of the same temple was a gift made to the temple in January 1790 by a British officer named Gillanders (O'Malley 1906: 215).

The Gayawal informants told me the names of several kings, princes, landlords, and other rich devotees, especially from Kashmir, Rajasthan, Bengal, Bombay, Mysore, and Baroda, who have financed the construction and repair of several religious buildings and temples. I do not include their vague and incomplete statements here as I feel the above evidences are enough to establish the interests of the religious and rich people of different parts of India in constructing religious buildings in the places of pilgrimage.

The Recent Transformation

In the present century, however, the enthusiasm to construct religious edifices on the part of even the rich devotees and "kings and princes" appears to be dampened. This, as I will examine later, can be understood in terms of the changing economic organization and religious attitude of the people. However, their place is being taken by organized secular agencies like government sponsored committees and organizations. At Gaya, according to the Pilgrims' Act of 1920, a committee, consisting of the representatives of the government, the priests, the city municipality, and the public, has been organized to look after all the affairs concerning the pilgrims as well as the religious buildings. During the last ten years, the Lodging House committee has completed several construction and repair works out of which I would like to mention three as typical examples. The first is the construction of a large dharmashala or pilgrims' resthouse; the second is the construction of a monument consisting of a park in honour of Shankaracharya; and the third is the laying out of two beautiful parks—Vishnu Park and Tulsi Park—at the back of the Vishnupada temple. When these constructions were ready, some political leaders and secular scholars were invited to inaugurate them. Of course, no work has been done by the committee to make any new temples but several repair works of temples and shrines have been undertaken. Moreover, all these constructions have been done in the neighbourhood of the Vishnupada temple in the Old Gaya. The Old Gaya was once a very crowded town but now it is being reduced to a town of ruins as many of the Gayawal buildings are in dilapidated condition. Owing to this, the Old Gaya provides ample space for semi-sacred constructions, such as parks, resthouses, and monuments.

In reviewing the materials on the sacred geography of Gaya from all these points of view, it perhaps becomes clear that though a place of pilgrimage is considered to be essentially Sanskritic and Great traditional in character, it includes sacred centres that have grown out of or around the folk or Little traditions. The study also refers to those indigenous elements that still persist in terms of the symbolic representation and ritualistic and motivational association as far as they are reflected through the sacred centres. The process of transformation of simple and folk sacred centres into complex and universal sacred segments or into a specialized sacred zone or sacred ground has been brought out from both the spatial and temporal points of view. The efforts and contributions of the rich devotees from all parts of India in developing such a sacred landscape at Gaya also have been documented. The loss of interest of such persons in this century has been indicated, and it has further been brought out that in order to fill this gap the government sponsored organization has come forward to take their place. Many of these factors are also reflected in the sacred performances, which is discussed in the next chapter.

CHAPTER II

THE SACRED PERFORMANCES AT GAYA

THE SACRED CENTRES are places where many varieties of ritual and devotional activities are carried on. They include several types of offerings, fire rituals, prayers and recitations, observance of some sacraments and festivals, sacred baths, water offerings, artistic and dramatic performances, etc. Singer (1955: 26-27) has referred to such activities as "cultural performances", arguing that the religious and ritual performances cannot be sharply distinguished in type from plays, music concerts, and lectures. In the larger framework of Indian civilization, perhaps, the similarity between religion and the rest of the culture might be a valid consideration, but for the present purpose, where only the religious aspect of the Indian civilization is under consideration, I describe them as "sacred performances".

TYPES OF SACRED PERFORMANCES

At the various sacred centres in Gaya, I observe sacred performances ranging from simple ritual salutation to artistic devotional music and dances, from offerings of flowers to offerings of gold and goats, from ritual utterances of the god's name to the reading of many types of religious texts, from a moment's worship to a fortnight's sacrifice (yajna), and from solemn and devoted meditation to the extent of fun and fairs. All these bewildering varieties of the sacred performances observed by the priests and the worshippers need no detailed treatment in the present context. However, before I proceed to describe a particular ritual-complex, it is appropriate by way of categorization to define and identify the sacred performances observed at Gaya.

A worshipper at any sacred centre at Gaya, as elsewhere in India, makes offerings of water, flowers, leaves, fruits, and grains of rice. The divinity present in the symbols is regaled with incense and earthen lamps. Burning camphor is waved before it. To the mother goddess a goat may be sacrificed and its blood smeared or offered at her shrine. Red sandal paste and vermilion are mostly offered to other vegetarian deities. Perhaps these red objects are substitutes for the blood of animals (Chatterjee 1953: 53). This form of worship of offerings to the deities may be called puja or floral worship, and it is usually performed under the guidance of the shrine priests. Some scholars of Indology consider puja to be essentially a non-Aryan ritual which was later accepted by the Aryans.[1] The puja may be followed by prayers (prarthana), appeal (astuti), reading and recitation of sacred texts (path), repetitions of sacred words or mantra (jap), and meditation (dhyan)—all of which are essentially forms of individual worship. Any or all of them may be performed by a worshipper with a view to attaining personal communion with the god. Such forms of worship may be verbalized or observed in silence as the worshipper desires. However, jap and dhyan need to be observed with complete silence, concentration, and solemnity.

The third form of worship is the fire offering (homa). I observed several worshippers making offerings of barley, rice, sesamum, and sandalwood mixed with clarified butter to the sacred fire. The Manglagauri, Pitamaheshvar, Vishnupada, and Bageshvari sacred clusters have several fire-pits (agnikund) for homa worship. It is said to be essentially the vedic form of worship, and it is believed that the gods feel the savour of the burnt offering and are pleased and give in return what is prayed for (Chatterjee 1953: 52). Though homa is taken to be the vedic form of worship, the puja form of worship, which is thought to be non-Aryan in origin, is doubtless more conspicuous and widespread in all the sacred centres at Gaya.

The fourth form of worship is the water offering known as arghya. When a worshipper performs a ritual bath in a river, he makes offerings of water to the actual sun. During the sun festival (Chhatha Vrata) arghya of milk and water, accompanied by fruits, flowers, and flour cakes (pakvan), are especially offered at the river Phalgu and Surya Kund. The Phalgu is also univercally efficacious for the libation of water (tarpana) and for the manes (pitri). Tarpana is an elaborate form of water offering; a particular form of it will be described in some detail elsewhere

[1] Dr. S. K. Chatterjee is one who holds to this opinion. In his argument for Aryan-non-Aryan synthesis, the combination of the floral ritual with the fire ritual constitutes an important factor (Chatterjee 1953: 53-4).

in this chapter. Like homa, arghya and tarpana are also vedic forms of worship.

The fifth type of sacred performance includes artistic devotional acts like sacred story recitation (katha), sacred group recitation (sankirtana), and sacred dramatic and musical performance (lila and gana). Katha includes the presentation of puranic and epic legends and myths by any Brahman well versed in this art of storytelling. Such kathas are frequently organized at the thakurbadi or other types of minor sacred centres and are attended by persons from that locality as well as from the areas around it. On the occasion of religious fairs, such performances attract large audiences from the surrounding villages.

Sankirtana is especially popular at some of the sacred centres, and at the Vishnupada it is a regular and relatively elaborate performance. The Gayawal priests in cooperation with some other interested citizens have organized an association for sankirtana performances. They have adapted devotional songs in the local dialect and regional language from the Ramayana, the Gita, the Bhagavat Purana, etc. (They showed me seven volumes of such compositions containing more than 1,000 songs of all types.)

Sankirtana is held at Vishnupada every evening, and on the eleventh day of the light half of every month (shukla ekadashi) the performance continues without pause for the whole day and night. Such continuous sankirtana, along with some dramatic performances, especially mark the occasion of marriage and birth anniversaries of Ram, the epic god. The sankirtana performance may be joined by any interested persons visiting the temple, but its most active and permanent participants comprise a team of about thirty persons. This team visits other places where sankirtana is held on a state or all-India level and gives its performances before large audiences. Locally, the party makes visits to the Gayawal families or to other invited households to give performances on the occasion of certain sacred domestic functions.

Performances of music by individuals are not very common at the sacred centres in Gaya. The Gayawal, in general, are noted for their musical talent but their performances remain confined to their own households except for certain musical sessions that are held at the courtyard of Vishnupada. At the minor sacred centres—especially at the thakurbadi—certain dramatic performances like Ram Lila,[2] Ras Lila,[3] Harishchandra Natak,[4] etc., are organized on the last four days of the month of Shravan. At some thakurbadi sankirtana parties, musical and dancing groups are hired to give performances.

On the occasion of the Durga Puja, in most of the localities in the city the image of Durga is temporarily enshrined usually near some permanent sacred centres, and for the four days the above-mentioned dramatic and musical performances are observed. The organizers of the different sacred centres and localities compete among themselves in an attempt to excel one another in the performances and to attract the larger crowds. The worshippers and visitors also make the rounds to all these places and watch the performances with a critical eye.

The sixth type of sacred performance finds expression in the philanthropic activities of the worshippers and sacrificers who give alms (dan) to the beggars and sadhus, gifts (dakshina) to the priests, customary presents (neg) to other sacred specialists, and who invite Brahmans for the ritual meal (brahmbhoj). The rich sacrificers also finance the construction and repair of religious buildings and donate land to run a temple or monastery, or money to enshrine a costly image in a new temple.

GAYA SHRADDHA: A RITUAL-COMPLEX

The most important single sacred performance at Gaya is the shraddha yajna (ancestor sacrifice) which is performed every year by more than 80,000 Hindus[5] coming from different parts of India. Shraddha at Gaya is essentially observed in honour of

[2] Ram Lila are dramatic performances depicting the life of Ramchandra, the epic god.

[3] Ras Lila are dramatic performances dealing with another epic god, Krishna.

[4] Harishchandra was an ancient Hindu king who made many sacrifices and went to the extent of selling his wife and son and accepting the servantship of an untouchable caste for fulfilling his promises and adhering to truth.

[5] It may be noted here that the untouchable sections of the Hindu also observe Gaya shraddha. The present investigator found several untouchables of different parts of India performing shraddha at Gaya.

the dead fathers and other progenitors and should be distinguished from the rites which immediately follow death (mrityu sanskar or death sacrament), subsequent anniversary ancestor worship (varshik shraddha), or the annual ritual calendric ancestor worship (mahalaya or jitiya). While there are several common elements among the four forms of ancestor worship, the very fact that Gaya shraddha is observed at a public sacred ground (kshetra) rather than a domestic and local sacred centre and that its success brings final emancipation to the ancestors and happiness to the survivors gives its performance all possible elaboration, seriousness, and sacredness. It is then a sacrifice (yajna) to which a name, pushkara, has been given (Vishnu Sutra n.d.: chap. LXXXV, vs. 1), and it should be distinguished from and compared with the death sacrament (mrityu sanskar), anniversary ancestor worship (varshik shraddha), and annual calendric ancestor worship (known by different names like mahalaya, jitiya, kanagat, etc.). Again, the person who performs Gaya shraddha of his father and other relatives is a sacrificer (yajna karta) and not a main mourner (karta) as in the case of the death sacrament, or a shraddha worshipper (shraddha pujak) as in the case of the anniversary or annual calendric shraddha worship.

The celebration of Gaya shraddha is first mentioned in the Vishnu Sutra (n.d.: chap. LXXXV, vss. 4, 22, 40) and then in the Vayu Purana (n.d.: chaps. 105-12), books which are believed to date from the beginning of the Christian era. Manu Smriti (n.d.: chap. III, vss. 122-285) also makes an elaborate reference to the rules that are to be followed in the observance of different types of shraddha, but no specific mention is made of any particular place for shraddha observance. The sacred specialists, namely, the Gayawal priests and the ritualists who guide and conduct the observance of Gaya shraddha follow several types of inexpensive books which are, in part, adaptations from the above-mentioned texts and, in part, practical reconstructions by the local priests.

On the level of observation, I found the shraddha sacrifice being modified to accommodate the regional practice as well as the economic status of the sacrificers. On the level of the analysis of the motives and expectations for making such a sacrifice,

I noted immense variations. Without making much reference to such variations but remaining conscious of them, let me first attempt to describe some of the important features of the Gaya shraddha.

The day a sacrificer embarks on the Gaya pilgrimage[6] he begins a period of austerity, self-mortification, restrictions, and prescriptions, which continues until the sacrifice is successfully completed. He avoids certain food that may pollute him; he abstains from sexual acts; and he must not be in a hurry or shed a tear. He is supposed to purify himself by avoiding wrath and banishing evil and impure thoughts. When he reaches the place of pilgrimage the process of purification becomes further intensified, and before he starts the actual performance of the rituals he observes fast for a day, undergoes ritual shaving and bath in the river Phalgu, and then puts on a sacrificer's ritual garments for this. His ritual garments consist of a new white shoulder cloth and a waist cloth. He now invokes his priest as the representative of his ancestors, worships his feet by making offerings of flowers and gifts, and thus seeks his blessings for the successful completion of the sacrifice.

Having completed the ritual of feet worship (charan puja), he starts the long series of water offerings (tarpana) dedicated to the divinities (devata, devi), to the ancient sages (rishi), to Yama, the king of the dead, and to the manes (pitri). The tarpana ritual is always performed at the river Phalgu and is usually guided by the Brahman ritualist (acharya) who acts as a secondary priest under the direction of the Gayawal. The acharya recites hymns from the ritual book, Gaya Shraddha Paddhati, which are appropriate for the various stages of the

[6] Incidentally reference may be made here to the importance of the river Punpun for Shraddha sacrifice. Though it does not fall directly in Gaya Kshetra, it has very close connection with Gaya Shraddha. The sacrificers who come to Gaya for Gaya Shraddha invariably drop in at any of the three points on the Punpun—Palmer Gunj Punpun (near Mogalsarai), Dehora Punpun (near Arwal in Gaya District), or Punpun railway station in Patna District. Within a day they observe the first Shraddha ceremony there and then come to Gaya. For these spots on the Punpun the Gayawal are also the high priests and they send their representatives to attend to their jajmans who come from all directions.

ritual and directs the sacrificer to make appropriate offerings and prayers.

The tarpana ritual lasts about five hours and consists of four main stages. In the first stage, called deva-tarpana (refreshing of the gods), water is taken in the right hand and poured over the straightened fingers. Special hymns are recited and water offerings (tarpana) are made for Brahma, Vishnu, Shiva, and then for the god of the universe (Vishva Deva). In the second stage tarpana is offered to the ten ancient holy sages, Marichi, Atri, Angiras, Pulastya, Ratu, Pullaha, Gautama, Kasyapa, Vasishtha, and Vishvamitra. Evidently, the names of the last three rishis are later appendages as they do not constitute a part of the traditional constellation of seven sages represented by the seven stars. In the rishi-tarpana the sacrificer faces the east as in the deva-tarpana, but the water is poured only with the forefingers.

In the third stage, tarpana is offered to Yama and his accountant Chitragupta. Yama is the guardian of heaven and hell and Chitragupta keeps an account of the activities of the mortals according to which they are placed in appropriate situations after their death. Special offerings are made to Yama and Chitragupta to be considerate to the ancestors. In the end, tarpana is offered to all the pitris. In both the stages of Yama-tarpana and pitri-tarpana, the sacrificer faces the south and puts sesamum seeds and kusha grass (botanically, *pao cynosuroides*) in water which is poured out over the side of the palm opposite to the root of the thumb.

In respect to the pitri-tarpana, the immediate paternal ancestors—father, grandfather, great-grandfather and other progenitors—are invoked, one by one, at the first instance. Next, the female relatives of the paternal lineage and then the immediate relatives on the maternal side are invoked. Special tarpana is offered to those relatives who have died of some accident or suffered a premature death. In many cases tarpana is offered also to such neighbours or distant relatives whose ghosts might be harmful to the sacrificer. It is believed that an offering of water will satisfy their thirst, refresh them, and thus lead them to peace.

The second type of ritual known as the pinda offering follows the next day. A pinda is a tiny ball usually prepared with the flour of rice, and it has been translated by British writers as rice cake. In addition to the pinda offering (pindadan), cooked rice is also offered to the manes at some sacred centres. Pinda offering is an elaborate ritual which is performed by a sacrificer under the guidance of the ritualist at many shraddha shrines. The first and the most elaborate pinda offering is usually performed in the neighbourhood of the Vishnupada temple. It consists of several stages of worship: dedication (sankalpa), vedic recitation (gayatri mantra), symbolization of gods and manes (sthapitkarana), joining of gods and manes (sapindikarana), and finally, pinda worship (pindapujan).

Through the vedic practice of sankalpa the sacrificer invokes his manes by their names and clan (gotra), discloses his identity, and defines the purpose of the sacrifice. With the ritualist, then, a few hymns from the Veda, known as gayatri, are repeated by the sacrificer. Next comes the stage of symbolization or enshrinement of the vishva deva (gods) and the pitri. The first is represented by a betal leaf to which offerings of nuts, flowers, fruits, and coins are made one after the other under the guidance of the ritualist. An earthen pot with offerings of barley, clarified butter, honey, tulsi leaves, etc., is also enshrined to represent the gods of the universe. Then the rice balls are enshrined to represent the paternal and maternal ancestors. Another earthen pot (chukka) is enshrined to represent the manes. Offerings of barley, sesamum, honey, tulsi leaves and clarified butter are also put in the pot. Thus, the sacrificer on the one side has enshrined the vishva deva and on the other side the pitri. Such an enshrinement is always guided by and accompanied with the recitation of the ritualist.

After this, each pinda representing a manes is invoked individually; offerings of sesamum, kusha grass, honey, and white flower are made, and a piece of thread symbolizing the dress of the pitri or manes is put on it. Such ritual offerings, accompanied by the recitation of hymns, continue for each pinda. Each pitri is individually propitiated and invited to partake of the food and clothes.

The last stage, sapindikarana, is the combination of the contents of the manes' pot with that of the gods' pot. This ritual joining of the two symbols is believed to unify the pitri with those of the vishva deva. The whole ritual concludes when the sacrificer has performed the ritual salutation by putting his head on the ground before the unified symbols. He then goes to the deity of Vishnupada temple and there makes the usual offerings and salutation. Later, rice balls are collected together and are left to be eaten by crows. Sometimes they are removed to be immersed in the Phalgu or in a tank.

These two types of worship—tarpana and pindadan—dominate the shraddha sacrifice. When a sacrificer goes to other sacred centres (noted for shraddha sacrifice) represented by an image or rock or tree, some form of pindadan is made; and when he goes to other sacred centres represented by tanks, tarpana becomes the important form of worship. But at many of the other places, the symbol as well as form of worship become largely oriented in terms of ghosts and spirits, hell and heaven. At Ramshila not only Yama is worshipped but also his two infernal dogs are offered pindas so that they might not bark at the sacrificer's ancestors and thus torture them (Vayu Purana n. d.: chap. 108, vss. 29-30).

At Pretashila the primary offerings are to the god and goddess of ghosts (Pretashila and Pretabhavani). In addition to rice balls, cooked rice also may be offered.

At another sacred centre, Kak Bali (crow's sacrifice), the crows of hell are worshipped. Besides pinda offering, powdered barley (sattu) and sesamum seeds are thrown in the air so that the spirits may partake of them. The Vayu Purana (n. d.: chap. 108, vss. 61-2) also mentions invocation for the worship of the vulture. At the sacred centre of Giddhkut (vulture's house), pinda offering was made in the past, but these days the shrine is completely abandoned.

A shraddha sacrificer also visits several tanks to offer tarpana; among them, Baitarani needs special mention here. The tank Baitarani mythologically represents the terrible river that flows between the earth and heaven. Baths and tarpana performed at Baitarani enable the ancestors to obtain emancipation from the horrors of hell. Some sacrificers make gifts of a cow or set free a bull in the name of their ancestors in the belief that it will help them in the passage of the Baitarani, the Hindu Styx.

A sacrificer also makes a visit to the sacred centres of Ram Gaya and Sita Kund where the epic hero Ram is said to have offered Gaya shraddha to his father Dashratha. Here, tarpana is offered in the Sita Kund and pindadan is performed at the temple of Ram. In a similar manner, performance of tarpana and pinda may be made at several other sacred centres, ideally enumerated to be forty-five. The performances should continue on each day of the week and on each date of the dark fortnight of a month for satisfying different types of desires and for achieving many kinds of happiness which each day and date are believed to offer (Vishnu Sutra n.d.: chap. LXXVIII, vss. 1-7, 36-49). In general practice, a sacrificer visits from three to ten sacred centres and completes his round in three to seven days. There are a few sacrificers, however, who make the ritual more elaborate, spreading it over fifteen days and over all the sacred centres.

When the round of sacred centres marked for visiting is completed, the final two rituals, sakshi shravana (witness-invocation) and suphal (success-declaration), are observed. These rituals are observed either at Akshayavat or at the residence of the Gayawal priest. Sakshi shravana[7] is dedicated to deities like Parpitamaheshvar, Gadadhar, Ram, etc., who are invited to act as witnesses for the performance of Gaya shraddha. Then, according to the suphal ritual, the Gayawal priest is worshipped as the embodiment of the ancestors and all types of gifts are made to him with the belief that they would be imperishable and would be enjoyed by the sacrificer's ancestors in heaven. This ritual is marked by a sacred conversation between the sacrificer and the priest. The sacrificer asks: "May you be satisfied?" The priest replies: "We are satisfied, the gods and the manes." Then the sacrificer seeks blessings for the increase in family members as well as in wealth. The priest replies: "Thus let it be." Such a conversation and seeking of blessing from the priest as the embodiment of "the gods and the manes" are also prescribed in the Brahmanical texts Manu Smriti (n.d.:

[7] See Chapter I, fn. 13.

TABLE 4

SOME VARIETIES OF ANCESTOR WORSHIP IN INDIA

Cultural Hindu groups	*Varieties of Ancestor worship*	*Purpose*	*Time*	*Ingredients of Offerings*	*Sacred Centres*	*Sacred Specialists*
The Hindu	Pushkara (Vishnu Sutra, chap. LXXXV) Tirtha Shraddha (Gaya)	Final anniversary ancestor worship (Varshik Shraddha); appeasement of the paternal ancestors; personal happiness and prosperity.	Pitripaksha Asin (1: 1-15) Chait (1: 1-15) Pus (1: 1-15) duration varies from three to fifteen days.	Rice ball (pinda), water (tarpana), sesamum, kusha grass, white flowers, cooked rice, objects needed as gifts for ancestors' comforts.	Rivers, tanks, temples, trees	Panda, ritualist, secondary shrine priest, barber, florist
	Pitri Parva (Mahalaya, Jitiya, Kanagat, etc.)	Partake of annual food and drink; reverence and gratitude to the ancestors; personal happiness and blessings	Annual Asin (1: 15); one day	Rice ball, cooked food, meat and fish by a few, tarpana, no shaving	Domestic; river or tank of the locality	Brahman priests by high castes
	Varshik Shraddha	Worship of an individual paternal ancestor; partake of food; expression of reverence.	Death anniversary.	Cooked food, tarpana, rice ball, milk.	Domestic; the local river or tank.	Brahman priests

	Mrityu Sanskar	Mourning and bereavement; food and drink to the prets; peace of the soul.	Just after death; usually for twelve days.	Tarpana, rice ball, milk, all types of gifts to the Brahman feast.	Temporary domestic shrine; local tank or river.	Brahman priests (Kantaha - barber, potter, etc.)
The Saora	Limma	Mourning and disposal of the body; cremation.	Immediately after death; three days	Turmeric, water, cremating objects	Cremation ground; household	Shaman
	Gaur	Help individual shade to meet gods and other dead ancestors.	Any time within a year or two after death.	Rice, wine, meat, buffalo sacrifice, menhir, feast	Household	Shaman and shamanin
	Sikunda	Provide food and drink.	Periodically by a group of families.	Rice, pulse, water, wine, (no meat)	Village ground	Shaman and shamanin
	Karja	Sharing of food and drink with the dead ancestors; expression of reverence, etc.	Every two years after the harvests by all villagers.	Paddy, wine, peacock's sacrifice, fasting	Village ground; village spring.	Shaman and shamanin
The Oraon	Funeral rites	Mourning and cremation; help the shade to meet other ancestors.	Immediately after death for three days.	Paddy, rice, copper, bread, cakes of rice.	Cremation ground; local river or tank	
	Har-bora	Token of gratitude to the dead ancestors; giving of food.	Annually after the harvest.	Half-boiled rice, pulse, offering of water.	Village pond; village ground	Pahan (village priest).

chap. III, vss. 251-9) and Vishnu Sutra (n.d.: chap. LXXIII, vss. 25-32).

On this occasion, however, the seriousness of the ritual is usually hampered by the haggling of the priest in an attempt to secure more and more gifts, and as a matter of fact this act has also become part of the suphal ritual. When the Gayawal priest is satisfied with what has been offered to him in the way of gifts and when the final blessings testifying to the success of the shraddha are granted by him, the sacrifice comes to an end. The sacrificer, touching the feet of the priest, makes a final ritual salutation, and the priest in return presents the sacrificer with a ritual garland and sweets as a mark of blessing for his sacrificial deeds and future happiness.

The shraddha, in general, can be observed on many occasions according to the months and days prescribed in the Vishnu Sutra (n. d.: chap. LXXVII, vss. 1-9 ; chap. LXXVIII, vss. 1-53). The Vayu Purana (n.d.: chap. 105, vss. 48-9) also describes several alternative ritual days and periods for the performance of Gaya shraddha. Owing to this wide choice perhaps, the flow of sporadic sacrificers to Gaya continues all the year round, but about sixty to seventy per cent of the total sacrificers prefer to observe Gaya shraddha during the dark half of the month of Asin. This period, known as pitripaksha (the fortnight of the manes), has become significantly established as the most effective period for shraddha sacrifice at Gaya. It is a common belief in Bihar and perhaps many other parts of India that during the month of Asin ghosts, spirits, witches, and mendicants (ojha) become very active and restless. The women take special care to protect their children from the evil spirits, and the sorcerers and witches observe rituals and vows to attain perfection. O'Malley (1901: 6-7) calls it a month for the Hindus to settle accounts with the bhut and ghosts. The Gayawal priests call it the period of their primary "harvests" (fasal), for to them "the bhuts and ghosts are their agents through which they earn wealth".

The two other periods when sacrificers prefer to come for Gaya shraddha are on the eves of two solstitial points, i.e., in the months of Chait (March-April) and Pus (December-January). These two seasons are considered efficacious for shraddha sacrifices in both the texts, the Vishnu Sutra (n. d.: chap. LXXVII, vs. 2) and the Vayu Purana (n.d.: chap. 105, vss. 46-9). Moreover, sacrificers from Bengal and Orissa after the rice harvest in December and the sacrificers from Uttar Pradesh and Central India after the wheat (rabi) harvest find it also economically convenient to come at this time on Gaya pilgrimage.

The significance of Gaya shraddha also might be understood in terms of the motives and purposes of the sacrificers. The sacrificers chosen for interview from different parts of India had very confusing statements to make regarding their purposes for observing Gaya shraddha. In most cases, a sacrificer had several objectives. The most common purpose for its observance was to implement the religious and social duty of a son towards his father and other paternal ancestors. A farmer from Sitapur, Uttar Pradesh, believed his most pious duty was to pay the debt of his fathers by observing Gaya shraddha. A landlord replied that when his father died and left some property, he asked that some of it be spent for his peace and welfare in his afterlife. A Tamil Brahman from Madras said that he did not know the state of the soul of his father and he must do all that was possible and which was prescribed in the Brahmanical shastra for the benefit of his father's soul. All these statements can be broadly understood in terms of filial piety, sentiments of love and attachment, and, above all, consciousness of the social and religious duty to one's father and other progenitors.

The second set of their replies is mainly fear oriented. A Brahman from Mithila said that unless Gaya shraddha was observed for one's ancestors, they would never let the survivors sleep in peace. A sacrificer from Saurashtra narrated how his father and mother appeared several times in dreams and asked him to observe Gaya shraddha as they were in great trouble after death. A farmer from Orissa told me that he came to observe Gaya shraddha to set at peace the spirit of his maternal grandfather at Gaya, as the spirit had visited his house many times. The dread-oriented motive of a sacrificer is also reflected in the following extract from the life-history material of one of my Gayawal informants (Vidyarthi 1955):

> I remember a very interesting event with one of my jajmans [sacrificers] . . . . He gave me Rs. 50 and many other things as gifts. But the next moment it so happened that the spirit (bhut) of his uncle came on him. He began to utter: "You have taken up all my wealth, you are enjoying all my property, and you have given so small an amount in my shraddha. I will not be satisfied if you do not give me a cow in alms. I will do you great harm if you do not fulfill this."

The same beliefs in spirit and dread for the ghosts of the dead find expression in the fear the Gayawal, as well as other Hindus, have for Andar Gaya as a place where numerous dissatisfied ghosts from different areas have settled down. For fear of being caught by them, very few people are seen in the lanes of Andar Gaya during the late night. A Gayawal reformer tells me about his awful experience with spirits (bhuts) which he encountered when he was returning from a marriage party with a friend at one o'clock in the night. They saw the bhuts clad in snow-white clothes, and when they came near by, the bhuts made a jump into the tank. Another adult Gayawal informant narrates how his sleep is usually disturbed in the late night when the bhuts begin to run about or to wash clothes in the tank near his house. Still another informant narrated an old incident about the continuous clapping by the bhuts when two of his Brahman acharyas were reciting the Ramayana. One of the Brahman became curious to know the identity of the "person". The other man, however, asked him to remain unconcerned and continue the recitation. But the first man broke the taboo and went inside to inquire about the identity of the "person", and the moment he did so, he developed diarrhoea and died after some time.[8]

As Andar Gaya is believed to be haunted by ghosts and spirits, the women take special care to see that their children are inside the house before dusk. The life-histories of all the Gayawal informants also reflect how they were not allowed to

[8] It is a general belief that one should not talk about or disturb in any way the ghosts or bhuts if one should happen to see them. Breaking of this taboo is said to bring calamities and even death.

stir out of their houses during their childhood. Perhaps this can be partially understood in terms of their fear of being affected by the evil spirits. I was also warned by some of my sincere informants not to walk alone after nine o'clock in the night since, as one informant put it, "nobody knows the expectation of a dissatisfied foreign ghost".

The third major motive of the sacrificer, though related to the other two motives mentioned above, is to achieve general prosperity, health, and happiness for himself and his family in this life and in the afterlife as well. It is the general belief of the sacrificers that the welfare and prosperity of the family depend upon the blessings of the manes as well as on the grace of the gods and goddesses. Gaya shraddha provides them with a chance to offer sacrifices to both. Such sacrifices bring to them punya, spiritual merit that improves the unseen condition of their afterlife. Such acts also grant them longevity of life, sons (vansh), freedom from disease, success over enemies, and thus satisfies all their desires. Such beliefs are not merely little traditional ; they are also mentioned in the Sanskritic texts, the Vishnu Sutra (n. d.: chap. LXXXVIII, vss. 1-53), and the Vayu Purana (n.d.: chaps. 109-12), as well as many others.

Only a few sacrificers that I met admitted the futility of ancestor worship. They took its performance lightly and they considered it a ritual that does not have to be observed. To them, the death sacrament was enough to set their parents' soul at peace. When asked about their reason for observing it, some said that they came to observe it as their parents believed in it and hence their shraddha sacrifice should be observed. However, they did not expect their sons to observe it when they were dead. A Madrasi officer from the Geological Survey of India told me that he observed the Gaya shraddha for his father not because of any serious belief in it but because he happened to pass through Gaya on official duty. A few professional specialists like doctors and lawyers told me that they also came to observe the Gaya shraddha not out of personal belief but mainly because of the insistence and persuasion of their mothers, uncles, or other orthodox elderly relatives.

The features and elements of Gaya shraddha are in many ways not at all unique (see TABLE 4). Similar offerings of pinda and tarpana are made by the chief mourner at the death sacrament of an adult Hindu (Srinivas 1952: 113-14; Dube 1955: 130-32; Pandey 1949: 464-68). In the different parts of Hindu India the death sacraments vary in their details (Pandey, 1949: 508-51), but it is predominantly common to provide the dead with all the materials and spiritual supports to complete his journey from pretayoni (the stage of manes), and then to svarga (heaven). In observing mrityu sanskar, the chief mourner has to undergo a series of austerities; the donning of a brief ritual garment consisting of a shoulder cloth and the ritual shaving are also important parts of the whole observance. Again, the Brahmans are invited for ritual food and they receive several kinds of gifts.

In addition to the mrityu sanskar, the Hindus in general observe annual worship on certain calendric days for the ancestors (Dube 1955: 103; Lewis 1956: 178; Srinivas 1952: 122). On these occasions also, tarpana, pinda, as well as cooked food are offered to the ancestors; Brahman priests are invited and worshipped as the embodiments of ancestors, and crows are fed. In addition to this collective worship of ancestors on a certain day of the ritual calendar, the Brahmans and other high castes in some areas also observe the death anniversary of some of their immediate relatives. Though the features of anniversary ancestor worship are similar to the annual calendrical ancestor worship, it is observed only for a particular individual and usually on a small scale. Since it is confined to a small section of the Hindus and is observed on a small scale by that section as well, we need not enter into its detailed description except to note that the features of the ritual observed on this occasion are also more or less similar to the other types of ancestor worship.

Annual and periodical ancestor worship are also observed in many parts of tribal India (Elwin 1955: 360-87; Roy 1928: 32-34, 186-87). The Saora of Orissa and the Oraon of Bihar, whose religious structures have been carefully studied, observe certain parallel elements of annual ancestor worship which are considered by the respective authors as indigenous to the respective tribes.

They make these offerings "as the shade is hungry, cold and naked" (Elwin 1955: 360) and "as a token of gratitude to their ancestor-spirits who have been providing food and clothing for their descendants and thus enabling them to continue their line" (Roy 1928: 33). In general, then, they make these performances as the Hindu do for the appeasement of the dead as well as for their own prosperity and satisfaction. Unlike the Hindu, however, their offerings include animal sacrifices and alcohol, their ritual is accompanied by shamanistic possession, and their motives are more or less free from the belief in rebirth and the conceptions of heaven and hell.

Even these basic differences, when considered in more general and diachronic perspective, appear to be quantitative. It is true that only vegetarian offerings are made to the Gaya shraddha, but some of the religious texts (Vishnu Sutra n.d.: chap. LXXX, vss. 2-14; Manu Smriti n.d.: chap. III, vss. 268-70) make explicit provision for meat offerings in the shraddha sacrifice. On the occasion of the annual ancestor worship or the anniversary ancestor worship of a particular relative, the Brahman make vegetarian offerings; but for other twice-born Hindus whose ancestors were non-vegetarians, offerings of goat-meat and fish are usually made. Professor Srinivas found the Coorgs of South India making offerings of even pork and arrach to the ancestors (Srinivas 1952: 169).

The shamanistic feature—in the sense of being possessed by one with the spirits of the dead and then speaking on their behalf (Elwin 1955: 372-75)—is perhaps unknown in the Hindu shraddha or ancestor worship. But the very belief that the priest is the embodiment of the manes and in his satisfaction lies the appeasement of the manes gives a shamanistic touch to the performance. There is another indication of the shamanistic element in one of the rituals of mrityu sanskar as observed by the Hindu of Bihar. On the eleventh day of the death ritual, a Kantaha (sometimes known as a lower form of Brahman), who is invited to represent the dead, is said to be possessed by the spirit of the dead. The statements that he makes are believed to be coming from the dead. I was told that such a belief was very widespread in the villages of Bihar, and had the opportunity of observing one such case of shamanistic possession in my village in the Patna district in Bihar. Moreover, the case of the possession of a sacrificer, as quoted earlier in this chapter, also reflects the fact that the shraddha sacrifice is not completely free from shamanistic elements.

The concepts of hell and heaven and transmigration of the soul are not fully developed among the tribal population of India. A vague idea among some sections of them about such beliefs has been noted by a few investigators (Dehon 1906: 135; Roy 1928: 36; Elwin 1955: 66-76, 437), but these ideas are generally thought to be borrowed from the Hindus. I do not want to enter here into the vexing question of the development of the conceptions of hell and heaven among the Hindus.[9] It is admitted that the Hindu, in general, have faith in all these concepts, and that their spiritual activities are influenced by the consideration of bettering their afterlife. On a more philosophical level, it is also accepted that all types of shraddha (ancestor worship) are observed to assist the soul of the dead in attaining a spiritual status that might lead it to escape the repetition of births and deaths. But in actual practice, as I have reviewed the motives and purposes of shraddha sacrificers at Gaya, their purposes boil down to merely expression of customary filial piety, appeasement of ghosts, and achievement of personal happiness and prosperity. Of course, there are a few who are primarily motivated to observe the Gaya shraddha or any other shraddha strictly under the influence of the philosophical formulation of achieving moksha (salvation) for their ancestors. But in most of the cases the influence of popular beliefs in ghosts and spirits, in the horrors of hell, and in the "crude" form of worship is reflected in their observance of shraddha. Taken broadly, these beliefs are not very different from the tribal and folk beliefs.

To summarize, I have attempted to give a typological description of the various categories of sacred performances that are usually observed in a place of pilgrimage like Gaya. I have also described the pattern of the Gaya shraddha sacrifice, bringing out its essential elements in points of ritual, occasion of its performance, purpose of its performance, as well as the extent of participation of priests in such a performance. Accepting

[9] A brief reference about the development of the concepts of hell and heaven has been made in my paper "Origin and Development of the Gayawal" (1954).

Gaya shradha as a case study of a Brahmanical sacred performance, an attempt was made to provide cross references to compare it with those of similar performances like mrityu sanskar (death sacrament), varshik shraddha (anniversary ancestor worship), shraddha prava (annual calendaric ancestor worship) of the Hindus, and with the annual and periodical ancestor worship performed by two of the important and most numerous tribes of Central and Eastern India.

In all these treatments, it was apparent that the present form of elaborate ancestor worship that is performed at Gaya is in continuity with the simpler forms of ancestor worship observed in the Hindu universe as well as in middle Indian tribal societies. Taking a simple developmental approach with Gaya shraddha as our point of reference, we can visualize the process of continuous growth and elaboration from simple indigenous form of worship into such complex and intricate forms of worship under the influence of sacred specialists and sacred intelligentsia. These latter are the subjects of my analysis in the following two chapters. Perhaps such a systematic and textual elaboration of some indigenous form of worship at places of pilgrimage later penetrated into their surrounding areas and exercised some modifying influence on similar forms of worship. It is likely too that the influence of such a sacred complex, as we shall see later, was keenly felt in the easily accessible peasant villages, although the tribal people living in the inaccessible hilly and forested areas remained comparatively out of reach of such influence.

This analysis of the shraddha sacrifice as observed at Gaya, in relation to materials on ancestor worship collected by students of rural and tribal India, brings to light the complex interaction of different levels of traditions. With some difficulty, we may discern them as great and little traditions. But for the sacrificers in general, paindadan or food offerings, tarpana, homa, and the many other types of performances constitute equally essential features of shraddha sacrifice and are observed without any distinction. "In other words, Gaya shaddha as it is performed today brings together ideas and rituals from diverse but mutually continuous levels of tradition and combines them in a sacred complex of universal importance."

CHAPTER III

THE SACRED SPECIALISTS: THE ORTHODOX STYLE OF PRIESTLY LIFE

AS IN THE MATTERS of sacred centres and sacred performances, I came across several types of sacred specialists at Gaya. Such specialists, who depend wholly or partially for their livelihood on their sacred services are many: priests and monks, members of the barber and florist castes, "pilgrim hunters" and the staff of the Gayawal priests, shopkeepers for sacred ingredients and objects, astrologers, palmists, sacred singers, reciters, musicians, and composers. Among these specialists, about which reference will be made at appropriate places, the priestly specialists need our special attention in this chapter.

The priestly specialists at Gaya are of many types, in terms of their association with a sacred centre and sacred performance and again in terms of their relationship with the worshippers. Then again, there are priests of different spatial importance—local and universal. Ethnically, as well, there are Brahman and non-Brahman priests.

The local Brahman priests officiate at the minor and major sacred centres of local importance. The temple priests at Manglagauri live in its neighbourhood and partly maintain themselves on the money given by the worshippers. At present there are six such families which have grown from an original single family. These six families officiate at Manglagauri by rotation on six of the seven days of the week. On Tuesdays the gifts received are equally divided among the six families. These families, in addition, have found other means to supplement their income. Three adults work as ritualists for the shraddha sacrifices of the Gayawal, two work in local offices as clerks, and another has taken over the adjacent temple of Go Prachar (cow preaching) from the Gayawal on a five-year lease at Rs. 475. This sacred centre is usually visited by the shraddha sacrificers, and it brings him an income of about Rs. 40 each month.

The Shiva temple of Pitamaheshvar is owned by a Shaiva priest who lives in front of the temple. He himself officiates at the shrine while the other members of his family sell the sacred ingredients to the worshippers. Several persons make annual donations to the temple as a fulfilment of their vows. The temple is said to have been sold to the father of the present owner by the Gayawal. At Bageshvari, two officiating prists who live in the house adjacent to the temple are employees of a local mahant who owns the temple. The income of the temple goes to the mahant and the officiating priests are paid by him.

In addition to the full-time shrine priests, there are priests who are employed by owners of minor sacred centres or thakurbadi for daily offerings. In such cases, a priest visits a number of these sacred centres and makes offerings to the deities on behalf of their owners. Then, there are domestic priests who officiate at sacred performances observed at the residences of some worshippers. Usually priests living in different localities of Gaya combine in themselves many priestly activities that might be needed by the local householders. In this way they enter into jajmani relationship with these families to whom they provide regular priestly services.

Besides these priestly specialists, there are at least three types of priestly groups that can be best understood in terms of their association with the shraddha sacrifice. These are the Gayawal, the Acharya, and the Dhami. The Gayawal caste is one of the universally known and socially well-organized priestly groups of India. Owing to the important roles it plays as an organized group of priestly specialists in the Hindu universe, it will be the subject of our detailed study. The Acharya, the ritualists, are Brahman priests of different linguistic groups who are employed by the Gayawal to assist them in their priestly services; they will subsequently be considered in connection with the organization of the Gayawal. The Dhami, whose sacred status empowers them to officiate at the shraddha ritual especially performed at five sacred centres—Pretashila, Ramshila, Kak Bali, Brahma Kunda, Ram Kund—share a peculiar position with the Gayawal who have a monopoly over the remaining sacred centres. The Dhami are said to be a survival of an ancient non-Brahmanical priestly order. They will be considered in some details in the following chapter in connection with the structural set up of the Gaya pilgrimage.

The Gayawal Style of Life

We turn at this point to describe and analyze the data on the Gayawal as a caste of priestly specialist. In general, the Gayawal present an orthodox style of life with a closed social system. Moreover, I find the Gayawal very much conscious of the ideals, expectations, moral values, and ethical way of life that are expected of it as a priestly caste of universal importance. On the other hand, when I analyze the data more closely, I find that in addition to their closed caste organization, the Gayawal are in wider relationships with the Hindu universe. Such system of structural relationships, even considered only in terms of their priestly profession, put the Gayawal in constant contact with a number of other local castes and priestly groups, many religious leaders and devotees, and, above all, with many poor and rich jajmans extended over the whole of the Hindu universe. Then, again, I discover that such a network of relationships has made a tremendous impact on the orthodox way of life as well as on the closed social system of the Gayawal.

Given the data, these problems of cultural persistence and change, unity and extensions of a social structure, as well as the questions of ideal expectations and real happenings in a cultural group, can be organized in many ways in terms of the interests of an author. For my present purpose, I propose to single out those categories through which the Gayawal may be identified as a unified caste of priestly specialists. Taking the most fundamental and enduring elements of the Gayawal style of life, my purpose here will be to describe them under certain categories that can be used for any type of comparative and cross-regional research. In the following chapter, then, I will examine the elements of priestly social organization that put the Gayawal in various types of interrelationships with the Hindu universe. Finally, I will turn back again to the consideration of the Gayawal style of life in so far as it has been modified by its contacts with the lesser communities of India as well as by western elements of culture.

The Gayawal style of life[1] might be considered as an operation of four major characteristics with several subcategories under each heading. Reserving their analysis for later, these are: (1) caste identification ; (2) ritualism and ceremonialism ; (3) the traditional profession of priestcraft ; and (4) orthodoxy. From the subsequent description, it would seem apparent that these categories are not mutually exclusive but are interrelated aspects of a single configuration. The functional interrelatedness of the various variables, however, have been isolated here to serve the purpose of convenient analysis.

CASTE IDENTIFICATION

Caste identification refers to those social and cultural elements which unite the Gayawal into a single historical, territorial, and kinship unit. Such a group identification refers to the high evaluation of the extended family, the clan groups, and the caste itself. Interests remain group-centred rather than self-centred, aspirations are based on the elimination of individual initiative rather than the development of self assertiveness, and ambitions are linked to social identification rather than personal accomplishment.

Such a group identification among the Gayawal finds expression in many ways. First, all the Gayawal are united by the same mythology which explains their single common origin by the hands of Brahma into fourteen clans (gotra). The purpose of their creation, it is said, was to assist Brahma in the performance of the great sacrifice that followed the killing of the holy demon Gaya Asur. The Vayu Purana which celebrates the mythology of Gaya Asur also sanctions the respect and worship of the Gayawal priests, especially by the shraddha sacrificers.

The second factor that denotes the caste identification of the Gayawal is the single-residence pattern. All the 120 families of the Gayawal inhabit the southern portion of the city on the bank of the sacred river Phalgu and around the famous temple of Lord Vishnu. This land of the Gayawal is more or less fortified on all sides, and the three gates on the north, the west, and the

[1] The term "style of life" has been used to suggest what is most fundamental and enduring about the ways of a group persisting in history. See Redfield (1953: 51-52).

south mark the entrances into their domain. The compactness of the whole locality, covering an area of about three square miles, is reflected in the narrow lanes and bylanes lined by the big, old buildings of the same architectural design. We find the same residence pattern among the pandas of Banaras and Baidyanath.

Third, the caste identification among the Gayawal finds expression in the specialization of a particular type of dialect. When they talk among themselves, the Gayawal speak a dialect which is a little different from the local dialect of Magadhi. The main difference between the two, as was reported to me, is the conspicuous presence in vocabulary and grammatical form of address of terms denoting respect and hospitality, while in Magadhi proper there is no particular word of respect for address. A name, Gayawali, has been given to the dialect to distinguish it from the main Magadhi dialect of the region.

Fourth, the unity of the Gayawal is expressed through the strict rules of commensality and through distinctiveness in food preparation and dress. An orthodox Gayawal does not eat kachcha food (edibles cooked in water) even when prepared by a respectable Brahman. However, he does make an exception in respect to the Brahman from South India and Maharashtra. To the Gayawal, lunch is a part of the daily sacrifice (nitya yajna), and several rituals are observed on this occasion. They are strict vegetarians and the use of garlic and onion is also tabooed. They are strictly non-alcoholic; however, they are well-known for the use of an intoxicating herb, bhang, which is said to be associated with Shaiva asceticism. Some of their food preparations like paranpuri, kesharbhat, kusumvi kadhi are unique dishes. In general, their food consists of preparations made of vegetables, milk, rice, wheat, sugar, etc.

The usual dress of a Gayawal consists of a half-shirt (namestin), lower cloth (dhoti), and a white shoulder cloth (chadar). The way a namestin is tailored is peculiar to the Gayawal. The dhoti they use is similar to that of the general Hindu, but the way they put it on is distinctly Gayawal in style.

Fifth, the group homogeneity and caste solidarity among the Gayawal finds expression in caste and family structure, customs of marriage, patterns of kinship relations, and group affiliations.

The Gayawal are divided into fourteen exogamous clans (gotra). Each gotra has been named after an ancient saint, and the Gayawal of each gotra believe themselves to be descended from this particular saint (rishi).[2] Traditionally each gotra is associated with a particular religious scripture (Veda, Upaveda, Sutra) and a particular system of worship (Sikha, Pund, Devata), but sociologically the primary function of the gotra is for purposes of regulation of marriage and identification at any family worship or sacrifice.[3]

The second unit of Gayawal caste organization is the lineage or vansh. A vansh to the Gayawal is more or less a professional title through which they are known to their patrons (jajman). A vanshnam, or lineage title, is patrilineally in. erited from generation to generation until it becomes unmanageable and may split into two or three. A relationship between families of the same lineage is known as bhaivi (brotherhood). In the past, several dominant lineages maintained their own club, known as Baithaka. The Baithaka, run by the eldest member of the lineage, was a meeting place for all the male members of the families connected with that lineage. Such lineage organizations also regulated interlineage relationships among the Gayawal. At present, the primary function of the lineage titles is to regulate the relationships among the Gayawal families in deciding rightful claims over the jajmans.[4]

The primary unit of Gayawal caste organization is the joint family, which consists of male members of three to four generations along with their wives and unmarried daughters living in the same household and sharing the same kitchen and domestic shrine. Their life-histories also indicate that they have very close relationships with their maternal relatives as well as with their fathers' sisters' families. Since all these relatives share

[2] Appendix III provides the names of all the fourteen gotra and their respective correspondence with Veda, Upaveda, Shakha, Sutra, Sikha, Pund, and Devata.

[3] When any offerings to gods and goddesses are made at the time of Yajna or other domestic ceremonies, the gotra of the worshipper is also uttered with the verse (mantra) by the priest.

[4] An analysis of such professional titles has been given in some detail under the section, Panda-Jajman Type, in Chapter IV.

the same locality, there is constant intercourse among them and exchange of visits, gifts, and consultations is very common. In addition to this structural arrangement which intricately interconnects all the Gayawal, the strict practice of local caste endogamy further fosters close kinship relations. Invariably, a Gayawal individual finds himself in kinship relationship with another Gayawal in more than one way.

Such structural cohesion and web of relationship find further expression in the collective and active participation by the whole joint family or lineage (or in many cases by the whole caste) in sharing the joys and sufferings, failures and successes, danger and difficulties, ritual and ceremonial performances of one individual or family. Several events and instances to illustrate this point are reflected in the life-histories of the Gayawal (Vidyarthi 1955). One of our informants became insane when he heard about the lethal attack on his mother's brother's son. Another informant developed an acute type of fit when he heard the news of the death of his married sister. Another female informant petitioned the gods to take away her life instead of that of her ailing granddaughter. And an old father offered prayer to the gods to grant him death before his sons and grandsons. We find the Gayawal social workers making constant efforts and sacrifices for the uplift of their caste. We find Gayawal individuals consulting not only their paternal kinsmen but as many other relations as they can before arriving at decisions or taking up actions. These are some of the specific instances which show the anxiety and restlessness a Gayawal individual feels in trying to achieve oneness with the other members of his family or the caste group by identifying himself with the trouble and sufferings, decisions and actions, joys and ceremonies of the others.

Caste identification, again, can be considered from the viewpoints of age and sex. Children are completely subordinated to the strict discipline of their parents and other elders of the family. Parents are considered and revered as gods, and the elders must be respected and obeyed. Any disobedience or breach of the rules of respect is considered an act of adharma, or "against religion". Their life-histories amply illustrate how, through the socializing mechanism, the idiosyncratic behaviour of a child that does not conform with the traditional group behaviour is curbed and the child is made to behave like his family or group. Qualities of obedience, submissiveness, and passivity among the younger to the elders are always appreciated. Even when a young person has grown up and in turn has children of his own, he works under the direction and experienced orders of his grandfather, father's elder brothers, father, and even his own elder brother. A person has his own say only when he is the eldest member in the joint family.

From the point of view of sex, the Gayawal woman considers herself to be the shadow of the male and lives under his subordination from the cradle to the grave. It is constantly believed and practised that before marriage she is under the discipline of her father; when she goes to live with her husband's family, she is under the control of her husband (and his father); and after her husband's death she is under the supervision of her sons. The husband, for a woman, is equal to God, and when he dies she never marries again. The life-histories illustrate the nature of the authority-subordination pattern that exists in the husband-wife relationship.

Ritualism and Ceremonialism

Ceremonialism refers to the religious and ritualistic orientation manifested in the observance of the initiation ceremonies, festivals, worship, pilgrimages, recitations, sacred baths, etc. They are observed with certain stereotypic formalities in the name of the gods, or social customs, or traditional beliefs, or a combination of all these. Ceremonial performances may occur in the sacred centres and may be motivated by socio-religious considerations. When we look at the activities of the Gayawal, we find them involved in several types of ceremonial performances—some for their own selves, some for their families, some for their community, and some for their pilgrims (jajman) and worshippers (darshaniya). They perform regular prayers to earn merits for their own salvation and for the happiness of their families; they participate in their own festivals; and, too, they participate in the ritualistic performances of their pilgrims and visitors.

The life-histories of the Gayawal indicate that as they grow in age their ceremonial activities and ritual practices multiply. There are at least two definite milestones in the course of their lives which especially mark the multiplication of their ritualistic activities. These are: (1) upanayan (sacred thread or second birth ceremoney); and (2) vivaha (marriage ceremony). Upanayan is performed between the ages of seven and nine, and it marks their initiation into a number of ritualistic rules of conduct, taboos, and "don'ts" regarding their behaviour. In all the biographies of the Gayawal, special and elaborate references are made to this ceremony. After this performance, everybody undergoes a rigorous training in sandhya mantra (hymns for prayers), observes prayers regularly, and recites sacred texts. Upanayan also gives a Gayawal professional status to officiate as a shraddha priest and attend the Vishnupada temple to assist his darshaniya in the performance of puja worship. In other words, as reflected in the autobiographies, the ritual responsibilities and status of a Gayawal increase with his formal initiation into the sacred rules of the Brahmanical life.

The second milestone in the career of a Gayawal, the marriage ceremony, further purifies the self and gives a Gayawal the status to participate actively in the ritual performances of his own family, of his extended kin groups, and also of other families of his community. When he has children, he, along with his dharma patni (wife-religious partner), acts as the functionary in the initiation ceremonies that his children undergo. During his old age, when his sons become mature enough to take up the responsibilities of the profession, he becomes all the more ritualistically inclined and devotes most of his time to worship of various types. The death rites, as well as shraddha, are also very ritualistically performed by the Gayawal. Incidentally, it might be mentioned that theoretically the Gayawal have to undergo a series of sixteen sanskar (literally, processes that make one cultured) in the course of their lives, but some of them are not very significant and in actual practice have been abandoned.

The other way of looking at Gayawal ceremonialism is to examine their daily activities. The daily routines of sixteen Gayawal males of different age-grades indicate a certain amount of uniformity in their daily activity pattern. In general, the morning is spent in personal and professional ritual performances, the afternoon in retirement, and the evening either in religious recitation or visits to temple or to relatives, or both. The ritualistic activities of an adult Gayawal might be sketched in the following way.

A Gayawal leaves his bed early in the morning uttering the names of his favourite deities and then recites pratahkali (hymns for the morning). He completes his elaborate toilet with the ritual bath. At the time of taking his bath, he always recites the names of gods and goddesses. Next, he puts on the sacred clothes (pitambar) and sits before the domestic shrine for his two-hour worship which includes offerings, recitation, and meditation. Now he is free to go to the temple or to guide the pilgrims in the observance of the shraddha ceremony.

Before taking his food, he utters the name of Annapurna (the goddess of food). His lunch is especially ritualistic as it is served by the eldest woman of the family. The first to eat is the eldest male member of the family who comes to the inner apartment dressed in his pitambar, the special silken dress particularly meant for this occasion. Before eating he makes offerings to Annapurna of a little of every item served to him. In the evening he performs musical recitations either in group or alone, either in the temple or in his home or at some musical gathering. His daily routine becomes all the more ritualistic when he is observing any vrata (religious vows) as prescribed in the ritual calendar.

Gayawal ceremonialism is also expressed in the distant pilgrimages they make, in their attendance at religious fairs, and in their giving of alms and charities to the poor and the needy They not only receive gifts from their jajmans but also believe in giving away part of these gifts to the beggars and other Brahmans, with a view to earning spiritual merit for themselves. At the time of the ritual calendarical days or on the occasion of illness in a family, charities are given to please the gods and goddesses.

Thus the caste, in general, is very much oriented to ceremonies and rituals. Both the male and the female in their respective spheres are ritualistically inclined. The men, owing to their religious consciousness and priestly profession, appear to be very ritualistic in public life. The women, though confined to their respective houses and having little to do with the priestly profession as such, are in no way less ritualistic than their male counterparts. In some cases they excel the male. They interpret the phenomena of nature, society, and the world in terms of the creation of God. For them, the children are the gifts of gods and goddesses ; wealth, property, success, failure, illness, and death all are governed by the will of the divinity. All such firm beliefs induce them to observe a series of ritual performances. To illustrate this point, I quote one example from the life-history of a Gayawal woman (Vidyarthi 1955: 20-4):

> When my children fall ill I become very nervous. I become impatient to see them cured. I go to the temples to make a vow for special offerings after their cure. I used to request my husband to call panditji for performing jap, and now I ask my son foı all this. Someties the women well-versed in mantra are called to make them cure by their jhar-phuk.

The Gayawal women also make frequent visits to the Vishnupada temple and undergo sacred baths in the river Phalgu. They have special interest in the performances of initiation ceremonies, special religious worship, and seasonal religious festivals. The eldest woman of the family is particularly responsible for looking after the ancestral sacred centre which is enshrined in each household. She takes great care to please these ancestral deities who are believed to protect the family and grant it prosperity. Elaborate worship and offerings are made to the family deities on the occasion of festivals and initiation ceremonies of some members of the family.

In addition to the domestic sacred centre dedicated to the ancestral deities, many of the Gayawal families have another domestic sacred centres devoted to deities like Ram and his consort Sita, Krishna and his consort Radha, or the whole joint families of these epic deities. Another domestic sacred centre, called agni kund (fire-pit), is also found in some of the Gayawal houses for the performance of the famous vedic rite, homa, in honour of fire.

Another feature of Gayawal ritualism is reflected in their

dependence on astrology. They firmly believe that the settings of the planets, determined according to the period of birth of the individual, control their destiny. At the time of setting forth on a journey, on the eve of marriage, at illness or childlessness, and on many other occasions, they consult the astrologers and act according to their expert advice. Rituals are performed to mitigate any evil effect of the stars and planets, and all the events in their lives are interpreted in terms of fate and the will of the gods and goddesses.

Thus, the Gayawal male and female are ritualistically oriented in their thoughts, actions, and ways of living.

The Traditional Profession of Priestcraft

The third major characteristic that gives distinctiveness to the Gayawal is their exclusive devotion to their own traditional profession of priestcraft. To them, the system of four-fold division of professions (varna vyavastha) is still a living Hindu institution and they strictly follow their own traditional occupation. Their adherence to the traditional occupation can best be understood from the fact that, except for two persons (not families), the whole caste still depends on the priesthood for its livelihood.

The Gayawal are full-time priestly specialists, and the priestly activities, as I have described in the previous chapter, are centred around two major rituals: the shraddha sacrifice and the worship at the Vishnupada temple. The Gayawal, as a priestly caste, have developed a net-work of sacred relationships with sacrificers and worshippers in the whole of the Hindu universe and also with many local caste specialists who provide them with sacred services as well as help in running the priestly organization. In the next chapter, I will examine these relationships in all their details.

Orthodoxy

The term orthodoxy refers to the state of exclusiveness, superiority, and ritual separateness that a particular group claims from the rest of the larger society of which it is a part. Such a claim and belief, acceptable to both the parties, perhaps can be interpreted in terms of the historical and contextual traditions on the one hand, and in the practice of ethical values, social customs, and ritual performances by the group on the other. Orthodoxy, incidentally, might be distinguished from conservatism which may arise owing to temporary factors and may not show consistency and continuity.

Orthodoxy among the Gayawal, as we have noted earlier, finds its sanction in the Vayu Purana and Gaya Shraddha Paddhati. In these religious texts, it is written that the Gayawal were especially created by Lord Brahma to assist him in the great sacrifice, that they are the custodians of the Gaya shraddha, and that only performance under their supervision and blessing would bring salvation to the deceased ancestors and happiness for the sacrificers and their families. These sacred charters placed the Gayawal at the apex of the caste hierarchy and gave them a high ritual status. They were regarded as the high priests, and even the Brahmans of high families and learning worship their feet and seek their blessings when they perform the Gaya shraddha of their ancestors.[5]

Along with these textual charters, the Gayawal have developed spiritual superiority over the rest of the Hindu population through observing the rules of commensality, the custom of local caste endogamy, the priestly code of conduct, etc.

Our inquiry through questionnaires further reflects the orthodoxy of the Gayawal. They have little social intercourse with the rest of the citizens of the town who are not associated with the priestly activities. Their orthodox beliefs and practices keep them apart from the rest of the civic life. They seldom go to the clubs and cultural gatherings of the cities; they very rarely go to the main market of the city; and they practically never visit their non-Gayawal friends except for a few of their jajmans. Their life-histories further explain how they have avoided modern schooling for fear their children might be spoiled in the company of boys of all types. One of the inform-

[5] "The Hindus of the whole of India, including Brahmans of all the countries who come to Gaya, worship the Gayawals in the same way as if they were worshipping Sri Vishnu Himself." Extract from the report on caste ranking during the Census of 1901. Also quoted by O'Malley (1906: 217).

ants tells me how he was discouraged by his elders when he wanted to go to the school with one of his non-Gayawal Brahman neighbours (Vidyarthi 1955: 21-3):

> I also expressed my willingness to go to the school with my Bengali friends. My father was reluctant. He consulted his elder brother about this. He completely opposed this idea. He was dead against sending me to the school. He... thought that there were chances to come in contact with characterless boys in the school. Such contacts might end in spoiling my character.

Some of the informants who went to such schools for a short time were always escorted by servants, and in case of any delay in their return their parents used to become suspicious and anxious. Another informant told me about his elder brother who was the first boy among the Gayawal to pass the school-leaving examination and to take admission in a college in a neighbouring town. He could not continue his studies there owing to his orthodox habits especially in the matter of food. All the life-histories indicate that the Gayawal get their schooling either at their guru's math or at their own residence.

The orthodoxy of the Gayawal, again, is reflected in the way they look at modern developments in their country. They consider all the changes brought about in the social, economic and educational spheres as harmful and detrimental to the cause of Hindu traditions. In reply to a question as to whether or not they thought Hinduism was dying out gradually, 92 per cent of the hundred respondents replied in the positive, 8 per cent could not decide correctly; not a single Gayawal answered in the negative. When asked about the causes of the gradual decay of the Hindu religion, most of them pointed to the defective system of education as its main cause. The Gayawal in general (94 per cent) think that the impact of western civilization has proved to be very detrimental to religious activities and family relationships in India.

The caste, as a whole, prefers education in religion to politics. Only 12 per cent feel the need for education in politics, while the rest (88 per cent) are for education in religion. A majority of them feel that the modern system of education, devoid of religious teaching, has proved fatal to Hinduism. In a group interview, some of them remarked that there was a time when their fathers and forefathers laid much emphasis upon brahmacharya and did not allow the mixing of boys and girls, but now free mixing and coeducation are encouraged by the government itself.

They were emphatically against the enactment of the Hindu Code Bill. When asked if it should be passed, 88 per cent replied in the negative. 12 per cent expressed no opinion, and not a single subject answered in the positive. Some of them vehemently criticized the contents of the bill, and one of them remarked that the moment it is brought into operation, the very backbone of Hindu society would be affected.

The attitude of the Gayawal toward the national government also deserves mention in regard to their orthodoxy. Whenever I asked their opinion about the activities of the government, their usual reply was: "Of what avail is a government that does not care for reviving our old cultural traditions (Vedic and Puranic traditions?) ?" The abolition of zamindari (landlordism) was not hailed by the Gayawal. In their replies, 80 per cent thought it immoral on the part of the government to snatch away land from those who had been its owners for generations. They also said that as the emperors Ashoka and Vikramaditya dedicated their lives and property for the religions they liked, so the modern government in India should also made proper arrangements for popularizing Hinduism.

Though the Gayawal are very conscious of the decline of the profession of priestcraft, still they are not in a mood to take up any other type of work. When asked about their choice between the priesthood and other commercial jobs, only 12 per cent replied affirmatively for the latter. In respect to their preference between such jobs as clerical employment and their traditional profession, a majority of them (78 per cent) prefer the priesthood. In the spirit of orthodoxy, they consider it beneath their dignity to take up other jobs.

Thus the orthodoxy of the Gayawal finds expression in their social usages, their exclusiveness from the urban population, their ritual performances, and above all in their attitude to modern developments. In general, their attitude is one of "no-change", and their state of mind is of "ritual superiority". But owing to their constant contacts with the pilgrims and visitors on whom they are dependent for their economic subsistence and the general secularization in India, they have not been able to live up to their expectations. Some of them have changed, and have changed to the extent of vulgarization. These changes in the Gayawal ways of life are the subject for discussion in Chapter V.

CHAPTER IV

THE SACRED SPECIALISTS: EXTENSION

IN THE preceding chapter it has been shown that the Gayawal as a caste of priestly specialists have their own orthodox style of life and a unified caste organization with certain isolable elements. In the present chapter, I propose to show how their very nature of the priestly socio-economic organization brings the Gayawal into relationship with many other systems that exist outside their caste organization. As a matter of delimitation, only such items of structural extension will be considered that concern the sacred and professional aspect of the Gayawal style of life.

In the course of a long history, the Gayawal has developed several types of relationship with the outside world. From contemporary ethnographic data and the few existing historical documents, five types of major persistent sacred relationships of the Gayawal with the outside world can be recognized. These are: (1) guru-shisya or spiritual teacher-disciple type; (2) panda-jajman or priest-sacrificer type; (3) mixed jajman-pauniya or master-servant type; (4) Gayawal-Dhami or Brahmanical-non-Brahmanical priest type; (5) pujari-darshaniya or shrine priest-worshipper type.

GURU-SHISYA TYPE

The first, the guru-shisya type, refers to the relationships that the Gayawal caste as a whole, or its members individually, enjoy with the spiritual teachers, religious leaders, and holy ascetics. Some of these spiritual leaders who are followers of Vaishnavism of the Madhava sect stay at Gaya permanently and are revered by the Gayawal as jati-guru or caste-teachers. Others known as Vairagi, or Vaishnava sadhu (ascetics), and Dasnami, or Shaiva sadhu of ten orders, visit Gaya, stay at their respective monasteries, and hold sacred sessions (satsang) with the Gayawal and other Brahmans living in Old Gaya. All such spiritual teachers, directly or indirectly, raise the priestly morale and religious life of the Gayawal in particular and other groups of people associated with the Gayawal in general. Moreover, visits of outstanding holy persons and their sacred sessions (satsang) attract large gatherings from the city as well as from the neighbouring villages. When these holy persons visit other places of pilgrimage or other parts of India, they hold similar sacred sessions, formally or informally, and speak about the sacredness of Gaya as a place for ancestor worship and the Vaishnava cult, thus helping to keep the current of pilgrimage flowing.

In the neighbourhood of the Vishnupada temple there are three monasteries—one dedicated to the Madhava sect, the second to the Shankara sect, and the third for accommodating any holy ascetics or religious leaders. In the course of my field work (1952-56), I found the Madhava math an active institution, whereas the Shankara math, while having a good collection of Sanskrit books, appeared on the whole to be desolate. I found some sadhus engaged in meditation in the third math.

The Madhava math is maintained by the Gayawal, and Madhava jati-guru, who is a full-time worshipper, scholar, teacher, and philosopher, is very well looked after by the Gayawal. He teaches Sanskrit texts and Gayatri hymn to the Gayawal, addresses private and public religious sessions at the Vishnupada temple, and holds disputations with such pandits and priests who come to him for these purposes. He keeps himself aloof from the factional disputes that arise from time to time among the Gayawal themselves but always tries to lift their morale with spiritual advice. In many ways he is a "sacred policy maker" and thus links himself with the series of sacred intelligentsia who have visited Gaya in the course of its long history and, perhaps, have been instrumental in developing priestly groups by, first, converting selected people to the priestly way of life, and second, providing them a living by popularizing Gaya pilgrimage in the Hindu universe.

It is unfortunate that we do not have even scanty documents for understanding the role of such sacred intelligentsia in developing a group of literati (Redfield 1953: 7, 36) as well as in communicating the great traditions to the masses. However, it can be conjectured with a certain amount of confidence that Gaya has been attracting sacred intelligentsia from the time it became universally known in India as the birthplace of Buddhism in the fifth century B.C. Since Gaya was the place where Buddha achieved enlightenment and began his first Buddhistic preaching, there emerged a large group of Buddhist literati, and in successive years several monasteries, temples, railings, etc., were built there (Mitra 1878: 229-48). Gaya attracted pilgrims not only from different parts of India but also from foreign Buddhist countries. Among them, two Chinese travellers, Fa-heien (A.D. 399-414) and Hiuen Tsiang (A.D. 629), visited Gaya during the period of decline of Buddhism and have left the earliest accounts about Gaya as a sacred place of pilgrimage.

A second great member of the sacred intelligentsia, Shankaracharya is said to have visited Gaya during his great religious conquest over Buddhism (Kashyapa 1952; Vidyarthi 1954). He is believed to have had a great part in establishing the importance of Gaya as a place of pilgrimage for shraddha sacrifice. He is also said to have converted the Buddhist monks to the Hindu priesthood and popularized them throughout India under the name of the Gayawal during his tour of religious conquest, popularly known as Shankara Digvijay. Recently a park, along with his image, has been installed in memory of his historic visit to Gaya. The desolate math with hundreds of Sanskrit books also reminds us that Shankara had great influence at Gaya.[1] There are numerous priests and householders who consider themselves to be followers of Shankara.

A third member of the sacred intelligentsia who had tremendous influence on the Gayawal is Madhavacharya[2] who flourished during the twelfth century A.D. The Gayawal caste as a whole is a follower of the Madhava Vaishnava sect, and, as we have noted earlier, the Madhava math is a living religious centre that wields a powerful influence on the Gayawal. It is believed that wherever Madhava went, especially in the south and west

[1] Shankaracharya, who is said to have flourished in the eighth century A.D., toured the whole of India and revived Hinduism after giving the death-blow to Buddhism. About his role at Gaya, Professor Kashyapa (1952 MS) writes: "There is no denying the fact that the present religious role played by Gaya kshetra is associated with the conquest of Shankarcharya over the Buddha's religion which had engulfed the Brahmanism if it was ever famous over here."

[2] R. G. Bhandarkar (1913-58) establishes his date of birth as Saka 1040 and death Saka 1119.

of India, he popularized the efficacy of shraddha and Vishnu at Gaya for earning spiritual merits and salvation. Some educated Gayawal suspect that the Dakhini (South Indian Brahman) first became the spiritual teacher of the Gayawal caste at that time. It is customary for one of the celebrated acharyas of the Madhava sect hailing from South India to reside at Gaya and act as spiritual teacher of the Gayawal.

A fourth outstanding member of the sacred intelligentsia stayed at Gaya and was converted to Vaishnavism there. This was Mahaprobhu Chaitanya (1485-1527). Fortunately, we know in some detail about this great spiritual leader because of an excellent biography which was written by one of his contemporary Bengali devotees (Kaviraja 1582).

Professor Sarkar (1922: xi ; *see* Kaviraja), basing his information on Kaviraja's biography, tells us that during Chaitanya's pilgrimage to Gaya he met Ishwar Puri, a Vaishnava monk of the order of Madhavacharya, evidently the jati-guru of the Gayawal, and accepted him as his spiritual guide. His acceptance of the bhakti cult and abandoning of the yajna cult brought "a complete change over his spirit, his intelligent pride was gone, he became a bhakta (devotee instead of a philosopher) and whatever subject he lectured on, the theme of his discourse was love of Krishna." The great master travelled for six years from Gaya to Banaras, Prayag, Mathura, Jagannath, and many other places of pilgrimage, and wherever he went he created a sensation. Millions of his countrymen began to come to the places where he held sankirtana, forming lines on both sides of the roads to see the great spiritual master.

Chaitanya thus took with him the sacredness of Vishnu at holy Gaya whose sight (darshan) produced such a wonderful change in his sensitive nature (Chariar 1909: 122), and Gaya became more widely known for its sacredness among the millions of followers of Chaitanya. It was hallowed as the place where Mahaprabhu Chaitanya (the great god) was converted to bhakti cult (devotional path) by the great Madhava teacher of the Gayawal. The Chaitanyaite call themselves Madhava Gaudiya and consider themselves a section of Madhavas (Ghurye 1953: 178-79). At Gaya they have a Gaudiya math dedicated to Hari, the eighth incarnation of Vishnu, and it attracts numerous followers of Chaitanya, Madhavacharya, and other types of Krishna worshippers. On the occasion of the birth anniversary of Hari held on Janmastami on the eighth day of the dark half of the month of Bhado, large crowds assemble to offer reverence to the epic god Hari.

Ramananda[3] in . e thirteenth century and Vallabha[4] in the sixteenth century, the other two great spiritual teachers of Vishnavism of North India, are believed to have visited and stayed at Gaya in the course of their extensive religious tours. It is quite likely that they might have talked about the significance of Gaya pilgrimage in the course of these tours.

In a later account, Buchanan (1811-12: 12, 93) refers to several sannyasis (ascetics) whom he met at Gaya. He makes mention of one "Dandi swami who adhered to the rules of Madhava as practised in the South from whence he come and retained all the pride of his country."[5] Evidently, Buchanan is making reference here to the jtai-gurus of the Gayawal who are usually quite orthodox and adhere to all the religious codes of conduct. He also writes about twenty-five other sannyasis who abstained from marriage. He further mentions three orders of Dasnami sannyasi (ascetics of Shankara's order) who act as shrine priests for the Gayeshvari temple. But he fails to give any detailed account about them as he was not allowed to enter into the math of many of these sannyasis. Monier-Williams (1891:88) describes the severe austerities and bodily mortification of Urdhava-bahu (a type of Shaiva ascetic) which he saw in the course of his visit to Gaya.

In recent times, the Gayawal have informed me about the visits of modern sacred intelligentsia like Ramakrishna, Dayananda, Vivekananda, and Guru Govind Singh, whose writings they claim to preserve in their professional record books. Swami Vivekananda (1955:729) also has written about his visit and the antiquity of Gaya. The life-history of one of my Gayawal

[3] Bhandarkar (1913:66-67) has attempted to ascertain the period of the Vaishnava teachers.

[4] See Bhandarkar (1913:77).

[5] The orthodoxy of such Gayawal gurus is reflected in the following incident that Buchanan describes: "When I attempted to enter the door leading into the outer of the house, it was shut in my face."

informants reflects the influence of modern religious movements like Arya Samaj and Brahma Samaj upon his religious thinking, although in the end he accepts his own traditional sanatan dharma (eternal religion) as the best among them.

To summarize, the sacred intelligentsia of one type or another—through their association with the Gayawal, with their sacred presence at Gaya, and with their sacred tours in the different parts of India—have lent purity to the Gayawal way of life, increased the sacredness of Gaya, and popularized the holiness of Gaya throughout the Hindu universe. These spiritual leaders and ascetics working with and through the organized group of priesthood (literati) and through their direct preaching, disputations, discourse, and slogans have kept the current of religion flowing in different parts of India. In addition to being connected with the sacred intelligentsia, the priests are in organizational relationship with the Hindu living in all parts of the Hindu universe. I now turn to the consideration of such a sacred relationship between the priests and their sacrificers or patrons.

PANDA-JAJMAN TYPE

The panda-jajman or priest-sacrificer type refers to the hereditary relationship and mutual obligations that have come to exist between the Gayawal families and many families of clean castes of different parts of India whose members come to Gaya for ancestor worship.[6] Traditionally the whole of India has been pracelled out among the several lineages of the Gayawal, and as a rule the pilgrims start from their houses knowing the names of their respective Gayawal pandas or priests. The caste organization of the Gayawal also provides effective mechanism to identify and regulate the priest-sacrificer system from generation to generation. Such mechanisms are (1) the inheritance of lineage designations and hereditary nicknames, and (2) maintenance and ownership of record books (khata) containing the genealogical details of all the sacrificers (jajman) who fall under Gayawal jurisdiction.

[6] For cross-reference on the jajmani system, see Lewis and Barnouw (1956) and Wiser (1936).

The lineage designation, first, regulates the inheritance of property as well as of the sacrificers in the patrilineal line. Second, such lineage designations (vanshnam) act as professional titles and thus enable the sacrificers to identify their hereditary panda. In case a lineage becomes extinct for want of a male heir, its title as a piece of property is inherited by another collateral relative who, in addition to his own lineage designation, also bears the adopted one. In other words, the lineage designations through which the panda are identified by the jajman theoretically never become extinct, and thus the panda-jajman relationship under such vanshnam is always maintained.

Several cases of combination of two vanshnam have been recorded. When Baddiha vansh was dying out, the only woman survivor adopted her daughter's son who was from Katariyar vansh (lineage). When she died, he became holder of two vanshnam—Katariyar and Baddiha. Such an adoption of two vanshnam gave him customary rights to communicate with all the rightful jajmans falling under the jurisdiction of the two lineages. Another informant of the Mahato lineage inherited the property rights of his wife's father and was known by two professional names—Mahato and Bhatt.

In general and common practice, the patrilineally inherited vanshnam is more important than the adopted one. But when the adopted title comes from a rich lineage or family, the patrilineal vanshnam becomes subservient or in some cases is completely abandoned for professional purposes, as is reflected in the life-history of one of the informants. He originally belonged to the Gayab lineage, but later when he inherited the property of his mother's father, he completely abandoned his patrilineal vanshnam and came to be known by the adopted title, Dhaukri.[7]

As far as my investigation goes, fifty-five such professional titles have been recorded. Among the fifty-five titles, about twenty have either become extinct, or are incipiently associated with other lineage titles, or survive in small dying families.

[7] The study of the Gayawal lineage and clan (gotra) provides an interesting problem of research. It is especially interesting because of their custom of local caste endogamy. For the present purpose, however, I have said enough to bring out the significance of lineage.

The origin of the names of these titles is not known in detail, and the Gayawal did not appear at all enthusiastic in giving me information (if they knew at all) about the significance of these names. However, a detailed list containing the names of these professional titles and their probable explanation, as reported by my informants, has been provided in Appendix II.

These vanshnam or Paddati (names of lineages and families), if considered in broader perspective, can be categorized in several ways (see Table 5). Out of fifty-five vanshnam, fifteen refer to certain religious, social, and political offices of their bearers within the caste group or pilgrimage's organization. Thirteen of them come from the nicknames or other personal characteristics of individuals after which the lineages were named and known. Nine of them are derived from the titles borne by several castes of Brahman varna, while six are after the caste titles borne by Vaishya castes in Bihar. Seven of the vanshnam might be identified with certain villages and regions from where their bearers are believed to have migrated to the city. Some of the titles as a matter of interpretation might belong to more than one category.

The problem is so complex and the data so meager that no satisfactory historical explanation seems possible. In the present state of knowledge, however, three hypothetical explanations might be suggested. First, these titles have been borne by the Gayawal lineage and families in the course of time to distinguish one lineage or family from another. Selection of such names are variously made by the unit concerned. Some took the names from the caste or territorial groups of the sacrificers to which they catered, and some distinguished themselves from other groups by their personal or familial characteristics. The Gayawal, in general, take this view to explain the origin and growth of the professional lineage titles. According to another explanation offered by several citizens, the present titles taken from the different caste titles or village names refer to the original affiliation of the Gayawal. Under the Vaishnava movement and with the rising importance of Gaya as a place of pilgrimage, it is quite likely that they might have migrated or have switched over to the work of priesthood at Gaya, still retaining their original caste or village names.

TABLE 5

CLASSIFICATION OF PROFESSIONAL LINEAGE TITLES OF THE GAYAWAL

Titles of Non-Brahman Castes	Titles of other Brahman Castes	Titles derived from Place Names	Titles after Social and Religious Offices	Titles Derived from Personal Characteristics	Origin Unknown
Ahir	Bhatt	Baddiha	Aginavar	Barik	Buhiya
Beldar	Bithal	Dihaur	Bhaiya	Bhogata	Devnar
Chaudhari	Chaube	Dubhaliya	Chariyari	Gayab	Dheri
Gupta	Gosain	Katariyar	Dhaukreshvari	Golivar	Hal
Mahato	Jhangar	Kohdauri	Dhakuri	Hunda	Polad
Sena	Mishir	Pahari	Garai	Judge	
	Pande	Parvatiya	Gurda	Kari	
	Pathak		Hada	Kharkharka	
	Upadhayay		Kolkat	Kutti	
			Mahata	Meharvar	
			Mauar	Nakphopha	
			Nayak	Pasera	
			Raja	Taiya	
			Sijuar		
			Tatak		

A third explanation, which I suggest, is a combination of both the above-mentioned explanations. In naming their lineage, the Gayawal at first retained their caste and village affiliations through names, and then later, when their lineages split into smaller units and when they felt the necessity of distinguishing one unit or family from another for professional convenience, they possibly picked up other types of names associated with their jajmans or with their own personal and familial characteristics. The second type of naming still continues ; in the memory of my informants, two cases of the acquisition of new titles have occurred. In the first case, the name, Judge, was given to a man noted for his honesty and later his family acquired this title from him. In the other case, the name, Golivar, was given to a man who possessed a gun and was efficient in firing it. His family also got this name and carried it for two generations until later when it was decided by the members of the family to go back to their original title, Gupta.

Whatever may be the historical implications of the vanshnam, its functional and professional importance is evident. It provides a mechanism through which the panda-jajman relationship extending over the whole of the Hindu universe is identified, remembered, and regulated.

The second mechanism that facilitates in establishing the rightful claims of the Gayawal on their jajmans is the record book (khata) in which the names of the jajman and their villages are carefully entered. When a lineage or a joint family of a Gayawal breaks into two or more, the area of jurisdiction as well as the number of patrons are likewise divided by the pages of the khata. When disputes arise over the claim of a pilgrim, these khatas prove a ready reference. In this way, the khata of the Gayawal is their most important property and it enables them to regulate the working of their "sacred estate". In the event of inheritance of the "sacred estate" of some collateral relatives, which actually means the transference of khata from one lineage to another, or in case of partition in a joint family, the members concerned keep at least their rich jajman informed about the changes. This was done in the past by touring in the area of jurisdiction by the Gayawal themselves or by sending their representatives. Now, they also take recourse to writing letters to them. One of the informants took special care to mention about such trips to Bengal after his partition with his father's brother's sons.

In spite of all these arrangements, however, every year some non-committed pilgrims whose jajmani relationship is not identified with any panda come to Gaya. According to one arrangement, such pilgrims are regarded as the jajman of the entire caste and all the sacred and secular services are provided them by a Gayawal organization called Vishnu Ashram (the resort of Vishnu). Profits received from such pilgrims go for the general welfare of the caste. A separate record book is maintained for such pilgrims, and the pilgrim is asked to transfer this temporary arrangement to a panda whom he likes. This is one of the many arrangements made to solve the conflicts that arise among the competing priests over the non-committed pilgrims. In the past, perhaps, it was easier to come to a decision on the question of non-committed pilgrims. But in the present time, as we will notice in the next chapter, all such arrangements for solving the problems arising out of non-committed pilgrims have failed, owing to personal conflicts and other modern developments.

The panda-jajman relationship based upon several obligations primarily finds expression on two occasions: first, when a panda and his party or his representatives make a visit to his jajman; and second, when a jajman and his relatives and attendants come on Gaya pilgrimage to observe shraddha sacrifice or offer special worship at the temple of Vishnupada.

The purposes of a panda in making a visit or sending representatives to the jajmans are manifold: to raise religious consciousness among the jajman for making a pilgrimage to Gaya; to renew relationships with old jajman and receive gifts or raise arrears for land or estate that he might have received in gifts; to approach the rich jajman to ask help in some domestic financial crisis; to recruit new jajmans and to guide all those jajmans who are willing to come on Gaya pilgrimage.

In the past when transportation facilities were limited and impediments in making journeys were many, it required elaborate preparations for a Gayawal to make a visit to the jajmans. A rich panda who made visits only to his wealthy jajmans was always accompanied by a host of attendants, guards, and musicians. He would take with him personal deities (thakurji), whose worship on the way and wherever he stayed would be a special feature. He would also take with him sacred objects like blankets, silken garments, stone and brass images, religious booklets and pictures, and, above all, varieties of sweets as prasad (token of blessings) from the Vishnupada. Such sacred objects were presented to the rich and poor jajmans.

In his visits to his jajmans, the panda would usually stay with a rich jajman who would extend all his hospitality and reverence. Wherever he would stay, religious gatherings would be organized, his thakurji would be elaborately worshipped, devotional songs would be sung, stories from Gaya Mahatmya would be narrated, and prasad brought from Vishnupada would be distributed among the gathering. During his stay, which might last from several weeks to several months, he would be honoured with all the rich food, comforts, and entertainments that his wealthy jajman could afford. When the panda with his party would move on, he would be given a royal send-off with all types of gifts consisting of jewels, clothes, horses, and even servants to assist him during his travels.

Though the panda would be especially inclined to contact rich jajmans during his jajmani yatra (visits to sacrificers), he would never lose sight of communicating with the common jajmans. In addition to his own trips, he would send special groups of his representatives to meet them, to persuade them to make Gaya pilgrimage, and then to escort them safely. For these many purposes he used to have several grades of servants, a travelling staff, and guides.

Such big and small trips were common in the past. Such trips undertaken by the panda and his travelling staff lasted from three to eight months, and he and his staff would return to Gaya with large groups of jajmans as well as gifts from old jajmans. In addition, he would arrange to wait upon the neighbouring highways to contact the pilgrims coming on their own accord.

With the introduction of cheap means of transportation, the trips by the representatives of the Gayawal have become almost out-of-date. They are no longer needed now to escort the pilgrims nor are the pilgrims desirous now of waiting until a large company of the panda's representatives arrives to accompany them. They can easily come to Gaya from any part of India without any transportation difficulties or without any fear of being robbed or harassed on their way. Owing to this development, the work of the panda's representatives has become concentrated on the railway and bus stations in the neighbourhood of Gaya. They also travel in the trains coming to Gaya and sort out the pilgrims belonging to their respective masters.

The panda, however, sometimes makes jajmani yatra for which he has to make very little preparation. Some of the life-histories of the old and young pandas also point out the emergence of a new type of jajmani trip wherein a panda takes along his wife, combines pilgrimages with jajmani trips, or conveniently goes alone from place to place within a few weeks and comes back with whatever gifts he can get from the poor and rich jajmans.

The second type of jajmani obligation occurs when the jajman and his relations arrive in Gaya for the performance of shraddha sacrifice. The panda makes all possible arrangements for his accommodation, cooking, and ritual performances with a feeling of cordiality, familiarity and age-old attachment. The panda tells him about the visits as well as the good qualities of head and heart of the jajman's ancestors who visited Gaya in the past, and how they gave him so much in gift. The jajman, thus, in a homely atmosphere performs all the rituals under the guidance of his hereditary family panda. He is entertained by musical performances for which the Gayawal in general are famous. He attends and participates in religious gathering like sankirtana, katha and other types of devotional recitations. He also may be advised to go to see some religious films that are usually shown in the local cinema houses. In addition to making the rounds of the sacred centres and participating in other secondary performances, some of the jajmans may choose to help in other types of religious activities—construction and repair of temples, feeding of Brahmans and beggars, giving gifts to sadhus and priests, and maintaining or aiding some religious institutions, etc. Such actions are believed to bring additional spiritual merits to the jajman and, moreover, also add to the prestige of his panda. The panda feels pride in those religious acts of special nature which his jajman does at Gaya and in whatever extraordinary gifts he may give to his panda. The Gayawal caste and even the citizens of Gaya long remember the royal visits of the great rajas, maharajas, and princes who made great gifts and held celebrations in the name of their ancestors at Gaya (O'Malley 1906: 68-69). My informants took great pride in making special mention of such royal visits that brought to them good fortune.

Such close and constant contact between the panda and the jajman have influenced the lives of both. The jajmans of the Gayawal come into contact with many other types of priests from other places of pilgrimage, as well as with the local and regional priests. Similarly, a Gayawal, though not always in contact with the same jajman, remains in close association with some jajman throughout the year, and his way of life has been evidently influenced by them. The Gayawal seem to have been especially influenced by the ways of life of the rich jajman. The rich gifts further help them in affording an aristocratic life. In the following chapter, I will examine certain of these modifications in the Gayawal lifeway.

Mixed Jajman-Pauniya Type

This type (master-servant) refers to the semi-hereditary relationship that the Gayawal themselves have entered into with several caste specialists primarily to provide adequate sacred and secular services to their jajman, and also to facilitate the smooth running of their priestly organization. The relationship between these caste specialists and the Gayawal is not merely that of employees and employers. Several socio-economic factors have brought them into closer association, and some of these "employees" have become part of the family organization and, thus, have influenced the Gayawal way of life.

A Gayawal family needs the services of several caste specialists in the organization of the priesthood as well as in the priestly way of life. First, in order to maintain his contacts with his jajmans and receive them at the railway and bus stations, he needs a group of attendants and travelling staff. Again, when these jajmans are housed, he needs several male and maid servants to provide them menial services. Moreover, for his own domestic work and comforts, he requires several attendants.

In order to meet all these requirements, a Gayawal employs several families of servant castes (especially of Kahar and Dhanuk castes). Cash payments are nominal, but these families enjoy many other privileges of free food, free clothes, free housing, special rewards during the celebrations at their master's house or from his jajmans, and financial aid when some celebration of rites takes place at their (servant's) houses. Several families of servant castes become attached to a Gayawal family and continue their relationship with the same family generation after generation. In twenty cases examined, 50 per cent of the families of the servants showed continuous connection with particular Gayawal families for the last four generations; 20 per cent for the last six generations; 10 per cent for eight generations; and another 20 per cent for the last three generations.

The life-histories of the Gayawal are full of examples of intimate types of relationship that they have developed with the servants' families. In general, a Gayawal child is reared by the maid servants; when he grows up he plays with his servants' children; and when he becomes an adult, in some cases, some closer relationship might develop with the girl servants. Concubinage is more or less a recognized institution among the Gayawal, although persons maintaining concubines are usually looked down upon. Such concubines, coming from servant castes, for many practical purposes become part of the family, though they occupy an inferior position both in the family and in the Gayawal caste. In general, the element of servantship has been a powerful influence in the domestic life as well as in the priestly life of the Gayawal.

Second, the acharyas conduct the jajmans to the various sacred centres and guide them in the performances of rituals. They are mostly Brahmans of Sakadvip, Kanauj, Shrotriya, and Maithil castes.[8] Brahmans from different linguistic regions —Marathi, Bengali, Tamil—also live in the neighbourhood of Vishnupada and are employed by those Gayawal who specialize in jajman from these linguistic areas.

Some Gayawal who receive many pilgrims employ three to ten acharyas; on the other hand, one acharya may serve two to three Gayawal families who receive fewer pilgrims. During the pitripaksha fair the Gayawal families employ many acharyas temporarily.

The relationship of the acharya with the Gayawal has become more or less contractual. The acharya employed on a permanent basis receives regular salary, though free clothes and occasional monetary rewards are also given. The families of the acharyas are usually on a formal relationship with their

[8] Hamilton Buchanan (1811-12: 317-21, 329) gives a brief description of such Brahman castes in his Patna-Gaya Report.

1. The famous Temple of Vishnupada which attracts pilgrims from all the Hindu world

2. The image of Lord Buddha in the famous Buddha Gaya temple

3. Shraddha ritual in action. With the sacrificers are seated the ritualist and the Gayawal Panda

4. On the Vishnupada Ghat of the Phalgu the *nai* (barber) is seen shaving the head of the Shraddha sacrificers

5. The image of Goddess Bageshwari

6. The bathing ghat on the Phalgu near the Vishnupada Temple

7. Sri Madhawacharya, the sacred intellectual, the *Jati guru* of the Gayawal. He lives near Vishnupada Temple

8. A pilgrim from Darjeeling is seen near Vishnupada Temple

9. The temple of rock-shrine of Gaya Asur has recently been renovated by one Motilal of Kanpur in 1953

10. The Bodhi Drum in the background of which is the famous temple of Buddha Gaya which is visited by the Buddhists of the world

masters' families, but there is more frequent social intercourse with them than with other families in the neighbourhood. Exchange of visits, gifts, invitations, and mutual help is usual on the family level. The acharya continues to serve the same master for his whole life, and there are even cases in which several generations of an acharya family serve the same master. But the element of hereditary service is not so strong with the acharyas as it is with the menial servants. Cases of frequent change in masters are not uncommon. The acharyas are also paid by the Gayawal for specific services rendered to their jajman.

Third, the munshiji, who belongs to Kayastha caste, maintains the Gayawal's khata (record book) and does other clerical jobs that may be needed for domestic and professional purposes. In case of disputes among the Gayawal over the claims of a pilgrim, he helps his own Gayawal master with ready reference. I was told that the entries of genealogical names are so complete and comprehensive that the khata has sometimes been required in court in order to establish rightful descent.

A munshiji works with a Gayawal family on a salary basis, but he enjoys many other benefits from a rich Gayawal family. I met several such munshijis who have been serving the same master whom their fathers and grandfathers had served. In case his master becomes poor or is poor, he takes up the work of other Gayawal families with whom his original master was on good terms.

Fourth, the pauniya class includes the Nai (barber), Mali (florist), Kumhar (potter), and Pindabechva (rice-ball seller). Pauniya means "one who receives", and such caste specialists provide service for annual payment along with special payments to be made on the occasion of festivals, *rites de passage,* and the annual pitripaksha fair. However, at the present time, instead of annual payment, piece work payment is also made by the Gayawal. One or two families of such specialist caste provide service to a group of Gayawal families. These caste specialists render services both to the Gayawal and to their jajmans who come to observe shraddha and require their services. Usually for both the services (rendered to the Gayawal as well as to his jajmans), payment is made by the Gayawal. The jajman, however, may make some present to a pauniya, especially the Nai caste who performs the ritual shaving. When a Gayawal family needs more services than its pauniya can supply, the pauniya is asked to make further provision for rendering service. Such a situation is usually encountered in the case of the Nai caste who are required in large numbers for the ritual shaving of the thousands of shraddha sacrificers during the pitripaksha fair. On such an occasion, the family barbers bring their distant relatives to work for them. The pauniyas thus provide service more or less on the basis of hereditary relationship.

Gayawal-Dhami Type

The Gayawal also maintain professional relationships with another caste of priests, usually called the Dhami or the Dhamin. The Dhami are guardians of the two sacred clusters—Ramshila and Pretashila hills—where shraddha sacrificers are escorted by the acharyas to make offerings in the name of Yama, his infernal dogs, and several gods and goddesses of ghosts and spirits. At these places, rituals are conducted by the Dhami who are entitled to three-quarters of the gifts that are made at these two sacred centres. The remaining share of one-quarter goes to the Gayawal panda. Thus, the relationship between these two priestly groups is one of partnership.

The Dhami comprise a community of about twenty-seven families who live in the rural setting of the foothill zones of Pretashila. Their locality, about five miles north of the city of Gaya, is joined by a metalled road. On the whole, they are an isolated, poor, and simple group of priests who are oriented to the rural way of life. As they are associated with shrines devoted to ghosts and spirits, they call themselves "Pretiya Brahman", or Brahmans associated with ghosts. However, I was told that the Dhami fall far short of what is expected of Brahman priests. Meat, liquor, palm beverage (toddy) are not tabooed to them. They are not so particular about their daily ritual bath, morning worship, and rules of commensality as I have noted in the case of the Gayawal. Cases of widow remarriage also have been reported. Such customs are almost unknown among the high castes in India.

It is generally believed by the Gayawal and the local citizens that the Dhami are non-Brahmanical priests. Some citizens identify them with the florist caste that inhabits a locality of Gaya named after the Dhami (Dhami Tola). Buchanan (1811-12: 323, 335) identifies the Dhami with the Dhanuk, low caste agriculturists, and suspects the present Dhami were their priests in ancient times. Moreover, their exclusive right to officiate over ghostly shrines and rituals further lends support to the view that the Dhami represent a survival of an ancient priesthood of a non-Brahmanical order (Buchanan 1811-12: 129-31; O'Malley 1906: 71-72).

Unfortunately, there is no way of knowing how this compromise between the Brahmanical and the non-Brahmnical priesthood evolved and came to be linked within the single ritual of Gaya shraddha. O'Malley considers it an old compromise between the more orthodox Brahmanical priesthood and the tribal priesthood that officiated at rites of aboriginal demonolatry practised on the jungle-clad hills. Taking a comparative and middle-range historical level, I will hypothesize that the two orders of priesthood represent two levels of development of the same complex. The Gayawal, owing to their shrewd art of priestcraft, resources, and connection with the sacred intelligentsia, etc., could make successful headway, while the Dhami, being isolated, poor, and simple, were left behind and later were consoled by their successful counterparts with the inclusion of their hill-shrine in the general routine of sharadha sacrifice. The Dhami, though without much result, still continue to raise jajmans, maintain khata, and carry on an independent priestly profession. In such efforts they come into conflict with the Gayawal, and several cases to this effect have been instituted in the local courts. To the thousands of pilgrims, however, who come here to offer shraddha, the two priesthoods are of equal importance in their respective contexts. Traditions have established that the Dhami should be revered and given gifts at the hill-shrines, and to many they are as important and as sacred as the Gayawal. They are an inseparable part of the same ritual complex.

PUJARI-DARSHANIYA TYPE

In the preceding four sections, we noted the structural relationship of the Gayawal with the outside world in respect to their roles as sharaddha priests. In addition to this status as shraddha priests, the Gayawal are also shrine priests. The pujari-darshaniya type refers to the relationship that a Gayawal, as a shrine priest, enters into with those local and regional worshippers who make ritual visits to a sacred centre at which he officiates.

The main temple over which the Gayawal officiate and which is largely attended by the worshippers is that of Vishnupada. Every Gayawal enjoys equal rights in entertaining worshippers and in receiving gifts from them during the daytime. In the evening, however, the right is restricted to the Gayawal of Bhaiya lineage. A representative of every family of this lineage, by rotation, goes to the temple in the evening, finances the special evening worship, and is entitled to receive all the gifts that are made there by the worshippers during his presence in the temple.

During the daytime, those Gayawal who want to escort visitors to the Vishnupada temple (which entitles them to receive the offerings made by the visitors at the shrine) assemble at the raised platform (darvani) at the gate of the temple. Here the Gayawal shrine priests watch for the arrival of the visitors. The priest who is first to see a visitor and prompt enough to declare his identity according to his dress or other such characteristics is entitled to serve as his shrine priest. At times, disputes and conflicts follow among the competing shrine priests on the issue of establishing rightful claims over a worshipper.

Ideally, the Gayawal in general do not like this job of shrine priesthood. Shrine priesthood is characterized by poor income, scanty gifts, continuous waiting, and undesirable competition. Moreover, the Gayawal, especially in the past, were so well off as shraddha priests that they cared very little for their rights as shrine priests. Only boys and a few adults of poor families attended to this job. Due to economic depression, however, the temple has attracted large crowds of competing Gayawal youths.

For the Gayawal boys, the temple provides a place for apprenticeship in the profession of priestcraft. Every day a Gayawal boy gets up early in the morning, takes his bath, decorates his forehead with sandal paste, puts on the typical priestly dress, and hurries up to the temple to hunt up darshaniya to get gifts. His attraction to the sacred temple is always greater than his attraction to school. My census shows that in 1953, out of 321 Gayawal of school-going age, only eighty boys had got admission into the schools, and very few of them attended regularly. Most of their time was spent at the temples watching and waiting for darshaniyas with a view to receiving some money.

The Gayawal shrine priests come into situational contact with more than 200 darshaniyas every day. On special sacred days and on the occasion of certain sacred fairs or an eclipse, the number of darshaniya goes up to several thousands.

To summarize, in the last two chapters I have examined some important features of sacred specialists with particular reference to the Gayawal high priests. First, the various types of sacred specialists that inhabit a place of pilgrimage were enumerated; next, the orthodox way of life of the Gayawal priestly specialist was described. Second, those elements of the social organization of the Gayawal sacred specialists that put them in structural relationship with other sacred specialists of Gaya, on the one hand, and with the Hindu world, on the other, were considered. In the next chapter, I will turn to the consideration of the Gayawal style of life in so far as it has been modified by its contacts with the lesser communities of India as well as with Western elements of culture.

CHAPTER V

THE SACRED SPECIALISTS: HETEROGENEITY AND PHASES OF CHANGE

In the preceding two chapters on the sacred specialists, a static, simplified, and ideal-oriented account of the unity and extensions of the Gayawal was attempted. Essentially, they give us an insight into the ideal values, style of life, and isolable elements of the Gayawal considered as a single caste unit. The present chapter promises an analysis of the Gayawal way of life in all its heterogeneity and dynamics. It proposes to examine the impact of "extensions" as well as of modernizing factors on the contemporary Gayawal society. On a diachronic level, it will be hypothesized that the Gayawal have passed through several cultural cycles in the past and have absorbed within its caste organization and way of life various heterogeneous elements which are essentially non-priestly in nature.

In the course of the ethnographic assessment of the Gayawal, I encountered several puzzling problems. On the one hand, many of my Gayawal informants give me a picture of a Gayawal way of life that is highly puritanical and orthodox, as described in Chapter III. In my own observation as well, I met a few persons and families who can approximate to that description in the sense of their ritualistic and priestly performances, though, being part of the caste, their social relations with the others have been a little strained. In order to distinguish this kind of Gayawal from the rest of the caste, I call them "sanskritic priests", in so far as they tend to observe the priestly pattern of life described in many of the sanskritic texts like the Manu Smriti and the Vishnu Sutra. Concentrating on their daily routine as well as on the general pattern of leisure, I find such sanskritic priests mainly devoted to religious acts and to practising high morals in all that they do.[1]

[1] The Buddhist text, the Dhammapada, translated by S. Radhakrishnan from the original Pali, devotes a full chapter (XXVI) to the characteristics of a Brahman. The term "Brahman" of the Veda is accepted by the Buddhists as a term for saint or one who has attained final sanctification.

The kind of priest described in the second section, in contrast to the first, leads a luxurious life, possesses a large number of attendants, and instead of engaging in religious acts spends most of his time in aristocratic pastimes like wrestling, music, bird-keeping, and sometimes entertaining prostitutes and concubines. Though his primary source of livelihood continues to be the priesthood (whose duties are mainly looked after by his servants), he also owns land (before the Zamindari Abolition Acts) from which he receives income and which is usually looked after by the jajmans who donated it. Lazy, aristocratic, exploitative, such priestly nobles, for our present purposes, might be termed "feudalistic priests".[2]

The third kind of priests that predominates in the present population maintains some elements of the sankritic and feudalistic priesthood but is mainly characterized by economic depression, competition, lip-service to priestly decorum, and a close association with the so-called "pilgrim hunters" who carry on the ceremonial trade. In other words, this type of priest has more or less ceased to live up to his traditional moral standards,[3] and is marked by economic, demographic, and spiritual degeneration. I propose to term such a large section of priests "proletarian priests".[4]

[2] In the European history, the term feudalism or feudal systems has been used profusely to indicate among many things a system of agrarian economy and land ownership. In the present context, this term has been used to denote a way of life, and refers to the aristocratic patterning of the life-ways of the priestly caste. In the absence of some other more suitable term, I find this term helpful.

[3] For a definition of 'moral order' which has been helpful in the present analysis, see Robert Redfield's *The Primitive World and Its Transformations* (1953: 20-21, 24).

[4] In the use of the term, 'Proletariat', for indicating the phase of disintegration of the Gayawal priesthood, I have been influenced by Arnold Toynbee. For definition and extensive use of this term, see Arnold J. Toynbee, *A Study of History*, abridgement of Volumes I-VI by Somervell (New York and London: Oxford University Press, 1947), pp. 11 fn., 377, 375-408. Also abridgement of Volume VII-X by Somervell (New York and London: Oxford University Press, 1957), pp. 1, 221. Redfield also finds the use of the term 'proletariat', very helpful in describing the heterogeneous characteristic of cities. See his *Primitive World and Its Transformation* (Cornell University, Ithaca, 1955), pp. 49, 81.

Thus, I have isolated three subcultural divisions—the sanskritic, feudalistic, and proletarian—among the Gayawal priests primarily on the basis of observation and interviews. These three types can be compared with what all the Gayawal at the present time believe to be their traditional or ideal way of life (Chapter III). From this comparison, the presently existing discrepancies between ideal and actual ways may be examined. These three subcultures among the Gayawal also seem to characterize three probable phases of development through time. The earliest is the sanskritic phase ; it is followed by the feudalistic or intermediate phase, and then by the proletarian or present phase. From a long-range historical perspective, a still earlier or formative phase can be conjectured—a phase in which the Gayawal would have been termed "folk priests". A present parallel might be seen in the Dhami priesthood which has been described in the preceding chapter. A suggestion of this phase is traceable today in the folk belief held by the Gayawal concerning ghosts, shamans (ojha), etc.

All four of these characterizations of the Gayawal priesthood—folk, sanskritic, feudalistic, and proletarian—postulated above as sequential phases, continue to exist among the Gayawal today, three of them as subcultures. Since all coexist in the present, one may assume that each earlier variety of priesthood persisted alongside of each later type without replacing it entirely.

The Gayawal in History

Unfortunately, there is a scarcity of historical evidence for documenting each of the four dominant elements of the Gayawal priesthood in the various phases of history. However, some handbooks and survey records of the British period tell us how the four elements have combined to make the contemporary Gayawal way of life. Buchanan (1811-12: 106), writing in the early nineteenth century, mainly recognized the folk characteristics of the Gayawal. In general, he notes the lack of learning and severity of asceticism in their conduct, and at another place he notes some of the sanskritic characteristics of some Gayawal (1811-12: 100). He does not make any specific reference to the feudalistic elements among the Gayawal of this time. Writing about one hundred years after Buchanan, Crooke (1907: 98) primarily emphasizes certain feudalistic elements among the Gayawal. O'Malley (1901, 1906), who seems to have firsthand knowledge of this caste, notes both the feudalistic and sanskritic elements of the Gayawal lifeway. In view of the contrast in the lifeway of the two orders of shraddha priesthood, the Gayawal and the Dhami, he calls the former "Brahmanical" (sanskritic) and the latter "aboriginal" (folk) priests (1901: 10-20 ; 1906: 71-72). All these sporadic statements about the Gayawal, though inadequate in terms of any conclusive significance, help us in understanding the heterogeneity of the Gayawal lifeway in the last century.

From the viewpoint of long-range historical depth, the heterogeneity of the Gayawal caste is again reflected in the conflicting theories regarding the genesis or origin of the present caste. Some scholars[5] (Buchanan 1811-12: 101, 322) suspect that the Gayawal, like the Dhami, are remnants of some ancient tribal priesthood, who have taken the title of Brahman and have "sanskritized" their ways of life. Other scholars (Kashyapa 1952 ; Mitra 1878: 10) have attempted to prove that the name, Gayawal, was given by Shankaracharya to those Buddhist monks who accepted Hinduism and adopted the profession of shraddha priesthood under the persuasion of Shankaracharya. Then, again, some citizens and authors, including the Gayawal scholars (Lal 1953: 21-22 ; Gurda n.d. 102-104), point out the resettlement of the Gayawal families at the present fortified locality in the late seventeenth century. To many citizens, this was the final orthodox recognition of the Gayawal caste. Some of these arguments regarding the theories of the origin of the Gayawal caste have been published by me elsewhere (Vidyarthi 1954), and I am convinced that they are inadequate for any decisive conclusion about the genesis of the Gayawal caste.

These evidences, however, decidedly reflect the heterogeneous and flexible character of the Gayawal priestly group. Though the

[5] Professor Nand Lal Chatterji, a social historian from Lucknow University, also expressed similar views in commenting on a paper of the author which was read under his presidentship. Partial reporting appeared in the Annual Report of the Anthropology Club, Lucknow University, 1953, as well as in *Spark*, Patna, Dec. 15, 1952.

contemporary Gayawal share the same mythology, practise local endogamy, believe in the orthodox way of life, and consider themselves as belonging to a single caste group, it seems, in the past, they passed through many diverse stages, and many new groups of persons belonging to other castes might have joined this professional group of priests. The fact that the Gayawal professional titles are derived from different caste groups and villages, as described in Chapter IV, might also be brought to bear upon the multiple origin of the present Gayawal. However, these historical problems need to be studied in all their historical complexity. It is sufficient here to say that some of these historical evidences indicate the heterogeneous composition of the contemporary Gayawal caste. Though the Gayawal of today are a well-organised caste, there are evidences to show that several other groups from time to time joined the profession of priestcraft and were possibly absorbed into the caste organization of the Gayawal.

The Feudalistic Phase

With this historical background, I turn again to my enthnographic data, life-history materials, and other such data that can tell me something specifically about the phases of change among the Gayawal. They can help me in understanding the last two phases—the feudalistic and the proletarian—which occurred during the last 150 years. The feudalistic phase seems to have spanned the years between 1800 and 1900, while the proletarian phase. the present one, might have begun after 1920 when the Bihar and Orissa Pilgrim Act of 1920 was passed and the effects of the world war and national movements were keenly felt in India. The feudalistic phase was marked by an increase in the number of pilgrims, bringing more frequent contacts between the Gayawal and their jajman as well as an increase in gifts. The accumulation of wealth and the consequent feudalization of the lifeway of the Gayawal can be explained under two heads: legal security and improvement in transportation facilities.

Legal security included the provisions of protection to the pilgrims and the efforts to terminate the exploitation which they had been suffering. Provisions for this security were embodied in the new regulations sponsored by Mr. Law, collector of Gaya district, at the close of the eigteenth century. According to these regulations, all the custom houses erected by landholders or petty government officials to extort money and harass the pilgrims at various places were abolished. Special officers were appointed to see that the pilgrims reached Gaya safely without harassment on their way. In order to regulate the visits of the pilgrims and to increase the resources of revenue to the government for combating the existing exploitation, a licence fee varying from Rs. 2 to Rs. 14 was prescribed for each pilgrim (Buchanan 1811-12: 103-104).

During the following century, the East India Company and later the British government made considerable improvements in transportation in many parts of India. Existing roads were repaired and improved, new interprovincial roads were constructed, rivers were bridged, river steamers were launched, and a network of railways was developed (Thorner 1950; Sanyal 1930). Gaya was especially favoured by its location on the Grand Trunk Road (thirteen miles from Gaya) which runs from Calcutta to Delhi and is joined by many other highways along its way. The Patna-Gaya road was improved, and through it Gaya was connected with water transportation on the Ganges. Railways from all parts of India converge at Gaya, and it has earned the reputation of being an important railway junction for many lines.

TABLE 6

RISE IN NUMBER OF PILGRIMS DURING THE FEUDALISTIC PHASE

Year	Pilgrims	Source	Remark
1798	17,670	O'Malley (1906: 68)	Licence Records
1805	31,114	O'Malley (1906: 68)	Licence Records
1811	100,000	Buchanan (1811-12: 106)	Licence Records
1906	300,000	O'Malley (1906: 66)	Approximate Estimate

With the increase in security and facilities for movement, the number of pilgrims continued to grow. The poor and the rich both began to come on Gaya pilgrimage in larger numbers. The increasing number of pilgrims can be best understood from Table 6.

While the number of pilgrims continued to increase, the government did not take any steps to curtail the sacred and secular roles of the Gayawal in dealing with the pilgrims. The Gayawal had a free hand in accommodating their pilgrims, in conducting them to different sacred centres, and in receiving from them as much in the way of gifts as they could. The monopolistic status of the Gayawal left them free to extort wealth either through persuasion or through compulsion. Whatever the mechanism, the Gayawal continued to receive fortunes from their rich jajmans and substantial gifts even from the poor ones. Buchanan (1811-12: 104) writes how the Marathas and the Bengalis, who were then the most numerous, would give them all types of gifts. He tells us:

> The Bengalese, in fact, give chiefly grains, brass vessels, silver coins, and clothes ; but sometimes they present cows. . . . The Mahrattas give money, jewels, plates, fine clothes, elephants and horses. The Bengalese who worship at forty-five places usually spend from 40 to 200 rs. ; some, however, spend as much as 500 rs. and some few great men have gone so far as 5000 rs. Almost all the Mahrattas worship at the forty-five places and several even give 5000 rs. while great chiefs expend 40 or even 50 thousand rupees. These expenses are exclusive of the charges of travelling, and of what is exacted by numberless solicitations to which the pilgrims are exposed.

Writing at the beginning of the twentieth century, O'Malley (1901: 15) makes similar statements about the income of the Gayawal:

> The rich pilgrims voluntarily give large sums. The pranami and gifts given are not only in cash. Landed property, jewels, elephants, motor cars, and other valuables are freely given, as freely received. One of the Peshwas of Poona is

said to have given a lakh of rupees in fees alone. Randhir Singh of Kashmir, it is said, gave presents in cash, ornaments and valuables to the value of three to four lakhs.

These concise statements regarding the number of pilgrims entertained and the amount of gifts received by the Gayawal give us a clue for understanding the factors that led to the feudalization of the Gayawal way of life. With all these sources of wealth, they rose to a position of affluence. From their rich jajmans they received not only wealth but also models of the aristocratic life that could be led by the use of wealth. The wealthy Gayawal way of life was patterned in part on the way of life of the landed nobility, with adaptations of course to the distinctive position of the Gayawal as priests.

During the feudalistic phase, the Gayawal put up palatial buildings not only for their own residences but also for accommodating their jajmans, and the employees that they needed in their service as well as in the service of their jajmans. They equipped their houses with luxurious and precious goods like wooden beds (palang), large mirrors, carpets, costly untensils made of gold and silver, embroidered clothes, ornaments, etc. Their food was very expensive and was cooked by Marathi Brahman matrons ; their clothes were gorgeous and especially meant for meeting royal patrons and English officials. For their transportation all the families are reported to have had carriage drawn by several horses and palanquin carried by bearers. A few families owned elephants, and in later periods cars were also owned by some Gayawal.

For their personal comforts as well as for doing sacred and secular duties for the jajmans, they maintained a host of attendants and representatives, both Brahman and non-Brahman. As the number of jajmans increased, the Gayawal employed other secondary priests to conduct their jajmans to the different sacred centres ; they accompanied a few wealthy patrons in person. In the course of time they became completely out of touch with the details of shraddha rituals, and it became institutionalized for the secondary priests to guide pilgrims in these matters. Ultimately, the role of the Gayawal was merely to get his feet worshipped at the beginning of the ritual and then, upon declaring the sacrifice to have been duly performed, to receive the gifts at the end. In sacred matters as well as in secular matters the servants became an important factor both as regards the organization of the "sacred estate" of the Gayawal as well as in domestic affairs. In addition, the Gayawal recruited guards and wrestlers for personal decorum, the safety of their property, as well as in dealing with the pilgrims. In essence, they became the functionless but all powerful heads of the "sacred estate" that were run by their deputies and representatives. The name, gaddi (throne), was given to distinguish their status, the areas from which they were entitled to receive pilgrims were named riyasat (estate), and the total number of jajmans that they received every year was called fasal (harvest). In other words, they borrowed certain feudalistic terms to define their priestly status.

With these "sacred estates" which brought plenty of sacred harvests, the Gayawal began to raise the status of their sacred throne by earning royal titles like Rai Bahadur, by accepting honorary posts of magistrates and jurors, and by participating in and making financial contributions to official functions. Their ancestors in particular and other caste members in general still remember the names of five Gayawal who were given royal titles, two who were appointed honorary magistrates, and many persons who were invited to serve as jurors. Many of the Gayawal who were invited and participated in the durbar celebrations held in honour of George V in the year 1911 felt pride in narrating their experiences to me. The Gayawal still preserve numerous pictures of their ancestors taken in company of well-known officials, rich patrons, or with great musicians and wrestlers that they used to hire from all parts of India.

Many Gayawal tried to raise their position by maintaining local clubs known as baithaka. They invited and maintained wrestlers, prostitutes, and musicians of repute to entertain visitors at these clubs and thus distinguished themselves among their neighbours and caste groups. Those persons running and financing a baithaka were called sardar of the baithaka. Being a sardar (leader) of a baithaka brought one special status and prestige which was recoguized by the Gayawal living in the locality in particular and by the Gayawal caste group in general. Nobody could give me the total number of such baithaka, but I was shown the ruins of buildings of three baithaka, and the names of five other baithaka were given to me by my old informants. Every male Gayawal was a regular member of one baithaka or another, and he used to attend many other baithaka on the occasion of special performances at these places.

These baithaka were centres where the Gayawal used to practise music, wrestling, or both. The Gayawal today still fondly remember the names of Gayawal instrumental musicians and classical singers who earned countrywide reputation for their performances. Moreover, such Gayawal artistes used to invite musicians and wrestlers to give performances as well as to train the Gayawal youth in their respective fields of specialization. Many of them settled down at Gaya under Gayawal patronage and their sons and grandsons still maintain their heritage of musical and wrestling performances. Dancing girls were also hired in some of the baithaka, and the Gayawal used to spend sleepless nights in "nach-watching, pan-chewing, and ganja-smoking", as O'Malley put it (1901: 16; also Crooke 1907: 98). In addition to these pastimes which kept them busy day and night, some of the Gayawal also borrowed the aristocratic habit of birdkeeping from the rich Muslims. Most of the above-mentioned expensive pastimes have seen their day among the present Gayawal, and radio is finding wide acceptance as a means of spending the leisure hours.

In their personal religious life, although the Gayawal maintained the rules of commensality and ritual baths, they were quite unmindful about their daily worship, their ritual visits to temples or domestic shrines, or about the observance of sacred fasts or calendaric worship. On the whole, they became quite unconcerned about the sanskritic rules prescribed for a Brahman. However, as far as my information goes, they abstained from eating meat and drinking liqour. Marijuana, drunk as bhang and smoked as ganja, were good substitute for the latter.

During this phase, it appears, concubines became a recognized institution and cases of sexual laxity and prostitution were not uncommon. One comes across many persons born of such unholy alliances. Family ceremonies such as marriage and the sacred thread sacrament became more ostentatious, showy, and expensive, rather than simple and solemn as before. In marriage, expenses ranged from Rs. 20,000 to Rs. 50,000 and similar expenses were incurred in the observance of funeral rites and shraddha sacrifice of their relatives.

I do not have much information about the activities of the Gayawal women during the feudalistic phase. Crooke (1907 : 98) found them occupied in preparing betel for chewing and doing trivial household chores ; the heaviest task, cooking, was left to the Marathi women who were found there in large numbers.[6] Nursing of the babies, as we have noted earlier and as it is reflected in the biographies, was entrusted mainly to the maid-servants. In several cases, they also suckled the children. The Gayawal women observed strict purdah, and except for visits to their neighbouring relatives, they had to keep themselves busy within their four walls in idle gossip or domestic squabbles. Their constant companions were the other female members of the household as well as male and maid servants, while their men folk were mostly busy in their baithaka. In general, being a part of the leisure class, the women, like the men, used to spend their time in unproductive and idle ways.

Proletarian Phase

The proletarian phase among the Gayawal marks its beginning in 1920 and is mainly characterized by economic depression and social disintegration. Such a transformation from a feudalistic to a proletarian way of life can be explained in terms of many developments both within the caste organization and within its extensions in the Hindu universe. These two sets of developments are so closely interdependent that they need to be considered in unison.

On the concrete level, I notice that the Gayawal are experincing hard times mainly because the number of pilgrims has gone down, those pilgrims who do come bring little gifts, and the gifts that are received, in turn, are distributed among many parties. In order to get a closer view of the whole situation and

[6] Crooke does not make any reference to the caste of Marathi women employed by the Gayawal for cooking. In view of the rules of commensality, it can be safely conjectured that such women were Brahman for kachcha cooking, and of some other clean caste for pakka cooking. I could not inquire about this point when I was in the field.

to analyze the matter further, some statistical observations may be helpful here.

Though it is very difficult to find out the number of pilgrims that visit Gaya, on the basis of figures collected by the Lodging House Committee during the last seven years, the average number of pilgrims per year varies from 50,000 to 80,000.[7] The annual fluctuation can be easily accounted for by the famines, droughts, and floods that sometimes hamper the visits of the pilgrims from an area. If we compare these figures with those of the late nineteenth and twentieth centuries, as given in Table 6, they fall short by more than two-thirds.

The decrease in the amount of gifts is all the more striking. Ordinarily, a priest of the sacred ground receives between Rs. 10 and Rs. 30 as his completion gift. In some cases, the amount may rise to Rs. 100, and in cases of princes and rajas it may go still higher. But such cases have become fewer, and the pandas now have to mainly depend upon commonplace jajmans. Those precious gifts they used to receive at the time of Buchanan (nineteenth century) and O'Malley (early twentieth century) are no longer realisable.

Even the little that a Gayawal does receive in the way of gifts does not go entirely to him. It is usually divided among the acharya, the rozgariya,[8] and the munshiji ; a part of it also goes to the government for procuring a house licence to accommodate the pilgrims. A typical case (see Table 7) copied from the record book of one of my Gayawal informants gives an idea of the partnership involved in the suphal gift if the pilgrim has come through a rozgariya. It shows that barely 20 per cent of the suphal gift is left to the Gayawal, while the major portion is taken away by the rozgariya and the government tax.

Returning to our original argument, I find that the number of pilgirms has dwindled, the amount of gifts has gone down, and several secular intermediaries have developed to share even the little gifts that the Gayawal receive. We also note that the

[7] The figures recorded by the Lodging House Committee do not cover such pilgrims who come by buses and other conveyances. Their figures are based on the issuage of railway tickets only ; hence they are approximate and low.

[8] Rozgariya means one who works for his livelihood, traders or wage earners. The Gayawal also call them dalal or touts.

decrease in the number of pilgrims is not striking as the decrease in the quantity of gifts and the breaking up of the monopolistic roles of the Gayawal in dealing with the pilgrims. I now turn to examine the factors and forces that have brought about all these changes.

TABLE 7

PARTNERSHIP IN THE SUPHAL GIFTS

Income		*Expenditure*	
Item	*Amount*	*Item*	*Amount*
	Rs. As. P.		Rs. As. P.
Charan Puja ...	... 1 0 0	Rozgariya ...	... 13 0 0
Suphal Gifts ...	... 25 0 0	Railway Fare for Rozgariya ...	... 3 0 0
Pinda Expenses ...	... 4 6 0	Shrine Priest ...	... 0 10 0
Total	... 30 6 0	Lodging House Tax ...	... 3 0 0
		Reward to Rozgariya ...	... 1 0 0
		Pinda Expenses ...	... 4 6 0
		Total	... 25 0 0

Proceeding historically, the beginning of the proletarian phase marked the decline in the number of pilgrims owing to several national and international factors. This period in Indian history is importantly marked by a series of civil disobedience movements and communal riots of large magnitude. Moreover, the impact of the world wars further added to the insecurity, economic crisis, and transportation bottlenecks in India.

Along with independence in the year 1947 came two important events that further hampered the economy of the Gayawal. The first was the partition of India, and the second was the integration of the princely states and the abolition of the zamindari system. Prior to the partition, pilgrims from East Bengal on the one side and West Punjab, Sind, and the Northwest Frontier Provinces on the other used to come in large numbers. Many Gayawal priests used to visit their jajmans in these areas, and some of the Gayawal families depended largely upon them for their livelihood. But owing to the obvious problems of refugees, loss of property and life, the "sacred estates" of the Gayawal in these areas were destroyed. Their approximate assessment indicates that in the year 1952, only twenty-five pilgrims came from West Pakistan instead of 2,000 as in former years, and only 300 East Bengal pilgrims visited Gaya while in pre-partition times the number usually came to 2,500.

The abolition of zamindari in the various states and the acquisition of the princely states that followed independence were further blows to the feudal economy of the Gayawal. It was brought out earlier that the Gayawal were very handsomely paid by rich patrons who did not hesitate to make all types of valuable gifts to them in the name of their ancestors to whom they felt so much obliged. Such payments were made not only at the time of Gaya shraddha but also on the occasion of their visits to the Gayawal, and, in some cases, as regular presents. Now, however, with their property gone and the imposition of Death Duty Acts, the jajmans cannot think of a costly pilgrimage for their ancestors, and this has very adversely affected the entire socio-economic organization of the Gayawal.

Besides these specific causes, there are several other factors which have brought about a change in the attitude of the people towards ancestor worship in general, and giving of gifts to the priests in particular. The breaking up of the joint family, the increase in modern needs and aspirations, and scientific and secular education, village uplift programme, etc., have all tended to develop a different state of mind, a new consciousness among the educated Hindus. They have begun to think it somewhat superfluous to spend money in "the name of the dead and gone" and completely unprofitable to give all types of gifts to the "greedy and characterless" priests. A sense of secularization and commercialization appears to have entered into their reasoning, and they have become doubtful about some aspects of the shraddha sacrifice, if not about the whole belief in the transmigration of the soul. Yet, under the pressure of the old customs and traditions and with mixed feelings of awe and reverence, many persons come to observe Gaya shraddha while at the same time they are loath to give any but the minimum fees to the Gayawal. The Gayawal no longer have the freedom to press their jajmans for more and more gifts, as several secular agencies are operating around them to help the pilgrims in case of any harassment.

In addition to these external factors which have forced the Gayawal into the phase of proletarianization, there are several forces and factors operating at Gaya and among the Gayawal themselves that need our consideration. We have noted how the Gayawal during the feudalistic phase became unmindful of their priestly responsibilities and left all the sacred and secular work to their servants and representatives. Moreover, owing to their monopolistic roles in dealing with the jajmans, they accommodated them in crowds in old, unhygienic houses, thus abetting epidemics like cholera, small pox, and the plague, which became usual features at Gaya during the pitripaksha fair. In the first decade of the present century a vehement form of plague and cholera took a heavy toll of lives. The population of the city went down by twenty thousand between 1901 and 1911 (India 1953: 18).

In view of these developments within the Gayawal caste, the housing conditions of the pilgrims, the epidemics etc., a great need was felt for the active participation of official and non-official organizations. In spite of the vehement opposition of the Gayawal, the government enacted the Bihar and Orissa Places of Pilgrimage Act of 1920 which curtailed the monopolistic role of the Gayawal in dealing with the pilgrims. Several provisions for the improvement of the pilgrimage and the accommodation of the pilgrims were made. Among other things, the pilgrims were to be accommodated only in licensed houses, duly inspected, assessed, and authorized by the medical men and the executive officers. Explicit and elaborate provisions were made to implement the regulations and conditions of the Pilgrims' Act. In this way, the district and city administrations became parties to the organization of the pilgrimage.

The Lodging House Committee, consisting of administrative officers and nominated members from the citizens, was formed to implement the provisions of the Act, as well as to make other policies that might be needed. It began to receive Rs. 3 per pilgrim from the Gayawal or the owners of the houses at the time of issuing the license. This authorized them to keep a specific number of pilgrims in a particular house. The old and unmaintained houses where the Gayawal used to accommodate their pilgrims were declared unfit, and the Gayawal had to rent houses in the secular zone of Gaya to accommodate the pilgrims. Owing to this, a large number of Gayawal houses were completely reduced to ruins, and the Gayawal were exposed to the money-minded house-owners as well as to the bureaucratic government officials and members of the Lodging House Committee. All this brought about a good many complications in the hitherto direct panda-jajman relationship. To entertain a pilgrim became expensive, and chances for exploiting a pilgrim became scarce.

Furthermore, various non-official social service agencies—the Boy Scouts, the Citizens' Associations, and the Pilgrims' Welfare Organisation—offered their services to the pilgrims in helping them get settled and saving them from the notorious squabbles and bickerings at the hands of the pilgrim hunters, the competing Gayawal, and the latter's representatives. Though these official and non-official organizations have been instrumental in curtailing the freedom of the Gayawal, they have not been able to solve the problems that arise out of the conflicting claims of the different Gayawal over the question of pilgrims. They are also not in a position to deal with the large group of unscrupulous pilgrim hunters who make their way by force, cunning, mischief-mongering, and, above all, by bribing the petty railway and government employees.

All these developments within Gaya, the Gayawal, and in India as a whole, brought about a considerable change in the feudalistic way of life that the Gayawal had developed during their days of affluence and constant contact with the feudal nobilities. As the situation in India changed, there was also a considerable change in the Gayawal style of life. Such changes might be conveniently studied under the four categories—caste identification, ritualism, the traditional profession, and orthodoxy—propounded in the third chapter. Such a comparison should bring out the range of differences between the sanskritic and proletarian priests, as well as between the ideal and real behaviour of the present Gayawal priests.

From Social Cohesion to Social Conflict

The Gayawal enjoyed a unique ritual position because of their mythological character, but in recent years the same mythological status was claimed by the Dhami who began to enter directly into a jajmani relationship with the pilgrims. Several cases were instituted by the Gayawal against the Dhami, but owing to the mutual rivalry among the Gayawal, the Dhami succeeded in some of their efforts. Some of the acharyas employed by the Gayawal to conduct the rituals now claim equal status and sometimes higher status than the Gayawal. They also make efforts to entertain pilgrims on their own initiative and to conduct their rituals in entirety. On the intellectual level, some of the scholars, as considered earlier (Mitra 1878), doubt the antiquity of the mythology, and consider the Gayawal a heterogenous group of priests which were later organized into an orthodox caste.

The compactness and homogeneity of the Gayawal locality are also breaking down. The uncared-for buildings, which were once occupied by the Gayawal families or used for accommodating pilgrims, have been reduced to ruins. A large number of houses have been sold by the Gayawal, and people of different castes have made inroads into their exclusive locality. Though all the Gayawal families continue to live in the same locality, the most important leader of the Gayawal caste, in a spirit of disappointment, left the locality with his wife to live in his garden-home two miles from the temple of Vishnupada. Another famous Gayawal author who has been nominated as a member of the Legislative Council of the State has left Gaya. He lives at Patna with his whole family and considers it a punishment next to death if he has to come back again to live in the ruinous locality of the Gayawal.

In matters of speech, food, and dress, the Gayawal also have been losing their distinctiveness. In addition to their own dialects, the different Gayawal speak the languages of the regions of their professional specialization—Marathi, Bengali, Tamil. Such regional influence is also reflected in their dress and food. Although the Gayawal were once extremely orthodox in the matter of food, now one family out of twenty has accepted fish and goat meat in their diet. Liquor also is no longer tabooed by a few families. (However, nobody publicly accepts such changes in the dietary pattern.) The nitya yajna at the time of eating lunch is no longer observed, and the rules of commensality have been relaxed, especially by the younger Gayawal.

As regards social relations, the Gayawal continue to practice local endogamy, thus confining their kinship relations to the local caste group. Recently, however, a marriage by a Gayawal youth to a South Indian Brahman girl was recorded. The marriage was arranged by the jati-guru who is a Dakhini, and owing to this it found acceptance in the caste. Incidents of divorce and widow remarriage are as completely unknown as in the past. Child marriage is still not uncommon, and owing to this, perhaps, the number of widows in the caste comes to forty-two, which is 17 per cent of the total women in the Gayawal caste.

Though the Gayawal continue some of the above-mentioned traditional practices, their social cohesiveness is being replaced by social conflict, factionalism, inter-family rivalry, competition, mutual suspicion, and jealousy. All these find expression, first, in the breakdown of the joint families. It was traditional with the Gayawal to be organized on the basis of large joint families in which male members of three to four generations along with their wives and unmarried daughters lived in the same household and shared the same kitchen. But these days, out of 120 families, only 45 per cent of the families can be said to be joint families of any size while the rest are natural families. There are also broken families (8·33 per cent) which consist of only one member each. Such families are made up of a widow or widower, which indicates that the care of the old is not being undertaken by other members of the society. In the course of my field work, I was shocked to see one of the renowned Gayawal counting his last days, uncared for and unattended. It was distressing to note that his son, so wealthy and living next door, did not take care of his father even at the time of his serious illness.

The other concrete expression of rivalry and factionalism is reflected in the efforts and failures of some Gayawal reformers and artists in organising social, cultural, religious, and professional associations. In the last thirty years, seven associations for various purposes were organized in which the organizers sought the co-operation of all the caste members. But, instead of getting support, the organizers had to override opposition

TABLE 8

ASSOCIATIONS OF THE GAYAWAL IN THE PAST AND PRESENT

Name	*Purpose*	*Membership*	*Period*	*Present Situation*
Baithaka	Social and recreational	Gayawal men. In some cases according to locality and lineage	Nineteenth and early twentieth centuries	Defunct
Sangit Samiti	Vocal and instrumental music	Gayawal musicians; musicians living in Andar Gaya; other invited musicians		Non-existent; now only informal friendly groups
Tirtha Vriti Sudharani Sabha	Professional and social	Gayawal men only	1930-1952	Defunct
Gayawal Sankirtana Samaj	Devotional group singing	Gayawal & other interested parties; attended informally by many	1935	Continues with a few members
Dvarka Troop	Scouting	Gayawal boys	1938-1947	Defunct
Chandini	Literary reading and discussion	Gayawal writers; other writers of the city	1946-1951	Defunct
Gayawal Nava Yuvak Samaj	Social, cultural, recreational forum for youth	Gayawal youth only	1950-1952	Defunct
Vishnupada Vriti Sidharani Sabha	Improvement in the temple priesthood	Gayawal men acting as shrine priests	1952-1953	Defunct

from many quarters, and when the associations were started, they could not function smoothly because of the internal rivalry, mutual suspicion, and factional jealousy. The life of such associations was miserably short, and at the present time, except for one, all the associations have died out.

Among the seven organizations whose important features are given in Table 8, Tirtha Vriti Sudharani Sabha persisted for a longer period than the others because of the unusual zeal of its permanent secretary who surrounded himself with good workers. It was organized in 1930 with its main objective being to devise ways and means to check the downfall of the Gayawal by freeing their business from the clutches of the agents and touts. Its other objective was to improve the social and religious life of the Gayawal. In 1932, this association reorganized the Madhava Math which was deserted by the Dakhini guru when he found the Gayawal in a state of feudalistic indulgence. Many other improvements were attempted under this association, but, again, it could not survive the burning disunity and jealousy, mutual suspicion, and rivalry of the Gayawal. It died out in the year 1953 when the secretary resigned in disappointment and shame and left the locality of the Gayawal to live in his garden-home two miles away.

Disunity, factionalism, and jealousy are also reflected in the number of litigations and family quarrels that have taken place. In the year 1953, I recorded seven civil and criminal cases that were being fought among the Gayawal themselves. My informants were shy in discussing the details of these cases, but many of the disputes concerned partition suits among some of their relatives. One such complicated case lasted for twenty-four years, and the man involved on one side had to spend about 75,000 rupees in defending himself.

From Ritualism to Pretence

The ritual and ceremonial orientation of the Gayawal has become a means for earning their livelihood. The commercial considerations in dealing with the pilgrims have become so predominant that one of my old informants did not hesitate to formulate his principle in the following phrase: first bread, then prayer.[9] In their daily routine, the Gayawal, especially the younger ones, have become very much secularized, and morning recitations and daily personal worship are not being practised. When I watched them in the temple or giving service to their jajmans or worshippers, I did not find them much moved with religious sentiments. I found them asking for money even before they had completed their priestly jobs. I found them ridiculing such worshippers who went there only for salutation or for offering flowers and not money. In other words, the commercial consideration to extort money in the form of gifts always dominates their spirit. One of my sensitive Gayawal informants rightly summarizes the attitude of the proletarian priests in the following words (Vidyarthi 1955: 21-8):

> In our Gayawal society we find a peculiar situation. Actually only a few practice religion sincerely, most of them are showy. They just pretend to be religious-minded people . . . . They do not have time to think as to how to attain heaven. They are mad after earning their bread. To them prayer, worship, spiritual merits, meditations, and shraddha all have become superfluous and showy—a means for earning their livelihood.

From Priesthood to Partnership

The truth of this statement becomes especially clear when I come to examining the changing pattern of the panda-jajman relationship. In the preceding chapter, the traditional pattern of the panda-jajman relationship has been described. It has been also shown how, in the course of time, a Gayawal needed a number of representatives to assist him in meeting those obligations. But during the last thirty-five years, the Gayawal have been put in a very peculiar situation. Owing to the economic depression, they were not in a position to maintain large groups of servants, nor were they in a position to dispense with them. The roles of servants and acharyas were almost institutionalized when the problem arose of finding alternative

[9] This is a translation of a commonplace proverb (pahale roji, tub roja) usually used to signify the importance of earning a livelihood before worship.

employment for them. So the Gayawal transferred their service from servantship to partnership. The Gayawal began to give them a reasonable percentage (20 to 30 per cent of the total gift) for their service. But the seed of partnership that was sown under the spirit of economic depression was further fertilized by the social disunity among the Gayawal and the commercial influences of the city, and later it played a devastating part in breaking up the traditional panda-jajman relationship. As a matter of fact, the traditional system was more or less replaced by a new system which might be called the rozgariya-panda relationship. Rozgariya is the name given to those wage-workers who deal in pilgrims with the Gayawal, bargaining to receive the maximum share from the suphal gifts.

Today the rozgariya-panda relationship dominates the scene, and Gaya as a matter of fact has become a great "ceremonial trade centre". At Gaya there are several types of gangs of rozgariya ; full-time, part-time, and seasonal. Again, there are rozgariya who travel from place to place ; there are some who wait at the points where the pilgrims enter ; and there are some who solicit the pilgrims in advance at other places of pilgrimage —Banaras and Allahabad. The rozgariya have their own mechanism to keep the pilgrims from going to their rightful panda. These are impersonation and bluff, telling about their characterlessness and unholiness, declaring them dead, alluring the pilgrims to take holier and more dignified panda, persuading them to pay less suphal gifts than their original panda would charge, etc. The rozgariya, thus, use all types of tricks to win over the pilgrims and make all attempts to take them to the panda who will give them the largest share. Such rozgariya have entered into trading relationships with the secondary priests like the acharya and the Dhami and with the house owners in an attempt to get the maximum share of the gifts by misleading the pilgrims to those priests who are ritually not entitled to perform suphal ritual.

With the development of the rozgariya organization, rough estimates by my informants indicate that more than 70 per cent of the pilgrims came through rozgariya of one type or another. The rest (30 per cent) are contacted by the respective panda through their own efforts. In the beginning, an attempt was made by a few Gayawal to check this development of the middleman between the pilgrims and the panda, but they could not succeed because of the lack of co-operation among themselves. These days, however, the rozgariya system has become organized on such a large scale that a Gayawal cannot think of maintaining a direct panda-jajman relationship. Every Gayawal has become part of this vicious circle and more than half of the suphal gifts go to such rozariya.

The emergence of the rozgariya has very adversely affected the sacred and social life of the Gayawal. The rozgariya are usually mischief-mongers, an unemployed and frustated section of the city's population. The Gayawal call them "goondas" or ruffians but admit them completely into the fold. In a spirit of frustration, poverty, and helplessness, the Gayawal have accepted "goondaism" as a means of earning their livelihood. One of my Gayawal informants, who is a famous Hindi author, tells me his reaction to the development of the rozgariya system in the following words:[10]

> Now the pandas are also becoming goondas in the company of the groups of goondas. It is unthinkable to raise the profession of priesthood to the traditional purity. The pandas can be saved only when they are removed from the profession of priestcraft. . . . Today priesthood means to practice goondaism and the result of goondaism is complete destruction. The Gayawal cannot keep themselves aloof from goondaism if they are to practice priesthood. They have to be in a closer brotherhood with the goondas to get pilgrims and earn their minimum living. Today the Gayawal pandas are slaves in the hands of the goondas whose number is increasing every day.

The caste endogamy among the Gayawal doubtlessly has been very rigid during the period under our present study. But even during this brief period of 150 years, one notes the emergence of a powerful new group, the rozgaria, who now tend to be included in the profession of priestcraft at Gaya. If we take

[10] My informant gave his impression about the rozgariya system in writing. This is an extract from his letter.

a long-range perspective of history, the titles of the Gayawal derived from different caste groups and the names of villages as discussed in Chapter IV, could indicate a similar inclusion of non-priestly groups in the pre-existing priesthood.

FROM ORTHODOXY TO DE-SANSKRITIZATION

Perhaps there is an overtone of pessimism in the above statement, but there is no denying the fact that the wholeness of the caste organization and its traditional way of life, as described in Chapter III and IV, have been badly affected by all these developments. The Gayawal style of life, which is essentially the sanskritic way of pious life, has become so degenerate that both the Gayawal themselves and the people in general are greatly concerned. The Gayawal who were once famous for their holiness and sacredness are now being labelled as a degenerate group of pandas, and their names are remembered with a certain amount of contempt and ridicule. In their social, religious, and priestly life, they now fall far short of what is prescribed for the Brahman priests in the sanskritic texts or what the Gayawal believe themselves to be ideally. Such conflicts are especially reflected in their attempts to appear wealthy and pious in public life. They are still shy about exposing their poverty and secularity to the outsider.

In spite of all these changes, however, the traditional orientation of the Gayawal is maintained in many aspects of life. The best illustration is their attitude to their own profession. With few exceptions the Gayawal do not attempt to take other jobs either to supplement their priestly profession or to supplant it. Some of them consider it sinful to take up other jobs. In the interviews, many subjects impressed upon me that service means subordination, lack of leisure, and increase of worries and responsibilities to which they were not accustomed. About fifteen years ago, a Gayawal, breaking his caste tradition, bought a chaff-cutting machine to supplement his family income. He became the object of vehement criticism and attacks by both his family and the community. In his life-history (Vidyarthi, 1955: 2J-9), he tells us of the attitude of other Gayawal towards his non-priestly action: "They began to hate me, rebuke me . . . . You claim to be a son of a Gayawal panda but have taken up a job of a labourer. You are a big black spot on the face of the Gayawal caste."

In spite of all these criticisms, he continued to run the machine. But in reaction to all these criticisms, he also became very much interested in religious activities and began to devote all his leisure to worship, organizing Sankirtana, and visiting temples. Another Gayawal who started a shop for selling coal in the year 1941 could not continue with it owing to severe criticism by his fellow caste members. Now, many more Gayawal are feeling the need to take up other jobs, but still not a single one has actually been able to do so. Perhaps in the future, as it has been done by pandas of other places of pilgrimage, the majority of the Gayawal will come forward to accept secular jobs in addition or instead of their traditional profession.

To sum up, the Gayawal pretend to believe in an orthodox way of life. The values and ideals to which they give verbal allegiance are enshrined in the teachings given to them by the sacred intelligentsia and prescribed for them in the sacred texts, the Manu Smriti and the Vishnu Sutra. But in actual practice the Gayawal always have been influenced by the ways of their jajmans and by other factors and forces that operate outside their caste organization. When they were in contact with the feudal nobles and when they accumulated plenty of wealth, they adopted several elements which were non-sanskritic for Brahmanical priests. And when, relatively speaking, factors of secularization and economic change began to dominate the Hindu universe, the Gayawal way of life again witnessed corresponding changes. At present, Gayawal culture is composed of many of these elements—folk, sanskritic, feudalistic, and proletarian—which have accumulated in the course of history.

CHAPTER VI

SUMMARY

THE PRESENT STUDY constitutes an ethnography of the sacred city of Gaya, a place of Hindu pilgrimage. The city is described in terms of three analytic concepts: 'a sacred geography', a set of 'sacred performances', and a corps of 'sacred specialists'. These three concepts, conceived collectively, are termed a 'sacred complex'. For a systematic description of such a sacred complex, it was necessary to formulate certain descriptive terms and concepts which could be useful for fuller studies of sacred complexes and, ultimately, for comparative work in this little explored field of anthropology.

Considered culturally, the sacred complex of Gaya is predominantly great tradition-oriented. It is great tradition-oriented in the sense that it represents the higher form of Hinduism as reflected in the predominance of sanskritic sacred centres, in the significance of the sacred performance of shraddha, as well as in the all-prevading influence of the Brahmanical priesthood and sacred intelligentsia. But in the course of analyzing these sacred features, the difficulties in isolating them from the lesser forms of Hinduism have been brought out. Persisting as an integral part of the same sacred complex, there are details and patterns of worship, as well as a type of priesthood, that have been shown to be essentially indigenous and folk-like in their characteristics. In other words, the sacred complex of a place of Hindu pilgrimage in India in itself is an intricate combination of the great tradition with the little traditions. In the larger universe of Hindu civilization, again, the significance of the statement is reflected in the continuity of the sacred complex with the religions of Indian peasant and tribal peoples. Viewed diachronically, it seems quite likely that a sacred complex could be understood as an elaboration and transformation of the simpler forms of original elements.

The textual materials used in the present study point to the same tendency towards combining traditions as do our contextual field studies. In the Vishnu Sutra (Chaps. LXXIII—

LXXXVI) and Vayu Purana (Chaps. 105—112) in which shraddha in general and Gaya shraddha in particular are celebrated, we note the incorporation of traditions that in no way can be called "great" in the present time. Isolated hills, rocks, trees, and ponds have been suggested as sacred centres for shraddha observances. Offerings of even beef and buffalo meats have been prescribed, and the purpose for observing shraddha largely for the happiness of the survivors rather than for the emancipation of the ancestors' souls has been emphasized. In other words, the little and local traditions of the folk and peasant societies have been continually accommodated at least in the puranic and ancient legal texts of the Hindus, and through this medium some of them have received universal recognition, acceptance, and also modification. Perhaps such a process of combination and compromise has helped in the past in developing a synthesis, a federation, a pattern for what today we call Hinduism.

In the larger framework of Hindu civilization, the sacred complex again may be considered in its structural extensions. It serves the local, regional, and the entire Hindu universe through sacred activities, and in turn, it is served by all of them in one form or another. It provides common symbols of worship, along with the universally celebrated ritual of shraddha, that attract people of different castes and sects, of distant linguistic and geographical areas, and of different economic and social status. The Gayawal priests have a jajmani relationship with all these people living in different parts of the Hindu universe. In making the sacred complex, all the devotees, irrespective of their economic status, have contributed their best, while the contribution of the rich devotees in developing the sacred landscape as well as in providing a living to the sacred specialists was outstanding. The construction of sacred buildings that help in developing the sacred geography have been mainly financed by rich persons of different parts of India; again, the sacred performances were elaborately observed by wealthy devotees who maintained the sacred specialists by giving valuable gifts. In other words, a sacred complex provided a meeting place for different kinds of peoples and traditions, of castes and sects, of class and status, and thus nourished a sense of Indian unity even when the spirit of nationalism was lacking.

Under the impact of western civilization, however, the sacred complex is witnessing a transformation. With the adoption of industrial technology and new means of transportation and with the acceptance of the principles of secularization and democracy, India as a whole is undergoing a series of social and economic changes. With all these changes, the sacred complex, which constitutes an integral part of civilization, is also in process of change. The three elements of the sacred complex—the sacred geography, the sacred performances, and the sacred specialists—are under a process of adjustment to the changing situation. While the secular zone of Gaya is expanding in population, area, and activities, the sacred zone is becoming more and more desolate, unimportant, and disorganized. The roles of secular agencies like the government and social service groups, as well as commercially oriented pilgrim hunters, are also increasing in the organization of the sacred complex. Some of the old buildings and dilapidated sacred centres are being replaced by parks, monuments to sacred intelligentsia, and rest houses. The sacred performances are becoming less and less elaborate to fit in with the changing pattern of leisure of the people. The importance of the priest is fast decreasing and his monopolistic right in dealing with the pilgrims is fast disappearing. As new types of people and institutions are becoming interested in the organization of the pilgrimage, the Gayawal are also slowly beginning to think of taking up other suitable jobs. It appears that the whole sacred complex is in the process of reorganization in terms of the general changes that are going on in and around India. In other words, the sacred complex is undergoing a secondary urbanization which remains to be studied in the future.

APPENDIX I

GAYA MYTHOLOGY: BRIEF EXTRACTS[1]

THE GREAT FATHER of the Universe, Brahma, born in the lotus-navel of Vishnu, created all living beings by order of Vishnu. From his fierce nature that lord brought forth the demon and from his humane disposition he produced noble-minded gods.

Among the asuras, Gaya was endowed with great strength and vigour. He was distinguished as a devout Vaishnava. With his breath held back, he practised the most rigorous austerities for many thousands of years on the noble hill of Kolahala. The devas were oppressed by his austerities and dreaded serious misfortune. They repaired to the region of Brahma and there prayed to the first Father of Creation: "Pray, protect us from the demon Gaya." Brahma said: "Let us proceed to Shankara [Shiva] for help." Preceded by Brahma, they all went to Shiva on the Kailasa mountain and saluting him said: "O Lord, protect us from the great demon." Shiva said: "Let us seek the help of Hari [Vishnu], the great god sleeping on the milky ocean; he will design some means of relief for us."

Brahma, Shiva, and the devas satisfied Vishnu by the following hymn: "Our salutation to Vishnu, to the Lord of all and the Creator of all and the Sustainer of all; to the Destroyer of all and the Extinguisher of all; to the Sustainer and the Supporter; to the Destroyer of Rakashasas and other spirits; to He who promotes the prosperity of the creation and is the Redeemer of yogis." Thus praised, Vishnu became manifest to the devas and inquired: "Why have you all come here?" They prayed: "Save us, O Lord, from the demon Gaya." Vishnu said: "Do you, Brahma, and others proceed to the Asura and I shall follow you."

Vishnu, mounted on his garuda, and the others, each on his exquisite vehicle, repaired to bless the demon. They addressed

[1] The accompanying material contains some relevant passages dealing with the origin of Gaya as a sacred city. It is translated from the Vayu Purana (Chaps. 105-106).

the demon, saying: "Why are you continuing your austerities? Well satisfied with your devotion, we have come to grant you any favour that you may desire. Say, Gaya Asura, what do you wish?"

Gaya Asura said: "If you are really satisfied with me, render my body purer even than that of Brahma, Vishnu, or Mahesh; purer even than all the deva and Brahman; purer than all sacrifices pools and high mountains; purer even than the purest of gods." "Even so be it," responded the gods and repaired to heaven.

[The result of this blessing was that] mortals who beheld or touched the demon at once ascended to the region of Brahma, and the domains of Yama were deprived of their inhabitants. Thus deprived of their subjects by Gaya Asura, Yama, along with Indra and the other gods, repaired to Brahma and addressed him saying: "O Father of creation, take back what you have bestowed on us [for we can no longer hold them]."

Brahma replied: "Let us repair to Vishnu, the undecaying." To Vishnu they thus addressed: "O Lord, by the sight of the demon whom you have blessed, all mortals are being transmitted to heaven, and the three regions have become empty."

Vishnu, thus implored by the gods, said to them: "Do you go and ask the demon to give you his body so that you may perform a sacrifice yajna thereon, and you will be able to overcome your difficulties."

The gods accordingly went to Gaya, the demon, who, beholding before him Brahma with his companions, rose from his seat, saluted them with reverence, and, having welcomed them in due form, said: "Blessed is my life this day; blessed is my penance; verily I have attained all my objects since Brahma has become my guest. Say, wherefore are you come, and I shall at once execute the task for you."

Brahma said: "Of all the sacred pools that have been seen by me in my rambles, there is none that is for sacrificial purposes purer than thy body, which has attained its purity through the blessing of Vishnu. Do you, therefore, O Asura, present me thy holy body for the performance of a sacrifice."

Gaya, the demon, said: "Blessed am I, O god of gods, since thou askest me for my body; my parental ancestors will be sanctified shouldst thou perform a sacrifice on my body. By thee the body was created, and well it is that it should be of use to thee; it will then be truly of use to all."

Having said this, Gaya leaning towards the southwest, fell prostrate on the ground on the Kolahala hill; his body lay on the north side, and his feet extended towards the south. Brahma then collected the necessary articles for the sacrifice, and having created from his mind the officiating priests (called the Gayawal), duly performed a sacrifice on the body of the demon. Having bathed and offered the concluding oblation to the fire, he gave adequate fees to the priests. On the completion of the sacrifice, he, with his divine companions was, however, surprised to find that the demon was still moving on the sacrificial ground. He thereupon said to Yama: "Do you go and quickly fetch from your house the stone of religion that is lying there and place it on the head of the demon by my order." Yama hearing this, immediately placed the stone on the demon's head to keep it immovable; but even after the stone was so placed the demon moved along with the stone. Then Brahma asked Shiva and the other gods to sit upon the stone to keep it fixed; and they did so as they were directed. But even after being pressed by the gods, the demon still moved. Greatly distressed, Brahma then ran to Vishnu and saluting that lord of three regions, thus addressed: "O Lord, Great Master of the Universe and Ruler of Creation, thou Master of virtuous beings and Giver of blessings and salvation, I salute thee." Vishnu asked: "From where do you come?" Brahma replied: "Lord of lords, on the completion of the sacrifice Gaya Asura began to move and thereupon we placed the sacred stone on his head, and Shiva and the other gods sat upon it, but still the demon moves. Now help us, O Destroyer of Madhu, to make him immovable."

On hearing the words of Brahma, Vishnu drew forth from his person a fierce form and gave it to Brahma in order to help him to make the demon motionless. Bringing that form Brahma placed it on the stone, but it nevertheless moved; so he again sought the aid of Vishnu. Vishnu thereupon came from the milky ocean, and under the form of the wielder of the mace (Gadadhar) sat upon the stone to prevent its moving. Moreover, he, in the five forms of Prapitamaha (the great grandfather, or the first), Pitamaha (grandfather), Phalgvisha (the Lord of Phalgu), Kedara, and Kanakeshvara rested thereon. Brahma, too, sat there; so did the elephantine Ganesh. The sun, in his threefold form of the sun of Gaya, the northern sun, and the southern sun, Lakshmi, under the name of Sita, Gaori, under the name of Mangala, Gayatri, Savitri, Trisandhya, and Sarasvati likewise sat there. And, since before sitting down, by playing his mace, Hari rendered the demon motionless, he is therefore called the first or sovereign wielder of the mace.

Gaya Asura said to the gods: "Why should you after I have given my sinless body to Brahma treat me thus? Would I not have become motionless at the request of Vishnu? Why then should he thus torture me with his mace, and the gods join him? And now since you all have treated me so cruelly, do you show your mercy to me."

The gods were delighted and said: "We are fully satisfied with you. Do you ask a blessing from us."

Gaya prayed: "As long as the earth and the mountains, as long as the moon and the stars shall last, so long may you, Brahma, Vishnu, and Mahesh rest on this stone. May you, the deva, rest on it too and call this place after me the sacred Kshetra of Gaya, extending over five krosa, of which one krosa would be covered by my head. Therein should abide for the good of mankind all the sacred pools on the earth, where persons by bathing and offering oblations of water and funeral cakes may attain high merit for themselves and transmit their ancestors, blessed with all that is desirable and salvation, to the region of Brama. As long as Vishnu in his triple form shall be adored by the learned, so long should this be renowned on the earth as the sacred place of Gaya Asura, and resort to it should cleanse men of even the sin of killing the Brahman."

Hearing this prayer of Gaya, the deva, headed by Vishnu, replied: "Whatever thou prayest, that shall for certain be accomplished. By offering the pinda and performing shraddha here, persons will transmit their ancestors for a hundred generations, as also themselves, to the Brahmaloka where there exists no disease. By worshipping our feet, they will attain the highest reward in the after-life."

APPENDIX II

SACRED CENTRES (VEDI) OF GAYA THROUGH THE AGES

Sl. No.	*Name of the Shrine (Vedi)*	*Reference in Sacred Texts*	*Approximate Location*	*Types of Sacred Performances*
1.	Kapildhara	G., V.		Ritual salutation
2.	Kapileshwar Mahadeo			Ritual salutation
3.	Koti Tirth Mahakoti	G., A.	South of Akchayvat Maranpur	Libation
4.	Kardmmalya	A., V.	Near Mund Prista	Ritual bath
5.	Kotishwar Kotish	G.	At Nawagarti on Variya	
		V., A.	In Gayawal garden	
6.	Kagshila		In the garden of Damodar Gayawal	
7.	Ram Gaya Tirth Madhu-shrwa is called Dasaswāmedh	V., G.	Bhiti	
8.	Keshonarayan		At Murcha	Worship salutation, ancestor sacrifice
9.	Kashi Khand Varanasi	V.	At Godawari	
10.	Kedar	G., V., A.	At Bavanighat	
	Kedar Pad	A.	At Bavanighat north of Vishunpad	
11.	Kankeshwar	V.		Salutation
	Kankesh	V.		
	Kankesh river	G.		
	Kankeshpād			
12.	Kaveri	V.	North of Nayli village on hill	Ancestor sacrifice
13.	Girikaran Mukh Girikaran Gokaran Mukh	V.	It is the rock of Akashganga Kund	

NOTE: A: *Agnipuran* G: *Mahagarurpuran* V: *Vayupuran*

APPENDIX II—*Contd.*

Sl. No.	*Name of the Shrine (Vedi)*	*Reference in Sacred Texts*	*Approximate Location*	*Types of Sacred Performances*
14.	Godwari Kund	V.	Hill in the south of Gridheshwar Mahadeo	
	Godawari	V.	Hill in the south of Gridheshwar Mahadeo	
15.	Gridhghat		Hills in the south of Gridheshwar Mahadeo and west of Gridheshwar Mahadeo	
16.	Gridh Vat	A., V.		
17.	Gridh Guha	V., G.	East of Patalganga there was a Kund which has been now filled up	
	Gridhkut	A., V.		
18.	Gridheshwar Mahadeo	G.	Famous	Ritual salutation
	Grisheshwar	A., V.		
19.	Gaya Nav	A., G.	At Vikula Ghat	
	Navi Tirth		At Vikula Ghat	
	Navi Kund	G.	At Vikula Ghat	
20.	Gajraj Tirth	G., V.	Behind Gadadhar Temple there is a pillar on elephant	
21.	Gaytri Devi	G., A., V.	At Gayatri Ghat	Ball of rice and curd
22.	Gaya Ditya	G., V., A.	At Bavnighat, south of Suryapad there is a small temple	Ritual salutation, worship
	Surya, Van			
23.	Gadadhar, also known as small Akshayvat	A., G., V.	Famous sacred centre	Ritual salutation, *Panchamrit* bath and *dupdan*
24.	Gadadhar		At the sitting Hall of Sagat Ghat	Ritual salutation
25.	Gadadhar		In the house of Chotan Upadhyaya Gayawal	Ritual salutation

APPENDIX II—*Contd.*

Sl. No.	*Name of the Shrine (Vedi)*	*Reference in Sacred Texts*	*Approximate Location*	*Types of Sacred Performances*
26.	Gadadhar		In the temple of Vishnupad near Vishadev	Ritual salutation
27.	Adigadadhar	G., A., V.	At Karshili	Ritual salutation
28.	Gan nath	V.	At sixteenth shrine	Ritual salutation
	Gann	G.	Five images of *Paschim* Ganesh	Ritual salutation
	Gajkarn	V.	Dandibag is called by this name	Ritual salutation
29.	Champakvan	G.	Dandibag is called by this name	Ritual salutation
30.	Hermitage of Chyawan Muni	V.	At Village Deokund, 18 miles south of Gaya	Ritual salutation
	Chyawan Bati		On Vāyu Kōn	
31.	Chandeshwar		Beneath the sitting of Krishna Dwarika or Bharkandeshwar	Ritual salutation
32.	Chandrabhaga	V.	A stream at the foot of Mandor Hill	Ritual salutation
33.	Jalashyaya	V.	Surya Chuan locality near Tinmuhani at Gayawal bigha	Ritual salutation
34.	Jamuna	V.	In the Sherghati-Patna road near Jambu Karan	Ritual salutation
35.	Jambu Karan		In the Sherghati road, west of Gaya on the bank of the Yamuna	Ritual salutation
36.	Tarkeshwar		Beneath the Vhishmakund	
37.	Trikut Parbat		Hill of Sambh Burj	
38.	Tirth-ke-Tirth		Rin Moksh on the hill of Gridh Kut	
	Gridh Kut Parbat (Rin Mochan)		Pap Moksh, Pichas	Bath

APPENDIX II—*Contd.*

Sl. No.	Name of the Shrine (Vedi)	Reference in Sacred Texts	Approximate Location	Types of Sacred Performances
	(Pap Mochan) (Pichas Mochan)		Moksh Mahadev	
39.	Devika (Devikasha Devikiwata)	V.	Annexed with Madhu Kulya	
40.	Darkshi		In Surya Kund	
41.	Devnadi	G.	A stream north of Amrit Well, i.e., north of Mangla Devi	Libation
42.	Dev Kund		West of Gaya at the same place where the hermitage of Chayawan Muni Kund and Budheshwar Mahadeo is	
43.	Dakshinark	V.	West of Suryakund	Ancestor sacrifice
	Dakshinmanas	V., G.	West of Suryakund	Ancestor sacrifice
44.	Dhenukarayana	G., A.	Gobachwa is called so	Ancestor sacrifice and libation
	Dhen Ban		Gobachwa is called so	
45.	Dhenupad	A.	Gowachwa	Salutation and ancestor sacrifice
	Dhenu	G.		
	Dhenu Prist		An image	
	Kam Dhenu Pad	V.	An image	
46.	Dharmarayana	G., A., V.	A famous sacred centre	Ancestor worship, libation
47.	Dhautpad	A.	One among the sixteenth shrine	Offering of rice-ball
48.	Dharmeshwar	V.	A famous centre	
	Dharmesh		A famous centre	
	Dharamraj		A famous centre	
	Dharm	V.	A famous centre	
49.	Mamkut Parwat Kronch Padadutratah		North of Kronch-pād Ram Gaya	

APPENDIX II—*Contd.*

Sl. No.	*Name of the Shrine (Vedi)*	*Reference in Sacred Texts*	*Approximate Location*	*Types of Sacred Performances*
50.	Narayan	G., A.,V.	Near Gowachwa, in the locality of Narayan Chuan	Worship
51.	Narmda	V.	Narayan Chuan Vihari	
52.	Narmadeshwar Mahadeo		In the garden of Lal Behari	
53.	Narsing	A., V.	Near Vishnupad Temple	Worship and ritual salutation
	Narhari	V., G.	Near Vishnupad Temple	
54.	Naumisaranya		Near Vishnupad Temple	
55.	Bhartha Kund, Mathan	G.	Near Hanumanjee of Southern Gate	
56.	Maheshwari Dhara Mahesh Dhara	G., V.	Mangla Devi	Ancestor sacrifice
	Maheshi Kund	V.		
57.	Mahanadi	A., G.	From Devghat to Uttarmanas it is called Phalgu Tirth	Ritual bath and ancestor sacrifice
	Phalgu			Ritual bath and ancestor sacrifice
	Phalgu tirth Phalgu tirthashram	G., A., V.		Ancestor worship
58.	Bhāv Sanrakshan		A famous centre	
59.	Mahi Kulya	V.	North of Akshyawat a small hill is made	
60.	Mahi Kulya		North of Pundarikasha	
	Dadhi Kulya		In the way to Kapildhara	
61.	Markandaye Markandeshwar, Mahadev		West of Vaitarni	Ritual salutation

APPENDIX II—*Contd.*

Sl. No.	Name of the Shrine (Vedi)	Reference in Sacred Texts	Approximate Location	Types of Sacred Performances
62.	Markandeshwar	G., A.		Ritual salutation
	Maha Lakshmi Lakshmi	V., G., A.	Near the gate of Vishnupada Temple	
63.	Mul Kshetra	A., V., G.	It is lying in a dilapidated condition, 20 paces from Vashistha Kund by the side of the road	Ritual salutation
64.	Mund Prista Devi	A.	At the Mund Prista	Offering of rice-ball
65.	Mund Prista	G.	At Karsoli	
66.	Mund Pristnam	A.	Annexed to the temple of Dhaneshwar	Ritual salutation to Mund Pristya Parwat
67.	Mund Prista Mahadeo	A.		
68.	Rudra Kapal Bhairo Asthan			
69.	Rameshwar Mahadev	V., G.	Near Ramgaya, according to others near the image of Ram on the Ramshila hill	Ritual salutation and worship
	Ramesh	A.	Near the image of Ram	
70.	Rathmarg	G.	On the southern way, the sixteenth shrine	
71.	Khadik		On the southern way to sixteenth shrine	
72.	Rukmini Kund Rukmini	A., V. V.	A famous centre	Ancestor sacrifice
73.	Lelihan	V., G., A.	10 paces west of Adi Gadadhar of Gaya	Ancestor sacrifice
74.	Lohdand		32 miles east near Nabadah near Sigra asthan	
75.	Lilawati Lilarjan		Near Saraswati	

APPENDIX II—*Contd.*

Sl. No.	*Name of the Shrine (Vedi)*	*Reference in Sacred Texts*	*Approximate Location*	*Types of Sacred Performances*
76.	Lomharsan	V.	At Mund Prista	
	Lom Dristi Kund	V.	At Mund Prista	
	Lomas Kund	V.	At Mund Prista	
	Mund Pristra Pad		At Mund Prista	
77.	Lomesh	G., V.	At Mund Prista	
78.	Somdhara		Kapileshwar Mahadeo	
	Som Kund	G., A., V.	Kapileshwar Mahadeo	
	Somtirth	G.	Kapileshwar Mahadeo	
79.	Savitri Kund		In the foot-hill of the Brahyoni	
	Savitri	G., A., V.	Near Agnidhara	
	Adi Savitri		On Brahmyoni Hill	
80.	Suwarn Dighika (Dighghi Tank)			
81.	Susumna Nadi		Near Susmneshwar Mahanadi	
82.	Susmeshwar Mahadev	A.		
83.	Sanak			
84.	Saunak			
85.	Sanandan	V.	On Nagkut Hill	
86.	Sanat Kumar	V.	On Ram Gaya Hill	
87.	Sanatan	V.	On Ram Gaya Hill	
88.	Sangmesh		South of Devghat sitting Hall	
89.	Sarswati	V.	Across Saraswati River on the way to Bodh-Gaya	
	Saraswati Devi	G., A., V.		
90.	Shwetark	V.	Near Suryakund	
91.	Sri Purusottam	G., A., V.	South of Koleshwar	
92.	Shila Nav		on several rocks	
	Shilav		South of Ram Gaya,	
	Bharatashram			

APPENDIX II—*Contd.*

Sl. No.	*Name of the Shrine (Vedi)*	*Reference in Sacred Texts*	*Approximate Location*	*Types of Sacred Performances*
93.	Shitla devi		On the Vekuta Ghat at Pitamaheshwar Uttarmansh	
94.	Agast Kund	V.	There is an image of Vyasjee at Murlighat	
	Agastshila Agastashram Agast Bharya Sah Agasta Say Sah Sukracharya Asthan residing there with his two sons			
95.	Akash Ganga	A., V.	A famous centre	Ancestor sacrifice
96.	Agnidhara	G., V.	50 paces ahead Maheshwaridhara is Sarswati Kund which is the abode of Sukra and his two sons. There are many feet of Rishis	
	Agnitirth			
97.	Amar Kantak	V.	The staircase which is south of Ram Gaya	
98.	Anar Keshwar	V.	A little south of Sankesh	
99.	Shyama River	V.	In the house of Devghat Pindbechwa	
100.	Alagiri		On the Karshili Hill	
101.	Udangiri Mritustak		Hill in the north of Brahmayoni	
102.	Uddaiguri		The hill of Bahadurgiri, beside the railway bridge on the River Phalgu	

APPENDIX II—*Contd.*

Sl. No.	*Name of the Shrine (Vedi)*	*Reference in Sacred Texts*	*Approximate Location*	*Types of Sacred Performances*
103.	Utarark	V.	Surya of Uttar-manas	
104.	Brahma Kund Brahmasarowar		Near Ghrit Kulya	
105.	Pretshila	A., V., G.	Pretkut, Pretparvat	Ancestor sacrifice
106.	Prit Kund	G., A.		Bramhkund which is also known as Pretkund — ritual bath, libation
107.	Ramshila		On Ramshila Hill	Ritual bath, libation and ancestor sacrifice
108.	Ramkund		Near Ramshila Hill	
	Ramtirth		Near Ramshila Hill	
	Rampad		Near Ramshila Hill	
	Ramjhap		Near Ramshila Hill	
109.	Sangam Mahanadi		Near Ramshila Hill	
	Prakash Adars Gaya Tirth		Near Ramshila Hill	
110.	Kagbali	V., A.	South of Ramshila	Ancestor sacrifice
	Yambali		South of Ramshila	Ancestor sacrifice
	Swanbali		South of Ramshila	Ancestor sacrifice
	Kakshila		South of Ramshila	Ancestor sacrifice
111.	Kankhal	G., A., V.	Suryakund, above Mundprista	Ancestor sacrifice
112.	Udichi	G., A., V.	On the Suryakund	Ancestor sacrifice
113.	Jihwal		Near Devghat, south of old Gadadhar Ghat	Ancestor sacrifice
114.	Saraswati Kund, also known as Saraswatidhāra	V.		Ritual bath, libation.
115.	Matangwapi Matang Kund	G., A.		Offering of rice-ball
116.	Buddha	G., V.		
	Budh Gaya		Behind in the West Aswawast tree	
	Bodh Shad			
	Maha Bodh			
	Baudh Taru			

APPENDIX II—*Contd.*

Sl. No.	*Name of the Shrine (Vedi)*	*Reference in Sacred Texts*	*Approximate Location*	*Types of Sacred Performances*
117.	Brahmsari Mulki	G., A., V.	East of Mangla-gauri	Ritual salutation of Brahma
118.	Brahm Sarowar Bramha Sari-mulki Bramhsar Bramhshad	A., V.		
119.	Bramhpad			
120.	Vishnupad (Pa-dankit padaswa-rup tirtham)	A., G., V.	In the temple of Vishnupad	Ancestor worship, ritual salutation, libation
121.	Rudrapad	G., A., V.		
122.	Kanwapad			
123.	Agstpad	A., V.		
124.	Matangpad	G., A., V.		
125.	Ganeshpad Ganpad	A., V., G.		
126.	Kartikpad	A., V.		
127.	Indrapad			
128.	Chandrapad			Ancestor sacrifice
129.	Suryapad Ravipad Adityapad			Ancestor sacrifice
130.	Garhyapatyagni Pad	A.		Ancestor sacrifice
131.	Gridhyapad			Ancestor sacrifice
132.	Dakshinagni Pad	A., V.		
133.	Awashyagni Pad	A.		
134.	Sita Kund			
135.	Gaya Shir			Ancestor sacrifice, libation
136.	Kup Dharm			Ancestor sacrifice, libation
137.	Gaya Kup Kup Gaya Tirth Kup Dharm Kup			
138.	Adi Gaya	V.	near Adi Gadadhar	

APPENDIX II—*Contd.*

Sl. No.	*Name of the Shrine (Vedi)*	*Reference in Sacred Texts*	*Approximate Location*	*Types of Sacred Performances*
139.	Bhim Gaya Bhim Kut Bhim Gora Pandu Shila	 G., A.		
140.	Bhishma Pad			
141.	Go prachar	G., A., V.	West of Mangla-gauri	
142.	Gadalol Gaya Lotam	G., A., V.		Ancestor sacrifice
143.	Akshayavat			Ancestor sacrifice
144.	Gayatri Kund			
145.	Prabhas Parwat			Ritual salutation of Prabhsheshwar
	Prabhas Khetra Prabhashekh Shila			
146.	Angust Shila	G.	According to one Puran, Angust-shila is a part of Pretshila, now called as Ram-shila	
	Shyam, Sawal—two dogs			Khanwali
147.	Kanwa Parwat			
148.	Nimishaditya Ishan Maheshwar			
149.	Karun Rudha		Bhadur Giri	
150.	Bhasmkut Bhasmakund		Manglagauri Hill	At Bhasma Kund
	Dharmraj, Agast with wife		Murli Hill, west of Mangla	
151.	Bateshwar Batesh	A., V. V.	Akshayawat	
152.	Par Pitamahes-war	V.	Near Akshayawat	
	Pitamah	G., A., V.	Near Singra Devi	
153.	Janardan Janardan Parvat	G., V., A.	Above Bhasmakut hill, near Mangla-gauri in the south	

APPENDIX II—*Contd.*

Sl. No.	*Name of the Shrine (Vedi)*	*Reference in Sacred Texts*	*Approximate Location*	*Types of Sacred Performances*
154.	Pundrikaksh Pundrik, Bhism bowed down here for salutation resting on his ankles	G., A., V.	Manglaga iri	
155.	Adyachal Hill		West of Bramhyani Temple	
156.	Vidyadhar Gandharv Maheshwar and Gauri live here		Here music is audible in the night	
157.	Ahichalgiri Adipal Ganpati	V.		
158.	Nabhi Gaya			Ancestor sacrifice
159.	Bhartashram Bharatjit had installed the images of Ram, Lakshman and Sita	G., A. V.		
160.	Dakshin Palām			
161.	Chup Kup, Kup Chup	A., G.	On Brahmyoni Hill	
	Brahma Chup	A.	On Brahmyoni Hill	
162.	Rampad			
163.	Madhushrwa			
164.	Kamakhyan	A., V.	South of Vishnupad	Ancestor sacrifice
164a	Kardmeshwar		Asmasan Ghat Road —in the house of a potter	
165.	Sankaya		Prapitamah south of Madhykala	
166.	Pitreshwar		West of Uttarmanas	
167.	Viranchi Narayan		Babhnighat, according to others Kashikhand	
168.	Vaikuntheshwar		North of Navi Gaya	

APPENDIX II—*Contd.*

Sl. No.	*Name of the Shrine (Vedi)*	*Reference in Sacred Texts*	*Approximate Location*	*Types of Sacred Performances*
169.	Virla Devi		Nāvi Gaya, north of Gayatri Ghat	
170.	Gaya Prist, Gadadhar		Adi Gadadhar	
171.	Vishal Tirth Vishal Hadi Vishala Vishalpad	 G. A.	Bisar tank	Ancestor sacrifice
172.	Sujan Tirth			
173.	Patal Ganga		Near Adi Gadadhar, according to others Godawari	
174.	Yamraj		Across the Phalgu in Bahuri bazzar	
175.	Sharkash Vahanayee			
176.	Ramsagar (Kuruksh̤etra)		Ramsagar tank	
177.	Pād Prakshalan Tirth (Gor-dhoi)		'Khajana' near Brahmyoni	
178.	Radhakund		Near Akashganga, according to others West of Akshayawat	
179.	Somesh Somnath		Near Kapil Dhara	Ritual salutation
180.	Agnish, Angaresh	V., A.		
181.	Lāt Bhairav		Near Brahmnighat	
182.	Baikunt			
183.	Batuk Bhairav		Babhnighat, according to others near Godawari	
184.	Madhu Sudan		South of Akshayawat	
185.	Dagdhashret, Dusoiya		Bishunganj, Sherghati Road	
186.	Nageshwar	G.	Sukhnama, West of Mahadeo according to others near Godawari	

APPENDIX II—*Contd.*

Sl. No.	*Name of the Shrine (Vedi)*	*Reference in Sacred Texts*	*Approximate Location*	*Types of Sacred Performances*
	Nag		Sukhmana, West of Mahadeo according to others near Godawari	
	Mahanag	A.	Near Godavari, according to others Nag Pristnag Tirth, Nag Parwat, below Ram Gaya	
187.	Krishna Dwarika			
188.	Nag Parwat Nag Tirth Nagadri			
189.	Pusp Dutteshwar		At Upddi	
190.	Barah		Near Nawada, according to others village Makhpa, Tikari	
191.	Anirudh	A.		
192.	Adityarath		Near Akashganga	Ancestor sacrifice
193.	Brajaditya			
194.	Kumar Kartikya	V., A. G., A.	Kagwali Darshan	Ritual salutation
195.	Swargdwar	G.	North of Pundrikaksh near Devnadi	
196.	Vayu Tirth		Near Gadadhar Temple	
197.	Matsyapad		South of Agast Kund	
198.	Tirtiya Kar	G., A.	Above Vaitarni	Ancestor sacrifice
199.	Mahakoshi	G.	Ram Gaya, South of Vishnupad, according to others east of Godavari tank by the side of the road	

APPENDIX II—*Contd.*

Sl. No.	*Name of the Shrine (Vedi)*	*Reference in Sacred Texts*	*Approximate Location*	*Types of Sacred Performances*
200.	Jagarnnath (Madhav Bhagwan)	V., A.	Image in the Bhartashram, according to others beneath Mundaprista	Ritual salutation
201.	Subhadra Madhav	G., A.	Image in the Bhartashram, according to others beneath Mundaprista	Ritual salutation
202.	Balbhadra	G., A.	Image in the Bhartashram	Ritual salutation
203.	Dwadshaditya	G., A.	Adi Gauri, Babhnighat	Ritual salutation and worship
204.	Vanhi	A., V.	At Gridheshwar	
	Awanih	V.		
205.	Lokesh	A.		
	Lokpal	A.		
206.	Rundresh	G., A.		Worship
207.	Bramheshwar	A.		
	Bramhtirth	G.		
	Brahmapa	V.	At Babhnighat	Ancestor sacrifice, libation
	Brahmeshwar			
208.	Astlinga, Somnath, Kalesh, Kedar, Parpitamah, Sidhaheshwar, Rudresh, Ramesh, Brahmkeshwar			
209.	Indresh			
210.	Kil Kalesh	A.		Worship, salutation
	Kilesh			
211.	Indresk			
212.	Bridhdhi Vinayak		Kashi Khand, according to others Gayatri Ghat	Ritual salutation and worship
	Bipish Vinayak			
	Bidhnesh Vinayak			
	Silidrahwa (Gaj)	V.		
	Kapish	G.		
	Gaj Vinayak			

APPENDIX II—*Contd.*

Sl. No.	*Name of the Shrine (Vedi)*	*Reference in Sacred Texts*	*Approximate Location*	*Types of Sacred Performances*
213.	Kaaleshwar	G.	Babhnighat	
	Kalesh	G., A.		
	Kalbhairav			
214.	Bhuvanaditya, Surya	G., A.		
215.	Kankark	G.		
216.	Ishwarnagasya			
	Ashwamedhesh	V., G.		
217.	Ashwamedh	A., G., V.		
218.	Swarg Dwaresh (Swarg)			
219.	Prareshwar	A., V.	North of Devnadi	
220.	Gomak			
221.	Goyanti			
222.	Ameye			
223.	Indratirth			Ritual salutation and worship
	Aindra	G.		
224.	Bramhrāy	G.	In the foot-hill of Brahmyoni	
225.	Vashistasharam	G.		
	Vashist Tirth			
	Vashisthi	V.	Near Godawari	Ritual salutation of Vashisthesh Madhev
226.	Mahakashi			
	Varanasi	G.	On Godawari	
227.	Kumardhara	G.	West of Godawari tank	Ancestor sacrifice, ritual salutation in the month of Kartik
228.	Sanwartwapi	G.		Offering of rice-ball
229.	Netra Gartak			
230.	Kronchpad Giri	V., A.		
	Kronch Pad	G.		
231.	Venswanar			
232.	Rewant	G., G.		Ritual salutation and worship
233.	Marenchak			
	Varenchak			

APPENDIX II—*Contd.*

Sl. No.	*Name of the Shrine (Vedi)*	*Reference in Sacred Texts*	*Approximate Location*	*Types of Sacred Performances*
234.	Garur	G., A.	North of Vishnu Temple	Worship
235.	Kshetraphal	G., A.	Near Godawari	
236.	Brahma	A., V., G.		Worship
237.	Brahmasen Ant Jagiri	G.		
238.	Adityagiri		Left to the hill of Maher Pahari Gauri	
239.	Dakshingiri Varch Vateshwaram		Near Pitamah	
240.	Urag			
241.	Anek Gir		West of Dakshingiri	
242.	Agastnath Agasteshwar	V.	On Murli Hill behind Manglagiri	
243.	Adipal Giri	V.	West of Akashganga	
244.	Alkanda (Alahknanda)	V.	North of Dhonheshwari	
245.	Ekadash Rudra	V.	In Jagmavari near Krishna Dwarika	
246.	Angiresh Angareshwar Angarkeshwar	A., G., V.		
247.	Amravan Amrasechan	V., A.		Libation
248.	Kanav (Kawey)			
249.	Kanki			
250.	Koshikik	G.	Across the road, beneath, east of Godawari tank	Ritual bath, libation
251.	Krishna	G.		
252.	Brahantarak Bharatashram		On the road near Bharat Ashram	
253.	Kachbra			
254.	Keyogasa		Mangla Gauri	
255.	Gomti			

APPENDIX II—*Contd.*

Sl. No.	*Name of the Shrine (Vedi)*	*Reference in Sacred Texts*	*Approximate Location*	*Types of Sacred Performances*
256.	Ganga Gangatirtha	G., A.	Near Senji Temple or at Uttarmanas	
257.	Gandki	V.		Ancestor sacrifice
258.	Mangladi	V.		Ritual salutation
	Manglagauri	G., A., V.		
259.	Chandna	V.	North of Putshila Gram Mahadev	
260.	Dharmwati Dharmra	G.		
261.	Jyesstha Jithiyan	V.		
262.	Gangakut			
263.	Pusa		North of Janardan west of Pundri-kaksh	
264.	Paina		Near Naimisharanya	
265.	Puskarini	A., V.	Puskarini tank	Libation
	Pushkar	A., V.	Puskarini tank	Libation
266.	Pankaj Van	V.		
267.	Champak Van, Bhim Pathanrewat Pandu Shila Arwand Van	G.	Located in the Vejri of Mundprista Hill	
268.	Kala			
269.	Karuvathi			
270.	Brihaspati	A.		
271.	Bhuvaneshwari			
272.	Bhasmnath	V.	East of Mangladevi	
273.	Mahant			
274.	Murtivaman	G., A., V.	At Ram Gaya	Worship, ritual salutation
275.	Mukhya Sakshi-karta Lukhya Sakshak Tirth		Janardan	
276.	Murtyastak	V.		
277.	Murtyastak Kund			
278.	Maunark (Maunyark) or Maunki		Dakshin Manas, according to others Uttarmanas	

APPENDIX II—*Contd.*

Sl. No.	*Name of the Shrine (Vedi)*	*Reference in Sacred Texts*	*Approximate Location*	*Types of Sacred Performances*
279.	Hari-Vishnu			Worship, ritual salutation
280.	Har			
281.	Yaksha			
282.	Yug			
283.	Yugdharmi			
284.	Yuprav			
285.	Yamrawali		On Ramgaya Hill, according to others south of Ramshila	
286.	Rukamkund Parijatwan	V.		Ritual bath
287.	Ramshita Sah		In the foot of Ramshila	Worship, ritual salutation
288.	Vahnab		In the foot of Ramshila	
289.	Vyas		In the foot-hill of Ramshila in the southern portion	
290.	Veni Prayag	G., V.		
291.	Vasistesh	G., A.		
292.	Saryu			
293.	Sindhutira Samudra Tirth Nirachchira Sangam Nirachchira Mandal Nirachchira Jla Shay Sangam	A., G., V	From Narayan Chuan to Khawa from Kraochad; North	Ritual bath, libation
294.	Saridwara			
295.	Saptarishi		Gandhar Hill near Gandharv Hill	
296.	Sideshwar	G., V.	Singhwahini Devi on Barabar Hill ; according to others near Sherghati	

APPENDIX II—*Contd.*

Sl. No.	*Name of the Shrine (Vedi)*	*Reference in Sacred Texts*	*Approximate Location*	*Types of Sacred Performances*
	Sidhdeshwari (Rachsiddhra) Swasidhara	G., A.		
297.	Phulvasi			
298.	Astwasu	V.	Near Koleshwari	
299.	Viswadev	V.		
300.	Aswini Kumar Aswniv	V.	Devkund	
301.	Marut	V.		
302.	Yuwki Kup Smriti Kup			
303.	Jangareshwar			
304.	Andhiyargiri		On Dhongeshwar Hill	
305.	Dhyotrawatti			
306.	Nimishahit			
307.	Maheshba Mahesh	A.		
308.	Mularstak			
309.	Uday Varun			
310.	Pusp Dantak (Ha, Ha, Hu, Hu)			
311.	Chirasthaditya			
312.	Valam			
313.	Munyopad		Near Agnidhara	
314.	Bhitti			
315.	Mhahrid	G.		
316.	Man Vidyadhar			
317.	Prachyagiri and Gauri			
318.	Phalgu Chandish Phalgu Chandi	A., V., G. V., G.		Worship, ritual salutation
319.	Rasbhayanvati Rasbahanadi	G.	The hill of Prachyagiri Mandaur	
320.	Punpuna	G., V.		Ancestor sacrifice, libation
321.	Mahachandi	G.		

APPENDIX II—*Contd.*

Sl. No.	*Name of the Shrine (Vedi)*	*Reference in Sacred Texts*	*Approximate Location*	*Types of Sacred Performances*
322.	Gaobhakt Gomar	G.		
323.	Gopatti			
324.	Nar Tirth	G.		
325.	Vasar Tirth Vaswa Tirth	G.		
326.	Vaisnav Tirth Vishnu	A.		
327.	Pitra Manas Uttar Manas	G.		Ancestor sacrifice
328.	Kagjala	G.		
329.	Bramhyoni Yoni Dwar	A., V., G		Ancestor sacrifice
330.	Matangeshwar Mahadev Matgesh	G.	At Bharatashram	
331.	Dharm Prist	G.	Dharmaranya	Ancestor sacrifice, libation
322.	Son Son-Nad Son Tirth	G.		
333.	Vidya	G.		
334.	Mal Pad	G.		
335.	Vidyadharpad	G.		
336.	Kothagiri		Koleshwari Hill is situated 32 miles south of Gaya. According to others west of Devkuli Hill	
337.	Mahendragiri		South Jar Brahmyoni, according to others on Mather Hill	
338.	Gangasagar	V.	Beneath Brahmyoni stream according to others, in the house of Bihari Lal Barik, Ray Bahadur, south of Susmana	

APPENDIX II—*Contd.*

Sl. No.	*Name of the Shrine (Vedi)*	*Reference in Sacred Texts*	*Approximate Location*	*Types of Sacred Performances*
339.	Rajgrihi			
340.	Devika			
341.	Adi Muktesh			
342.	Naimik	V.		
343.	Baina Desh Nami Kup	V.		
344.	Devdar Van	V.	At Mundprista, according to others at Karshili	
345.	Panchlok	V.		
346.	Saptlok	V.	At Mundprista, according to others at Karshili	
347.	Rishikesh	A.	At Mundprista, according to others at Karshili	
348.	Debrun Char Rudra Char Surya	V., G.	Near Putshila	
349.	Vaitarni Mahavaitarni	G., V.	Yuth Madhye	Libation and gifts of cows
350.	Dharmchup	G., A.		
351.	Shilo	G., A.		
352.	Swapusta	G.		
353.	Arvind Parwat Arvind Adira			Ritual salutation
354.	Maspad	G.		
355.	Janwartak	G.		
356.	Aaw Rahma Brahma	V.	Near Goprachar	
357.	Vat	A., V.	Near Gadalel	
358.	Aadi Maharudra	G.		
359.	Matasyapad	G.		
360.	Kurm	G.		
361.	Ram (Dashrathi)	G., A.	In Kashikhand	
362.	Urjit			
363.	Kalanki			
364.	Nagarjun	A.	In Barabar Hill	

APPENDIX II—*Contd.*

Sl. No.	*Name of the Shrine (Vedi)*	*Reference in Sacred Texts*	*Approximate Location*	*Types of Sacred Performances*
365.	Ardan	A.		
366.	Val	A.		
367.	Kam	A.		
368.	Krishnadityapad	A.		
369.	Gayaprach-chalan	A.		
370.	Vodlipad			
371.	Vanarak or Vanrak	A.		
372.	Mukhyatirth	V.		
373.	Gayakut	V.		
374.	Gayapad	A.	Near Choadhari Ghat	
375.	Arunaditya			
376.	Arunadityapad			
377.	Karunadityapad	A.		
378.	Amodhpad			
379.	Muketa	V.		Ancestor sacrifice
380.	Hanstirtha	V.	Near Ramgaya	Ancestor sacrifice
381.	Ramgaya		Sitakund, east of Devghat	

APPENDIX III

PROFESSIONAL LINEAGE TITLES OF THE GAYAWAL

AGINAVAR: It is said that these Gayawal were once agnihotri (fire worshipper) Brahmans. The title, Aginavar, they say, has been derived from this. Only one family bears this title. There is now no family specializing in fire worship among the Gayawal.

AHIR: Said to be used by those Gayawal who in the past kept several cows and distinguished themselves in wrestling. This title is usually borne by a caste whose traditional occupation is dairy farming in Bihar.

BADDIHA: Named after the village Badi Dih, where the family is believed to have taken shelter when the city of Gaya was attacked by some Muslim king.

BARIK: Means subtle. The family which was noted for intelligence was named "Barik." "Barik" is also the name of a caste which makes leaf plates.

BELDAR: "Bel" means creeper. Those who decorated their houses with creepers were called "Beldar". This is also the title of a labourer caste. There is no family with this title now.

BHAIYA: Princes of royal families in Madhya Pradesh are titled "Bhaiya". These Gayawal are believed to have borrowed this title, as that family specializes in their patronage.

BHATT: This Sanskrit title, meaning "learned", was given to a family noted for its learning.

BHOGATA: He who indulges in luxury. There is now no family with this title.

BITHAL: An orthodox family.

BHUIYA: *No information.* Perhaps the name of a village from where the family came.

CHARIYARI: Four Gayawal families of four friends (char yar) combined to carry on the work of priestcraft. Each of these families was called "Chariyari".

CHAUBE: Derived from "chaturvedi," which means "those who know all the four Vedas". A Brahman title.

CHAUDHARI: Persons famous for marketing were called by this name. Usually this title is borne by business castes.

DEVNER: *No information.* No family by this title now.

DHAUKRESHVARI: Those whose dhaukri or pilgrims' rest house was considered as superior were called Dhaukreshvari.

DHAUKRI: This title is the word for the place where pilgrims stay. As the dhaukri of a few persons remained vacant for some time, they were called by this name.

DHERI: *No information.*

DIHUAR: "Dih" means village. Those who protected the village from the attacks of the Muslims were called by this name.

DUBHALIYA: Named after the village, Dubhaliya, where they took their shelter at the time of Muslim attacks.

GARAI: Those who got pilgrims from the hills were called by this name, which is perhaps derived from the word "garva" or hill.

GAYAB: Persons who lived in a secret manner were given this title. In the local dialect, "gayab" means "to disappear".

GOLIVAR: Persons of a family efficient in fighting with guns. Seems to be a modern title.

GOSAIN OR GOSVAMI: A Brahman title.

GUPTA: A title borne by several Vaishya castes.

GURDA: Someone who received a large part of the king's property.

HADA: There is no Gayawal family of this name now. Title given to that family whose members were priests of the Hada Rajput caste.

HAL: The plough is called hal. No information from the Gayawal about any association of this family with the plough.

HUNDA: Name given to a miser Gayawal who hoarded money in a hunda, or large vessel. No family by this title now.

JHANGAR: Said to be the title of certain Brahmans in the Punjab. The Gayawal who specialized in Punjabi patrons called themselves by this name.

JUDGE: To a Gayawal, the late Laljee Guput, people gave the title of "judge" for his honesty.

KARI: Those who used to do hard work to make the pilgrims comfortable were called "kari," an abbreviation of hard worker, "kari vriti".

KATARIYAR: Some say they were named after the village, Katari, where they took shelter at the time of Muslim invasions. Others say the name comes from the family's having once been narrowly orthodox, "Kattar".

KHARKHAUKA: As they loved "khar," straw, they were called by this name.

KOHDAURI: Those who migrated to Kohdauri Village at the time of crisis.

KOLKAT: Those who defeated the Kol tribes. No family by this title now.

KUTTI: Those who preferred to live in a "kutti," or hut. No family by this title now.

MAHATA: A royal position especially in South India. These Gayawal are said to have borrowed this title from their pilgrims.

MAHATO: The family which was originally the head of the Gayawal village was called "Mahato". "Mahato" is at times used for the head of a village. However, it is a very popular title for the people of several agricultural castes like Govala, Kurmi, etc.

MAUAR: According to the Gayawal, this title is said to have been derived from "mira" or "malik," which literally means "master".

MEHARVAR: Some Gayawal family which was generous to the pilgrims called itself "meharvar", a Persian word meaning "generous".

MISHIR: A common Brahman title. The family interested in the reading of religious texts was called "mishir".

NAKPHOPHA:—Name given to a family which felt pride in their wealth. "Nak", they say, is the distorted form of "nag" (serpent), while "phopha" means "pride", with reference to the jewel which each serpent allegedly carries.

NAYAK: The man who had the capacity for community leadership was called "nayak" (leader), and his family was named after it.

PAHARI: The family that took shelter at Pahatpur during a

crisis has this title. Some say that their title came from the fact that this family used to entertain pilgrims mainly from the hilly regions of Central India.

PANDY: A common Brahman title.

PARVATIYA: It is said that before their arrival, the families bearing this name lived on "parvat" (hills) at Kirshilli.

PASERA: Descendants of a noted Gayawal wrestler whose meals consisted of things weighing five seers (panch ser) bear this name.

PATHAK: A Brahman title. Those who remained absorbed in ritual studies.

POLAD: *No information.*

RAJA: Means "king". The Raja protected the Gayawal during the attacks.

SENA: The family of a man interested in the army (sena) was called by this name. This is the title of a caste in Bengal which is said to have been formed by persons born of the concubines of the Brahmans in Bengal.

SIJUAR: Distorted from the word "shrijuar", which means "those who receive wealth in terms of tides". "Shri" means "wealth", and "juar" means "tide".

TAIYA: Means "tactful" in the Magadhi dialect. Those who took away the besieging army tactfully were called "Taiya".

TATAK: "Tat" is a word which the Gayawal use for payment. It was reported that the man who organized the panchayat was called "Tatak", and later his family was called by this name.

UPADHYAY: A Brahman title. Those interested in the study of the Veda.

APPENDIX IV

THE GAYAWAL GOTRA (CLANS) AND THEIR CORRESPONDING DIVISIONS

S. N.	Gotra	Veda	Upa Veda	Shakha	Sutra	Shika	Pud	Deota
1.	Gautam	Yajhuah	Dhanur	Madhnindni	Katyayan	Dakshin	Dakshnin	Vishnu
2.	Kashyapa	Sam	Gandharva	Kauthumi	Govil	Bam Bam	Shiva	Vishnu
3.	Kaushik	Yajhuah	Dhanush	Madhyandhini	Katyan	Dakshin	Dakshin	Vishnu
4.	Kaushika	Yajhuah	Dhanuah	Madhyandhini	Katyanan	Dakshin	Dakshnin	Shiva
5.	Kanva	Yajhuah	Dhanuah	Madhyandhini	Katyanan	Dakshin	Dakshnin	Shiva
6.	Bhardwaj	Yajhuah	Yayuah	Madhyandhini	Katyanan	Dakshin	Dakshnin	Shiva
7.	Ausanasa	Yajhuah	Dhanush	Madhyandhini	Katyanan	Dakshin	Dakshnin	Shiva
8.	Vatsya	Sam	Gandharva	Kauthumi	Govil	Bam	Bam	Bam
9.	Parasar	Yajhuah	Dhanuah	Madhyandhini	Katyayun	Dakshin	Dakshim	Shiva
10.	Harit Kumar	Yajhuah	Dhanuah	Madhyandhini	Katyayun	Dakshin	Dakshim	Shiva
11.	Madhlya	Yajhuah	Dhanuah	Madhyandhini	Katyayun	Dakshin	Dakshim	Shiva
12.	Laungakahi	Rig	Atharyan	Aswalayan	Aswalyan	Bam	Bam	Vishnu
13.	Vashistha	Yajhuah	Dhanuah	Madhindhi	Katyayun	Dakshin	Dakshin	Shiva
14.	Atreya	Yajhuah	Dhanuah	Madhindhi	Katyayun	Dakshin	Dakshin	Shiva

APPENDIX V

SEVEN LIFE-HISTORIES OF THE GAYAWAL

A

NAME: C. L.
AGE: 72
FATHER'S NAME: K. L.

(Though old, with very robust body; when interviewed, was sitting on his cot on the first floor of the house; no interference; three sittings in two days; in autobiographical narration very frank, however an attempt to exaggerate such events as may appear gratifying and conceal others that may affect his prestige.)

Childhood. I was born in a big family. At the time of my birth my grandfather and grandmother were alive. I was the first issue of my father. My father was the second son of my grandfather and his eldest brother also lived with him. My uncle had one son and one daughter when I was born, and they used to give me company during my childhood.

My family was economically very well off then Rs. 15,000 per annum, perhaps, was the income. In addition there were several horses and three elephants maintained by the family. There was a group of servants and maid servants. I was looked after by the maid servants. But my mother also used to take special care of me. After the retirement of my grandfather, my uncle, as the eldest member, was the head of the family. He used to love me very much and he never distinguished me from his own sons. (*Question.*)

During my childhood I was attached more to my uncle than to my father. I used to live in close association with my uncle. My father did not talk to me much. He was shy even of taking me on his lap and speaking to me affectionate words. This was mainly in the presence of my uncle. Owing to his neglect, and the encouragement of my uncle, as far as I remember I became very attached to my uncle and not at all to my father. My uncle used to keep me always with him. Among the women, my mother was specially affectionate to me. I was her first child and that also a son—how could she afford to neglect me! She always kept aneye on me and never beat me. Of course, I remember one event in this connexion. When I was four, there was some quarrel with my cousin (5 years). We used to play and quarrel all the time but this time, perhaps, I called him by some vulgar name. My mother did not like it at all. She beat me and I began to cry very loudly. This moved my mother very much. Tears came in her eyes and perhaps she took a vow not to beat me any more. My aunt also was not less affectionate to me.

Four years and after. My education started very early. My mother who was somewhat literate began to teach me the three R's when I was only four and a half years old. She used to teach me with great affection and by six and a half years of age I learnt quite a bit of "books and arithmetic". My uncle used to give me lessons in worship, prayers, mantras, etc.

I was never allowed to go out of the house, and I used to play inside the building with my cousin, brother and sister, and with the children of the servants. Our plays were very peculiar. We used to make deities out of stones and mud and we used to offer them prayers. We used to take the images of god and goddesses in procession. We used to beat 'drums' and pots to make noise and then used to throw the images or deities in the well. I was also interested in kites and tops. My cousin was interested in bird-keeping. There was a couple of servants to look after them. I used to look at these tiny birds which appeared to me very beautiful. At times my father also used to feed them.

At the age of six, I was enrolled in the neighbouring upper primary school and continued to go there up to the age of ten. In the school, I did not feel much interest. The teacher was not kind to me. He used to threaten to beat me with a cane. I was very afraid of him.

At the age of eight the Sacred Thread ceremony (Yajnapabit) was observed. It was a big function and thousands of rupees were spent (*Ethnographic*). Now I was initiated to the Brahmanic way of life and uncle began to watch my activities very carefully.

A special panditjee began to come to teach me both Sanskrit and *Sandhya.* The panditjee, whose name I cannot recollect, was attached to the Gayawal *Thakurbadri* (the centre of religious performances). At that time there was no trace of *Math.* I began to observe Sandhya (worship) the day I wore the Sacred Thread. A number of restrictions were associated with the Sacred Thread (*Ethnographic*) and at the beginning I had some difficulties but later it became a matter of practice. Now I was not allowed to eat when the servants' children were with me. I also started to attend the *Akhara* (a place specially prepared for wrestling and physical exercise), which was located in the garden adjacent to the house. During that time, children of even one year of age used to go to the *Akhara* with their relations and used to see the wrestling. I also attended it from the very beginning of my childhood and began wrestling when I was about 9 years old. This continued till I was 40 years old. At this age, I underwent a hydrocele operation and I had to discontinue all types of physical exercise.

Ten years and after. I was married when I was 10 years old and my wife was six. The marriage was finalised by my grandfather. He took a great interest in the performance of the marriage ceremony. More than ten thousand rupees were spent. Sweets were distributed in the whole of Gaya, and even the servants of the family were presented costly shawls.

Some time after the marriage, I fell ill. I got a poisonous abscess which continued for about a year. This marked the end of my schooling. After my illness, I continued my studies at home. Two teachers used to teach me at two different times every day and they used to teach me everything. All types of things—Bengali, Hindi, English, religions—were taught to me. It continued till I reached the age of 18. I became the least interested in education when my wife came to my house (when I was sixteen). At that time she was about 12 years old.

I became also interested in song and music when I was about 12 years old. My cousin used to learn music (harmonium and tabla) from a teacher. I used to sit beside him and enjoy the musical sound. I was specially interested in vocal and not in the instrumental music. There were a group of *Kathak* servants in my family. They are traditional singers of devotional and genealogical songs. They were specially employed by my grandfather to entertain our pilgrims who used to visit Gaya. They also used to go to our 'Desh' (territory from where pilgrims come) to recruit pilgrims. They were good singers, they used to entertain the pilgrims throughout the way. At that time pilgrims generally used to come on foot or on horses or elephants. So, I learnt a number of devotional songs from them and thus was initiated to music. But I did not feel much interest in this line though it continued till my thirtieth year. Later, I left it, though I remember some of the songs even today.

When I was twenty, I became specially interested in bird-keeping. Besides, *Lal, Lava, Tithar, Maina, Sugga,* a number of other varieties of birds were under my possession and I used to get delight in feeding them. Sometimes I used to keep birds of different types and used to watch their "fight". I got costly cages of different designs for them. For ten years, I was mad after them, but later the interest dwindled. (*Question.*)

When I was of eighteen, my grandfather died. After two years of his death, partition occurred between my father and my uncle. With this partition, my friendly activities also decreased. Till now, my uncle in co-operation with my father used to look after the affairs of the pilgrims. But now my father was alone and being his only son, I had to take care of the pilgrims and look after their affairs. This also affected my studies.

At the age of 35, I could not check the temptation of going on a pilgrimage. My father also gave his approval. We thought, we would also meet our *jajman* (votaries) in different parts of India. The auspicious day for starting on the pilgrimage was finished. I, along with my wife, *Tharkurjee* (our personal deity) and four servants, set out on the journey. Father took on himself all the responsibilities of home and pilgrims. From Gaya we went to Bengal and stayed at Calcutta. A *jajman* arranged everything for me in a *Dharmshala.* From there we went to Jagnath Puri in Orissa, then to Rameshwaram in Madras. We spent about eight months in all these places. From extreme south we went to west and after visiting Dwarika, Bombay, Bindhyabasini, etc., we came back to Gaya. This pilgrimage of South, East and West India took about one year.

After two years, we again went on a pilgrimage to north- and north-western India. After staying at Kashi, Prayag, Mathura, Brindaban, Rawalpindi, Karachi, Peshawar, we went up to Kabul in Afghanistan. We used to meet and stay with our *jajman* in all the places of pilgrimage. This time my long stay was in Sindh and Baluchistan. We were specially invited by rich pilgrims of these places. They met all our expenditures and escorted us to their respective places. I was very much impressed by the functioning of the village councils of these places in Sindh and Baluchistan. We used to eat very rich food consisting of fresh fruits, dry fruits, vegetables, bread, ghee, etc. At the time of departure, they used to give us all types of clothes, money in cash and a large variety of things. Wherever I went, I was very much respected. I used to talk to them on religious matters. In the village councils, I usually went to sing and talk. The Kathak servants used to sing devotional songs very well. I used to devote about four hours of the day in religious worship.

On my return from my second pilgrimage I became more and more inclined to religious activities. Most of my mornings and evenings were spent before the deities in worship and prayers. Once a month, and on the occasion of the festivals and religious functions, I used to go to the Vishnupad temples for *Darshan*. My worship was usually concentrated before our own *Thakurjee* (family shrines). But during the last six years, every morning I go to the temple. Though it is far ($\frac{3}{4}$ mile) and I am old, still in no case do I fail to go there.

I never went to the temple for securing gifts from the visitors. Though 'Bhaia' families are specially privileged to attend the shrine in the evening for securing gifts, I never enjoyed this traditional privilege. (*Question.*). There is no particular reason for this. But mainly temperamentally and partly owing to distance, I did not exercise my right for the same. My priestly profession (*Vriti*) has been continuing for the last 20 years. I have faced several types of experiences during my career as a priest. The people who come to offer Shraddha are very sincere but now they are very much exploited by the priests and their servants. Only yesterday, a group of five pilgrims came from Barelly in Uttar Pradesh. Originally they were from West Punjab (Pakistan). A *dalal* (agent) misled them and took them to a separate place and convinced them that they were in the hands of their own *Panda*. Anyhow, they offered the *Pindas* and other things at two places. But they were doubtful about the identity of the *Panda* and enquired about me from my nephew. There were quarrels on this issue and ultimately the men have come to me and today they will again begin their *Pindadan*. At this age of 72, I do not want to enter into all these disputes, but our profession has become so commercial that there is no way out. I had to take entire responsibility of the profession after the death of my father when I was 45.

I have not been blessed with any issue. We are very dissatisfied on this account. After my death nobody will be left to perpetuate my or my father's name. It is very unfortunate. But what can we do? In spite of our combined worship and pilgrimage, we could not modify the effect of the planets that rule in the 'house of children'. I am under the influence of *Mangal* and in no case was there any likelihood of the birth of a child.

Owing to this, I discontinued sexual intercourse at the age of 40 years. I thought that when there was no chance of conception for my wife, it was immoral to indulge in sexual intercourse for the sake of pleasure. I preferred strengthening my body to sexual enjoyment.

I had to undergo a good deal of rigour and trouble to live up to the vow. At times, the sexual desire used to become very strong and I was very restless. But my promise not to meet my wife in the night was never broken. I never went to her. In order to sublimate my sexual urge, I used to wash my penis and used to distract my mind by reciting or reading passages from the Ramayana. This sort of repression and conflict continued for several months. Fortunately I met a Brahman *sadhu* at Vishnupad temple. He came here on pilgrimage from Haridwar. I visited him several times and in the course of a conversation, he suggested to me a very simple 'medicine' for this. He suggested that if I drank the juice of the red flower of banana along with sugar candy, my sexual passion would vanish. He further stated that if I wanted to revive it again, I may eat the flower of *Tulsi* along with honey. I acted according to his advice and since then the sexual urge does not disturb me. It is perfectly under control. (*A delicate question about sex.*) I never engaged a young maid servant in my house. There were several aged maid servants. These maid servants used to live just like the members of the family, and when they died, I had not only to observe their death rites but I had to marry their sons and daughters at quite an early age. At present, there is only one domestic servant who looks after me. My wife has one maid for her comfort.

Regarding my religious beliefs and practices, they might appear to you very strange. You will never find a Gayawal doing in the manner I am going to narrate to you.

At the age of 17-18, I went to the fair of Harihar Kshetra. You know this is even today the biggest fair of India and perhaps also of the world. This was my first visit to this fair and I was very curious to know and see all the things there. When I reached there, I went to the *Pandal* (stadium) of Arya Samaj. Some person was delivering a speech about religion. I sat down to listen. When the lecture came to an end, and the people dispersed, I slept on the carpet there. This was mainly for want of any other suitable space. In the morning I had conversation with some of the members of Arya Samaj. One of them enrolled me as the member of Arya Samaj. I paid him Rs. 51 and I got accommodation to live in a small tent. I stayed at the site of the fair for about twenty days. I read some of the small books published by Arya Samaj and bought books worth Rs. 200 from them. Now, I was a full-fledged follower of Arya Samaj. I began to preach the gospel of Arya Samaj at Gaya. The same year, I organised a three-day function of Arya Samaj at Gaya and invited five learned members of Arya Samaj from Patna to deliver speeches. I was very much criticised by the Gayawal and other people. They rebuked me in all the possible ways and charged me with the sin of leaving *Sanatan Dharma* (the eternal religion). But I remained adamant and continued my affiliation with Arya Samaj. My father also did not like my activities but he did not interfere in this matter.

At the age of 35, I got a chance to listen to the speeches of the members of Brahmo Samaj. I studied its literature and was influenced by its liberal ideals. I continued to go to the temple of Brahmo Samaj for about four years and used to discuss religious matters with enlightened people and then used to think about them.

Thereafter I came in contact with a Maulvi Sahab (a Muslim teacher). I read Koran with him. I attended the mosque near by. Maulvi Saheb thought that I would adopt Islam. But my aim was altogether different. I wanted to know about the basic foundation and function of every religion. This strong curiosity to know about the teachings and function of other religions impelled me from religion to religion.

At the age of 30, I also began to attend the Sunday prayers of the Roman Catholic Church. I read some of their literature which they kindly gave to me. The Christian girls used to accompany me and they tried many means to convert me to Christianity. But I stood firm on my old religion.

In the end, at the age of 45, I came to the conclusion that the essence of all religions is the same. I considered *Sanatan Dharma* to be the best among all and began to do worship and prayer according to the systems prescribed by it. I had no doubt now about the validity of this system of beliefs. During this period I was also convinced that we should never think of death and we should do our work with alertness and optimism.

At the age of 45, I became interested in a different type of work. This was to work for the protection of the cattle. I used to collect the old cows and bullocks from the cattle fairs held twice a year on the Phalgu. The two fairs, as they are held today, occur on the full moon of Kartika (September) and 20th day of Chait Bishuad (May). During these two fairs, we used to collect about two to three hundred heads of cattle which we used to bring to the Gaya Cow-Protection House. Hundreds of such cattle were sent to Nepal Cow-Protection Centres. I still continue this work during the fairs. But now I can only collect 40 to 50 cows. People do not give them to me without substantial payment. I was always responsive to this activity for the development of our community. When a few Gayawal took the initiative to organise an association of the Gayawal community, under the name of Trith Vriti Sudhanni Samiti (Society for the Improvement of Pilgrimage Profession) for certain improvement in the profession, I joined them. Actually, the step that I took at that time was economically unsound for me. The main aim of the Samiti was to end the *Rojgari Pratha* or the commercial (agency) elements that entered our profession. I was very much benefited by this new introduction of *Rojgari Pratha.* I had my influence on a number of *Rojagaria* (commercial agents) who used to bring a large number of pilgrims in my fold. The porters of the local railway stations, the police and the goondas (mischief mongers), all used to help me. I hired a big house at Sahebgunj (New Gaya) adjacent to the railway station to deal with them and the pilgrims. But when I found a number of Gayawal brethren active in stopping it I decided to give up *Rojgaria Pratha.* I left the house at New Gaya, and came back to Ander Gaya (Old Gaya) to enjoy my rightful share and help the people in eradicating this evil. Since then I have always planning to improve my society (*Ethnographic*). I have written two or three books in this connection, the manuscripts of which you can examine. These days, I am busy in framing certain rules regarding the Gayawal priestly profession. I want to reorganise the *jajmani* on a new model. The old records are no longer very useful. Moreover, it brings about complication and bitterness. So in my new scheme of things, I totally want to remove "registers" as records of reference. We want to regulate the numbers and territory of pilgrims through the Gayawal *Panchayat* (Council). We are taking the consent of everybody. Let us see how it works. I am very doubtful in view of the disunity among ourselves.

I have been living in this house alone for the last thirty years. My wife lives on the second floor and I live here on the first floor. In the night, the servant and maid servant go to their respective homes. I do not ask them to sleep here. As we are afraid of thieves, I do not sleep much in the night. I always keep a gun and torch within my reach at night.

On the whole, I like this quiet and peaceful place. I never prefer to be in the midst of crowd and noise. I have been thoughtful and meditative from the very beginning of my life. I am proud of making certain chemical things. I can make a digestive drug out of *Nuni* (a type of saline soil), and separate the "bitterness" of *Khira* (a type of fruit). I hope to live longer to see my society on a higher ethical level. But I am very doubtful that my efforts would succeed. But one has to make efforts, the result lies in the hands of the gods.

B

NAME: SRIMATI J. D., wife of the late M. L.
AGE: 65 years.
FATHER'S NAME: B. L.

(This is the mother of one of my chief informants, Sri N. L. K. On my request he persuaded her to give me some information regarding her life and activities. She agreed to our proposal but did not come in my presence. She replied to my questions staying in the room while we were out on the verandah. N. K. her son, acted as the mediator.)

I was born in a very rich family. During that period the average annual income of my family came to be about 50 to 70 thousand rupees. I was very much loved and cared for in my father's family as well as in the family of my mother's father. As I was the first issue of my parents, the extent of affection for me knew no bounds. My uncle and aunt had no issue at that time. They also loved me very much. My grandmother was exceptionally good to me. She used to entertain me for all the time. It was her exclusive duty to take care of me. She continued to look after me till I was eight. At my mother's father's place, I was specially attached to my mamu (mother's brother) and mamani (mother's brother's wife).

Four and a half years after my birth, I was blessed with a brother. Now, I had to leave mother's milk. It was a painful experience but my grandmother used to satisfy me. My parents continued to love me as usual.

During my childhood, I was specially interested in dolls. My usual playmates were my maternal cousins. They used to live close by and sometimes I used to go to them or sometimes they used to come to me. Though both houses were almost side by side, we were not allowed to go alone. I used to go to them with my old servant. My special interest was in the "marriage of the dolls". Every month or so, I remember, we used to celebrate the marriage ceremony of the dolls. Sometimes I owned the male doll and my maternal sister owned the female ones and vice versa.

We used to spend a sum of Rs. 5 to 10 on such a celebration. I also used to go with the old servant to play at the house of my father's sister (fufu).

I began to read and write at the age of seven and owing to that coaching, I even today read passages from the Ramayan and keep accounts.

I was married when I was nine years old. About five thousand rupees were spent in the celebrations. Marriage did not bring any change in me. As usual I lived with my mother and continued to share her domestic work. My special work (there) was to play with my younger brother.

At the age of 18, my "second marriage ceremony" was performed. Now, my relation with *swasural* (husband's family) began to increase. The first time, I lived at swasural for one day; the next, I stayed there for three days and the third time I stayed there for one week. In this way, my association with my father's family began to decrease and that with the husband's family began to increase. After three years, I began to live for years at my husband's place. I used to get all types of things from my mother. Some were in the shape of personal gifts and some were given ceremonially at the time of my departure from her place.

. . . Now my domestic and family life began at my husband's house. I was received in the family quite well. My mother-in-law liked me. I tried to please her and I did what she liked me to do. But this created jealousy in my eldest *gotani* (husband's brother's wife) who was not on good terms with our mother-in-law. Owing to her jealous and greedy nature, I also could not become agreeable to her. Later, my differences with her increased and with this her cruelty towards me also increased. My mind always remained disturbed owing to this tense relationship but there was no way out. It was next to impossible for my husband to propose a partition to his eldest brother. All types of quarrel and exchanges of words continued for eight years. Later, they proposed a partition and my husband's eldest brother began to live separately with his wife.

I was on a very good relationship with my *Majhali jethani* (husband's second brother's wife). She used to take my side at the time of my quarrels with *Bari Gotani*. She along with her husband continued to live with us. But after one year, they began to live separately. However this partition was not based on any misunderstanding and quarrel. It was just a matter of convenience.

My first issue was a daughter who was born when I was 18 years. After an interval of two years, another daughter was born. The third issue was a son who was born after another two years. I got two more sons and one more daughter, each at an interval of two years.

My whole-time work was to look after the children. They were very dear to me and I loved them very much. I never made any distinction between a son and a daughter. But I confess that I have liked the eldest son the most. Still I am more affectionately attached to him than the others.

With affection, I also exercised my control over them. I never allowed them to go out of the house without my permission. When they used to break my order (*Aghya*), I used to express my anger to them. I also wished that my children should get education and learn music. I used to take special care of them in this connexion. I used to pay the teacher extra money to coach them carefully.

When my children fell ill, I become very nervous. I become impatient to see them free from any trouble. I go to the temple to vow to make special offerings for their immediate cure. I used to request my husband to call *Panditjee* for (jap) special propitiation and now ask my son for all this. The women well-versed in *Mantras* are called to exercise their "magical utterances" to cure them. I also asked the servants and my husband or son to call doctors.

My husband died at the age of 62 about three years ago. His death brought to me all the pathos of widowhood. I wished I could have died before him. However, I consoled myself by looking at my three sons and their children. But after one year my grand-daughter (16 years, married daughter of the eldest son) also died. She was suffering from fever and cough for several months. All types of worship and medicine were tried. But she was not cured. I happened to take her to Patna. Her mother, myself and her father accompanied her to the hospital. We hired quarters in the paying ward of the hospital. Later her husband's relations joined. Her condition improved for a while but later it deteriorated very much. She died within a month.

Her death has left a very painful impression on me. Though this cruel event took place about a year back, I still continue to weep for her for days and days together. I made all prayers to God. I propitiated Him to take my life instead of hers, but my prayer was not heard. My life has become a burden to me after seeing two deaths. Still I am alive. But I am alive only because God is not granting me death. Disease does not come to me, though I have become so lean and thin. This is all the illusion of God.

C

NAME: G. L.
AGE: 59.
FATHER'S NAME: N. L.

My father had two brothers and all of them lived together at the time of my birth. My father was the youngest of the three brothers. My elder uncle had no issue while the eldest uncle had three sons and one daughter at the time of my birth. I was the fourth issue of my father.

The economic status of my family was fairly good at the beginning. But six months before my birth, my family was involved in a criminal case that badly affected the economic conditions of my family. The case that our family had to fight was against another Gayawal, named U. The quarrel started at the Vishnupad temple between members of my family and that of U. on the issue of worshippers and gifts. The quarrel became complicated and both the parties became very much involved in it. It culminated in physical fights and deadly weapons like sword and *bhala* lethal weapons were used. Among others U. was heavily wounded and a case was instituted against our grandfather and his sons. My grandfather won the case but more than a hundred thousand rupees were spent in the case. He had to sell his property—land, Zamindari and house—and also take a loan. Owing to all these the economic status of the family deteriorated considerably. My grandfather was not in a position to maintain the status of the family. He was one of the respectable men of the community and was in charge (*Sardar*) of the Deoghat *Baithaka* (Gayawal Club). But now he was not in a position to maintain the expenditure of the *Baithaka*. He used to remain very unhappy. He fell ill and deliberately did not take any medicine. My uncles and father left no stone unturned to persuade him to undergo treatment. But partly on religious grounds and partly because he wanted to die, he did not take any medicine. Ultimately he died.

Two years after his death, partition took place in my family. At that time I was six months old. After partition we shifted to this house. At that time, the income of each family was reduced to one thousand rupees. The grandfather also left a loan of Rs. 46,000 which was divided among the three brothers for payment.

The economic condition of my father was very bad and in a mood of despair and depression, he gave me away in adoption to Sri K. L. In my family there was no precedence either of taking or giving a son in adoption. But, due to the pressing poverty, my father was compelled to give me in adoption. He was under the impression that this relationship would keep the two families on good terms in many matters. He also thought that after the death of K., I would become the legal heir to his *throne* (gaddi).

But in course of time, the economic condition of K. began to deteriorate while the economic conditions of our family began to improve. Now K. fell under heavy debts. My father always helped him in securing loans. But in the meantime misunderstanding grew between my father and K. and ended in inter-family tension. At this time I was twelve years old. When K. died, I refused to go to his house to take possession of his property. As a matter of fact this question did not arise owing to differences between our families that arose two years ago. His nephew (brother's son) became the owner of his property.

My mother was of a very simple nature but she never remained in good terms with my father. The main reason for their differences was the liberal attitude of my mother towards the servants and maid servants. She used to give money, grains and other things to them very benevolently. This, she used to do very liberally specially with the servants and maid servants of her father's family. They used to visit her regularly and used to get all types of things from her. My father used to impose restriction on her doing so. He was deeply concerned with the declining economic conditions. But my mother was the least concerned with all these practical matters. She was the only daughter of her father and on the slightest provocation, she used to escape to her father's place. (*Question.*) My mother was especially attached to the maid servants mainly because she was looked after by them during her childhood after the death of her mother. Her mother died when she was only three years old, and since then, she was in closer association with them.

Owing to all this there was great tension in my family. My mother never cared for her children and used to escape to her father's place. My father used to keep me there in the house with a view that she would not go without me. But she was such a strong-minded woman that she used to leave me for many days and used to live with her father without me. As a result of all this, I was completely neglected by my mother. In her absence, my "grandmother" (father's father's brother's wife) used to look after me. I was never left to the maid servants for nursing. After one year, I began to be fed completely on cow's milk. I used to drink about four pounds of milk. Now, my mother began to live in her father's place for still longer periods, varying from two to four months. My father never allowed me to take me with her. So I could not enjoy her company and affection for longer periods. My two elder sisters used to entertain me. My father also used to pay attention to me but he was not very much attached to me.

My father was fed up with the affairs of my mother. He engaged a concubine. She was an inhabitant of Kahal Gaun village in Bhagalpur district and was Kayastha by caste. At that time she was 19 years old. She used to live in the house adjacent to ours. At that time I was only 3 years old. My mother was not at all furious for this deed of my father. She was also not at all cruel to the concubine. After one year the concubine gave birth to a son who is still alive. My mother also loved her son, perhaps more than myself.

After this incident my mother began to live at her father's place for still longer periods. I was the least attached to her and now I never cared for her company. But again a turning point came in her activity. This was, with the death of the concubine when her son was only 3 years old. My mother was very much moved by the pitiable condition of the boy (Gopal). She could not see him being neglected. She began to live with us to look after him. But at the time, he reached the age of six, she again began to escape to live in her father's place.

I was admitted in the Primary School at the age of five. A teacher of the same school, Gopal Babu, also used to coach me at home. My father wanted me to go to school as he felt the best education could be had there. But I was not interested in studies and after three years, I discontinued. My father did not press me much owing to his belief that a Gayawal cannot get an education. I was very much interested in all types of outdoor games and at times I used to go to the school with my eldest brother and Gopal just to play in the field. The drill master used to persuade me to read and write. He also spoke to my father in this connexion and I was again admitted to the school at the age of ten. But I was more interested in play than in studies. In the course of time, I became good at football, hockey and cricket. I was counted as one of the best players and was captain of the hockey and football teams for several years. In the classes, I failed twice and at the age of 17, I reached the tenth class. Then I discontinued my studies for ever. My elder brother was very intelligent and after passing the matriculation examination, he went to Bhagalpur for his college education. He took his admission in the intermediate class but owing to difficulties in the matter of food, he discontinued his studies after eight or nine months of his admission. He was the only man in the Gayawal society to have passed the matriculation examination and got admission in the college at that time.

My Sacred Thread ceremony was observed at the age of seven. After that I was initiated to learn *Sandhya* (prayer, hymns). A Brahmin from the south (Dakshni Brahmin) used to teach me *Sandhya*. He also taught me Sanskrit.

I was married at the age of 12. The marriage was settled by my father. At the time of the marriage my wife was about 9 years old. About Rs. 2,500 were spent in the marriage celebration. The second marriage ceremony took place when I was of 17 years. I never met my wife for sexual intercourse before this ceremony. After my marriage, I used to go to my father-in-law's place on the occasion of festivals but I used to come back to my own house in the night.

I did not know anything about sexual matters before my wife came to my house. At the school, I had to maintain my position, as I was the captain and I did not mix with the students loosely and talk to them on sex. At the home, my father used to keep strict supervision on me and all of us used to sleep in the same room. Under the circumstances, my first intercourse was with my wife at my own place. At the end of the first year of her stay in my house, she became pregnant. During that period, plague broke out in Gaya. My family along with 20 others moved to Baidhyanath Dham. My wife gave birth to a son there. But the baby died only within ten hours owing to excessive bleeding from the umbilical cord. It happened because of the mistake of the *chamain* (local midwife) in cutting the umbilical cord.

Regarding my childhood games and companions, I was not allowed to go to play out of my house. I used to play with my sisters and brother in the house itself. Running from pillar to post, *jhula,* etc. were our favourite games. My father was a famous wrestler and under his direction we (myself and my eldest brother) also started physical exercises in our childhood. I continued these till last year when I was not in a position to get a suitable diet.

When I began to go to the school, I began to play outdoor games in the field of the school. As the captain in the school, I had to make all the arrangements for the play of football and hockey. I was also interested in physical exercise at the school and once I stood first in gymnastic performances. I was mostly friendly with the students of higher classes. This was caused mainly because (M. Bhaie) my elder brother was two classes above me and all his friends were my friends as well. On the whole, however, I was friendly with all my classmates. I was not very intimate with any of them.

I was not attached to my priestly profession or with the affairs of my *jajman* till I was a student. During that period, however, I used to go to the Vishnupad temple with my *jajman*. Out of five pice that usually was offered, I used to take one pice and the other four pice I used to give to my grandmother. I also used to get 2 annas every day for my refreshment in the school. I used to save some money out of it. This money, I used to spend either in travel or in investment on interest ; I used to get a chance to go to places like Allahabad or Banaras with some of our relatives. I used to give the money also to some of our relatives after charging interest.

At the age of 17, I began to look after the major affairs of *Vriti* (profession). My father entrusted upon me all the works regarding the *jajman*, and the family. I was now responsible to attend all the social functions like marriage, death, etc., in the community. I was also given the accounts for loan and credit, etc. At that time, the net income of the family had risen to fourteen thousand. I was carrying on the work successfully.

Social service: From the very school career, I became interested in social service. When I left the school and engaged myself in priestly profession, my interest in social service became still stronger. I used to attend and take special care if someone became sick among our relatives in the community. I also began to help and make visits to the members of the Baithka. I was determined to remove some of the evils of our society. This vow reminds me of a funny incident in school. The subject of it was the hobby of bird-keeping of the Gayawal. I was very much ashamed to see this and I felt that the Gayawal were doing things that were subjects of social ridicule. Since then, I have made up my mind to uplift the society. But how to make things acceptable? How to enter into the society? I was neither interested in music nor was I a very wealthy person nor was I an accomplished wrestler. However, I continued my efforts to get into them. There was a group of Gayawal dominated by Sri Bihari Lal Barik. I tried to associate myself with this group. I was invited by him on the occasion of Holi festival. I went to his musical group. All of us were mad after religious and vulgar musical performances suited to the occasion. I was accepted there with respect and goodwill. My association with them continued. I was not interested in music but my aim was to use the group for the work of social uplift.

The first important work that I could do was the re-establishment of the *Math.* I requested the Dakhini Swamijee to give me some competent men to run the *Math.* A *pandit* agreed to stay in the *Math.* He began to teach the Gayawal youths *sandhya* and Sanskrit. The Gayawal accepted my proposal to give maintenance to the *panditjee.* At that time my age was 34 years, i.e., the *Math* was started about 25 years ago.

In the same year, a big meeting of the Gayawal was convened to oppose the endowment bill that dealt with the curtailment of powers of the priests or temples or *Maths.* I was elected by the people to conduct the proceedings of the meetings. With this, I also put before them other problems of our community and made a special appeal to devise ways and means to improve the priestly profession (*Vriti*). Sri Matho Laljee Katariar seconded my proposal and we decided to make an organization for the improvement of the *Vriti.* Then persons offered themselves to work for this. But some of them strongly opposed the idea. They were in favour of maintaining the status quo and did not like any change. In order to win them over, a number of persons offered passive resistance. Persons began to offer *Satyagraha* at the doors of those who opposed the proposal. It was really unexpected. Could the Gayawal undergo self-torture during the scorching sun of June (*Jeth*)! In the end they gave their approval, signed the petition and the Organization was officially registered (*Ethnographic*—function of the Organization, etc.).

Now a group of three or four persons began to launch a movement to minimize the expenditure at marriages which used to be to the tune of Rs. 25,000—30,000. Such a heavy expenditure was usually met by selling land, zamindari, house or by taking a loan (*Ethnographic*). We prepared a detailed history of the items of expenditure indicating that the marriage could be performed in Rs. 500. Madho Babu also gave his consent and we began to go from door to door to canvass its acceptance. We were very badly and widely criticised by most of the Gayawal. The first marriage on this pattern was performed in the family of Munni Babu and the second was performed in my own family.

Some of the people boycotted this type of marriage and showed their resentment by not attending the function. However, gradually they began to accept it mostly under the pressure of economic conditions; the growing public opinion was also in its favour.

We also started a night school and began to gather Gayawal children to teach (*Ethnographic*).

When I was of 46 years, I started the scouting movement . . . . Bihari Babu made vehement opposition . . . however with the active co-operation of Dwarka Nath, it was successful (*Ethnographic*).

D

NAME: S. L.
AGE: 45 years. Birthday (Shravan, Krishna Ekadeshi, 1967 Sanbat), September, 1910.
FATHER'S NAME: Sri B. L.; died at the age of 70.

(Interviewed the subject in his dilapidated house where he lived alone. Two sittings on the same day (June 16, 1955). The subject dictated his autobiography under the headings suggested by me. Questions of clarification asked as indicated in the content. The informant was alone and we were never disturbed or interrupted.)

Just before I was born, there was a partition in my family. My father and his only brother (elder) decided to live separately. (*Question.*) I will not be able to tell you in detail the cause of separation, but as far as I have heard, and remember, it was specially because my father was fortunate to have many children (three besides me at the time) while his brother had none. Perhaps this created jealousy in him and specially in his wife, and they decided to live separately. However, the oldest member of the family, my father's uncle (father's father's brother) continued to live with my father. At the time of my birth, there were three children in the family, viz., my brother and two sisters. My brother was 6 years old, while my two sisters were of 4 and 2 years respectively. During that time, the economic condition of the family was fairly good and my father used to get an income of Rs. 35,000—40,000. My father was a devotee of Lord Shiva and used to spend his time in worship, and in visiting temples. He was considered well-versed in religious knowledge.

I was left mostly in the care of two maid servants. One maid servant, who is still alive, used to suckle me while the other used to take care of me. In all, there were twelve maid servants in the family to look after my elder brother and sisters as well as other domestic comforts. The maid servant, Suraji, suckled me for five years. Off and on my mother also used to suckle me. I used to sleep with Suraji. But at the time of my illness, my mother used to take special care and, I was mostly with her. She loved me very much and she used to admonish the maid servants to look after us very carefully. Besides my mother, I was very much loved by two sisters of my father who used to come frequently to see me. My maternal grandmother (mother's mother) also used to pay special attention to me.

During my childhood, I used to play with my brothers and sisters as also with the children of the servants. We used to quarrel among ourselves. But we also used to play together. We were in the habit of beating the children of our servants. However, I used to avoid further quarrel with my brother and younger sister by keeping myself aloof after the (?) first quarrel. I used to say, "Boycott—I will not play with you." However, I never quarrelled with my elder sister, and we always used to live together. From the very beginning of my infancy, I have been sickly. Cough and dysentery were my perpetual illnesses. Perhaps owing to this, and the consequent weakness, I was irritated on the slightest pretext, and in anger, after leaving their company, used to sit aloof.

My father used to remain very busy in religious performances as well as priestly activities. However, he used to keep a very strict watch over me. He always asked me to live and play inside the house. He always expected that I should do nothing against his directions. (*Question.*) Sometimes he used to take me to the temple. I also used to go to my maternal grandmother with a servant or the watchman. When I was four, my eldest sister was married. At that time she was eight years old while her husband was about 12 years old. At times he also used to come to play with us. There were no restrictions as such and in spite of age, relationship, and sex, we used to play together.

When I was crossing five, the servants, instead of the maid servant, began to look after my comfort. My mother also used to look after my two younger sisters. However, my maternal grandmother used to be very affectionate. She had no issue except my mother, and she lived in her house alone. She wished me to inherit her property after her death. My father's sisters as well as my mother's grandmother were also very affectionate to me. They used to give me their clothes, money, etc., and used to feed me in their laps with great affection. I used to play the whole day. My favourite game was spinning the top. My father engaged a tutor when I was about 5 years old. But I always used to avoid him. Mostly, I used to hide myself in some corner of our big house or at times I used to manage to escape to the place of my maternal grandmother. Owing to all this, I was able only to pick up the alphabets of Hindi and English by the time I was nine years old.

I was initiated to the Brahmanic mantras (Sacred Thread ceremony) at the age of six. After this ceremony, I was directed to follow the strict rules of the Brahmanic life. My association and freedom with the children of the servants began to be restricted. For one year, Kanahiyajee, who was a well-versed Brahman in Vedic hymns, used to come to my house to teach me *Sandhya* (mantras and prayers). That also marked the beginning of my daily regular prayer. I was also initiated to Priesthood (*Vriti*) after the Sacred Thread ceremony. I began to perform the Suphal ceremony and Charanpuja ceremony for the votaries that came to maternal grandmother. She used to pay me at the rate of one rupee per votary as a token of my 'gift' from the votary. I used to give half of it to my elder brother. I also used to accompany some of the pilgrims of my father to the temple (Vishnu) and the river, Phalgu.

I was very much interested in talking with the pilgrims and took keen interest in watching their differing behaviour. From my father, I also learned how to play cards. Card playing was the favourite game of my father's and I could pick up this play by the time I was six or seven years old. My father was also interested in chess. I also developed interest in chess in my twelfth year. At this age my father also asked me to begin physical exercises. My elder brother was specially interested in it and he used to go to his cousin (Sijuarjee) for both physical exercise and wrestling. I could not develop much interest in it owing to my poor health.

Ten years and after: My illness also affected my education. At the age of ten, I was admitted in class IV of Haridas Seminary School. But I was very irregular in the class. In the period of seven months for which I continued to be a student, I could attend the classes only for a month and a half. After this, I never went to school. However, my education at home continued. Two teachers, one for Hindi and the other for English, used to come to teach me at home. During this period a Sanskrit Pandit also used to come to teach me *Sarswati*. But on the whole, I could not work more than ten days a month with them. This was partly because of my unwillingness to read and partly because of my poor health. However, owing to all these irregularities I could not make any progress in studies. In priestly activities, there was also not any progress, except that I was now more used to persuade the prilgrims to offer me money. Interest in games was as usual. I picked up another game. I used to throw (a tennis ball?) on the wall, it used to come back again, and then I used to throw it repeatedly and by myself. Every evening, I used to play like this alone. I learnt chess from a non-Gayawal friend of my father, named Chrotujee Khatri and began to play chess with Panna Babu. 'Kite' and 'tops' were my other favourite pastimes. Bird-keeping became another hobby. I became interested in buying birds like *Tuti, Lal,* and thus I kept myself busy in looking after them.

At times, especially during festivals, I used to go to the Vishnupad temple for a 'ritual visit'. On many occasions, I used to go there with my 'pilgrims'. I never went there to collect gifts from 'ritual visitors' or worshippers. A large number of boys and adults used to go to the temple exclusively for this purpose. But there was not so much of bickering, rivalry and competition then.

By and by, my circle of Gayawal friends increased and with them, my interests also multiplied. In my association with Ram Babu Buddhia, I developed an interest in listening to music. I also made the friendship of Matho Lal Deri. He was related to me. I began to go every day to play badminton with him. Now I began to give up other sport like 'top' and 'kite' and began to develop interest in these things.

Marriage and sex: I was married at the age of fourteen. At that time, my wife was only 10 years old. The marriage was performed with the usual grandeur. An amount of Rs. 20,000—25,000 was spent on this occasion. At that time money was spent like water. The 'dancer' (prostitute) who was hired from Banaras charged Rs. 1,000 for her performance.

Even before marriage, I was curious to know about sexual life. When I was young (4 years to 8 years), several times S. hired 'dancers' (prostitutes) and I used to go to see their dances. At times, he used to place me in their laps, jokingly. Out of shame, I used to run away very hurriedly. At that time, I did not feel anything in terms of sex, but the 'fun' was entertaining. However, after 12 years of my age, the absorbing talks regarding the experiences of my married friends, used to make me feel very sexy. I used to feel a strong desire for the sexual act and in order to satisfy it I used at times, to embrace and kiss the daughters of the servants and maid servants of the family. But actual sexual intercourse was impossible owing to several facts: first, I did not know how to get into it; secondly, I was afraid of facing the situation; thirdly, I was very fearful about the reaction of my parents; fourthly I did not get a solitary place for the act.

Even after marriage, I could not get a chance to satisfy my sexual desire, firstly because I was not allowed to meet her in the night, and secondly because she was brought to my home several years after our marriage. The Second Marriage ceremony was performed after four years of marriage. Then she came to my place and I could get a chance to mix with her.

In the meantime, a very unfortunate event happened in my family that further affected my life. Just after one year of my marriage, my elder sister died. I was very much attached to her. The moment I heard of her death, I was very much shocked. I developed an acute type of fits. I did not attend her funeral ceremony. I was put under medical treatment but it continued for about eleven years and my father spent about Rs. 25,000 to get me cured. But it continues in a diminished form—and even these days, I get mild attacks.

After one year of the death of my sister, we started on an all-India pilgrimage. My sister's husband also accompanied us. For four months—Kartik (September), Aghan (October), Push (November), Magh (December)—we visited all the religious places like Banaras, Allahabad, Dwarkajee, Rameshwaram, Puri ; and big cities like Bombay, Calcutta, Madras, Ahmedabad, etc. (*Question.*) This pilgrimage was arranged to console us in our time of grief. It could not be planned just after my sister's death, because of her Barshi Shradda (death rite) which was, as usual, observed six months after her death. This shradda is observed only in case of a married woman whose husband is alive.

After my return from the pilgrimage, I began to spend my time in the company of my friends. My special interest was now in music. I began to learn to play on *Tabla,* in which my elder brother was well versed. I also tried *Israj,* and Harmonium as well as vocal music. But I could not become competent in any branch.

On the suggestion of my friends (as I was weak), I again started physical exercises, under the guidance of Khaira Pati (a member of the Thatera caste). He began to train me very conscientiously. Later, I also became interested in wrestling. But it also did not continue long.

After twenty years: When I was reaching 21, I was inspired by G. L. to study Sanskrit. I started to attend Utteradhi Math where regular classes in Sanskrit were held by Pandit Parddhumnacharya. This time, I felt interest in studies, and I am still continuing my reading in Sanskrit. In the meantime, I picked up some knowledge of Hindi literature. When erate with me in some religious activity. I began to organise class for teaching 'special' prayers (*Sandhya*) to the Gayawal ys. The class continued for some time and later I had to p it as I could not get the co-operation of the people.

Now, I had nothing to do but sit at home idle like the other yawal. Most of my time was spent with P. L. He was sincerest friend. I also began to assist my father and brothers priestly activities. This continued up to my fortieth year.

My father died when I was forty-one. This brought a great deal domestic responsibilities to me. My brothers made me the ad of the family and entrusted all the responsibilities to me. this kept me busy for two years. Then, there were domestic arrels and misunderstanding among all of us. All the five others decided to live separately. Property and estate were ided. I did not like to involve myself in all these priestly d 'estate' affairs. I entrusted my property to the eldest son my eldest brother and he (Mahadeo) began to look after my grims and property.

These days, I spend all my time in the study of Sanskrit. My y place is *Math* and my solitary association is with khini Guru (the Gayawal priest.) I seldom go anywhere. ive quite aloof from my family in this old building. For d, I go to Mahadeo's place. Till the end, I was in friend-p with P. L. But his misbehaviour with me also broke s relationship and now I do not go to him.

neral attitude: I feel strongly that religion and morality fundamental elements of any social group. The members a society must be educated and they must be of strong moral racter. We cannot think of such a society unless there is ity among themselves.

This is also my feeling that by and by religion is losing its portance in India. This is primarily because of the policies the Government. The Government are not giving attention the protection of cows and the slaughter houses are still ive. The Government are enacting laws to allow divorce d are checking untouchability.

The religious community like Gayawal is also fast undergoing degeneration. Disunity, pride, truthlessness, professional

I became a regular student of *Math,* all the s very close to me and I found myself with a friends. My religious activities also found elab in the habit of offering prayers (*Sandhya Banc* in the day ; now I also started to do it in the ev to go to the Vishnupad temple both times ev my devotion to Vishnu, perhaps because of my began to offer prayer to and attend the templ this way, most of my·time was devoted to reli (*Question.*) Work pertaining to priesthood was More and more pilgrims were coming but my look after all types of work. I was left without to attend the *Math.* But as the *Math* was a Vishnupad temple, I, along with my class-fellow to go to temple with a view to receiving sor worshippers.

Regarding my relationship with my wife, I was attached to her and I used to spend only a little She was intelligent but temperamentally she was and wilful. She used to refuse to act accordin When I was 23 years, I was blessed with a daug time my wife was about 19 years old. After some T.B. and died at the age of 21. After four daughter also died.

At the age of twenty-six, I took the initiative recreational club. Sri G. L. and D. N. took th was started. Gayawal Athletic Club was one o of which I was the secretary. Later, it was decide thing for the general development of the Gayawal came out with the suggestion to organise a scout Gayawal boys. The troupe was named Dwarka T selected to train the Bal-scouts Dal (scouts below 1C After three years, we started an evening school a in charge of it. I shifted to the building of the sc we could not get the co-operation of the Gayaw both the movements failed within six years. By th about 30 years old.

Even with the failure of these undertakings, social service was not dampened. I thought the

I became a regular student of *Math,* all the students became very close to me and I found myself with a new circle of friends. My religious activities also found elaboration. I was in the habit of offering prayers (*Sandhya Bandare*) only once in the day ; now I also started to do it in the evening. I began to go to the Vishnupad temple both times every day. With my devotion to Vishnu, perhaps because of my father, I also began to offer prayer to and attend the temple of Shiva. In this way, most of my·time was devoted to religious activities. (*Question.*) Work pertaining to priesthood was on the increase. More and more pilgrims were coming but my father used to look after all types of work. I was left without any such work to attend the *Math.* But as the *Math* was adjacent to the Vishnupad temple, I, along with my class-fellows, was tempted to go to temple with a view to receiving some 'gifts' from worshippers.

Regarding my relationship with my wife, I was not very much attached to her and I used to spend only a little time with her. She was intelligent but temperamentally she was very arrogant and wilful. She used to refuse to act according to my will. When I was 23 years, I was blessed with a daughter. At that time my wife was about 19 years old. After some time, she got T.B. and died at the age of 21. After four months, my daughter also died.

At the age of twenty-six, I took the initiative in starting a recreational club. Sri G. L. and D. N. took the lead and it was started. Gayawal Athletic Club was one of its branches of which I was the secretary. Later, it was decided to do something for the general development of the Gayawal boys. B. L. B. came out with the suggestion to organise a scout troupe of the Gayawal boys. The troupe was named Dwarka Troupe. I was selected to train the Bal-scouts Dal (scouts below 10 years of age). After three years, we started an evening school and I was put in charge of it. I shifted to the building of the school. But, as we could not get the co-operation of the Gayawal in general, both the movements failed within six years. By this time, I was about 30 years old.

Even with the failure of these undertakings, my spirit of social service was not dampened. I thought they would co-operate with me in some religious activity. I began to organise a class for teaching 'special' prayers (*Sandhya*) to the Gayawal boys. The class continued for some time and later I had to stop it as I could not get the co-operation of the people.

Now, I had nothing to do but sit at home idle like the other Gayawal. Most of my time was spent with P. L. He was my sincerest friend. I also began to assist my father and brothers in priestly activities. This continued up to my fortieth year.

My father died when I was forty-one. This brought a great deal of domestic responsibilities to me. My brothers made me the head of the family and entrusted all the responsibilities to me. All this kept me busy for two years. Then, there were domestic quarrels and misunderstanding among all of us. All the five brothers decided to live separately. Property and estate were divided. I did not like to involve myself in all these priestly and 'estate' affairs. I entrusted my property to the eldest son of my eldest brother and he (Mahadeo) began to look after my pilgrims and property.

These days, I spend all my time in the study of Sanskrit. My only place is *Math* and my solitary association is with Dakhini Guru (the Gayawal priest.) I seldom go anywhere. I live quite aloof from my family in this old building. For food, I go to Mahadeo's place. Till the end, I was in friendship with P. L. But his misbehaviour with me also broke this relationship and now I do not go to him.

General attitude: I feel strongly that religion and morality are fundamental elements of any social group. The members of a society must be educated and they must be of strong moral character. We cannot think of such a society unless there is unity among themselves.

This is also my feeling that by and by religion is losing its importance in India. This is primarily because of the policies of the Government. The Government are not giving attention to the protection of cows and the slaughter houses are still active. The Government are enacting laws to allow divorce and are checking untouchability.

The religious community like Gayawal is also fast undergoing a degeneration. Disunity, pride, truthlessness, professional rivalry have become the important characteristics of our society. All these have encouraged rivalry and competition, jealousy and backbiting in our midst. The following may bring the situation under control:

(*i*) Spread of the right type of education among the Gayawal youth;
(*ii*) Stopping toutism in pilgrimage;
(*iii*) Unity and pure fraternal relationship among the Gayawal;
(*iv*) Purity in thought and action.

E

NAME: SRI N. L.
AGE: 42; Birth: Jayast, Purnima 1971 Sambat, Monday morning at 4 A.M.
FATHER'S NAME: SRI M. L.
(Rationalization here and there; uninterrupted interviews, sense of pride in the informant.)

I was born in the joint family of my father and his three brothers. I was the eldest son of my father. As I was born after two girls, I was very much loved in the family. The family's economic condition was fairly sound with an income of Rs. 70,000—80,000 annually. My uncles and father enjoyed very respectable positions in the Gayawal society.

At infancy and in childhood, both my father and mother used to care for me. Two servants (one of 9 years and the other of 10 years) were also specially employed to look after me. They remained attached to me till I became 15 years old. For two years, I was suckled by my mother. After two years, when my next brother was born, I had to depend entirely on cow's milk and other tood. Even after the birth of the next child, the affection of my father and mother for me remained constant. I was loved by them so much that I doubt whether any Gayawal has had the like of it from his parents. When my eldest uncle used to come in the inner apartment to eat, he used to entertain me for an hour before his dinner and then for another hour after it. The other uncle was also very affectionate to me. My father's sisters and their sons were also very attached to me. After one year of my birth, there was partition among my father and his three brothers. After that their attachment with me was very much reduced. (*Partly based on his mother's information.*)

Childhood: My father never encouraged me to go out of my house. I was also not very much inclined to go out of my house. My father wanted to keep me in his company and even a few hours of my absence used to make him restless. He earnestly wanted me to spend my time in studies. When I began my studies, there was a brief religious performance for the god of learning, Ganeshjee. This function took place at my maternal grandmother's place. When I was performing *Arti* (a ritual of lamp showing) the clothes of the deity (domestic shrine) caught fire. There was a great confusion. It was extinguished. I was very much ashamed and felt extremely offended. This incident took place when I was five years old. Anyway, I began to read and write from that very year. A very old teacher of 80 years who was associated with the Gawalbigha Primary School used to come to coach me in the morning from 7 A.M. to 9 A.M. My two other sisters also used to learn with me.

I was not very much interested in studies but my memory was very sharp and I used to prepare the home task for the teacher. Most of my time was spent in plays which were confined to the house itself. I was specially interested in kite and pigeon-keeping. My usual playmates were my younger brother and the servants. Some children of the neighbourhood also used to join me. I was very particular about cleanliness from the very childhood. I never liked to put on a cloth which was once used by me. I always preferred to wear laundered clothes. I had a special liking for white clothes.

My Sacred Thread ceremony was observed at the age of eight. I was not very particular about learning prayer hymns even after the ceremony. I was not asked to go to *Math* for this. My father, however, taught me something to utter after the daily bath. I was also not encouraged to go to the temple. As far as I remember, I went to the temple for the first time on the occasion of the weaning ceremony of my younger brother, at the age of five. At the age of four my father's father's brother's wife adopted me, and with this adoption I was entitled to her property (Baddiha). Before the age of nine, however, I was the least concerned with the *Yatris* (pilgrims).

Ten Years up to Marriage: With the years, more attention was being given towards my education. Two teachers were employed. The first used to teach me history and arithmetic in the morning, and the second teacher used to teach me geography and English in the night. I became more interested in my studies than before. I was also in close contact with the children of my manager who was a Bengali. From his sons I learnt to write and speak Bengali. I also expressed my willingness to go to school with them. My father was reluctant and he consulted his eldest brother. My eldest uncle completely opposed this idea. He was dead against sending me to the school. (*Question.*) He was of the opinion that the school provided a chance for meeting all types of good and bad boys. The chances for being friendly with characterless children were many. This might end in spoiling my character.

After the age of twelve, I began to attend religious classes in the *Math.* There, I learnt all types of prayers, hymns, etc. in Sanskrit. The Acharya also used to give us lessons in the method of worship and shraddha. This continued up to the age of nineteen years. I remembered by heart three or four religious books (*Hanuman, Vayuastuti, Vishnu Astuti*).

The *Math* moulded my religious feeling. The whole atmosphere of the *Math* and its surrounding was compelling. I was personally very much influenced by the teaching and action of Sri 108 Pradumnachara. I was one of his pet pupils. He liked me very much because of my good memory. I used to commit to memory all types of hymn or *Astoka.* Now I began to observe regular prayer and worship. I began to observe "fast" worship (Ekadasi worship) on every 24th day of the month. It continued for four months. I also began to go to the temple for *Darshan*. I never went there with a view to secure some money in the shape of gifts from the worshippers. At times, I used to go there with my *jajman* to collect the offering that they would make at the altar.

My oldest friendship was with B. He used to come to my family with his parents when I was a child. My family has been on very friendly terms with his family for the last three generations. Perhaps, I was encouraged to find in him the first and the last friend owing to this age-old traditional tie. The second life-long friend is Sri B. L., whose warmth and affection for me is indescribable. He became my friend when I was eleven. I am reminded of the incident that brought both of us together for the first time. It is very interesting. I was very fond of the bicycle. When my father went to the fair of Harihar Kshetra, he brought a bicycle for me. B. was also fond of cycling. I came in contact with him owing to our common interest. He taught me how to ride a bicycle and we used sometimes to go out together on the cycle. I also began to play cards with him

I was married at the age of fourteen. My marriage ceremony was accompanied by that of my second younger brother. For the first time, my marriage negotiation was going on with another family. It continued for about four years and everybody knew that I would be married there. But my father had to change his decision in view of the choice of his eldest brother and I was married in the family which was selected by my eldest uncle. At the time of marriage my wife was about nine years old. In the performance of the marriage ceremony about Rs. 23,000 were spent. Perhaps this marked the last in the big series of expensive marriages in my community. I think after this no such amount was spent at the time of marriage (*Ethnographic*).

My studies continued even after marriage. But after two years, the tutor was disengaged for economic reasons. Now, our financial condition was going from bad to worse. That period marked the beginning of the economic decline in our family that went on increasing, and that still continues. However my studies of Sanskrit in the *Math* continued.

In the meantime at the age of eighteen, I became interested in physical exercise and wrestling. My interest in it continued to increase and for six years, I used to spend most of my time at it. In the morning, in addition to other physical exercises, I used to practice wrestling with three or four persons.

Owing to excessive indulgence in exercises, I fell a prey to constipation which later resulted in piles. It was very serious and my health was very badly affected by this. All types of local treatments were tried but without any success. It was cured by the medicine given to me by a saint of Banaras. The saint originally belonged to Ajodhya and had been a judge in the civil court. But later he became very much involved in religious activities and gave up his job. My father knew him and when we went to Banaras, he took me to him. He was very kind and gave me some Ayurvedic medicines which cured me. However, weakness continued and I did not dare take exercises.

I became interested in music from my very childhood. My uncle (Sri M. L.) was a very accomplished musician and he was specially famous for his performances on the harmonium. From him I developed an interest in it and began to learn it. But it did not continue for long. When I became interested in wrestling exercises, I did not get any time for my harmonium practice.

My "second marriage ceremony" took place when I was twenty years. At that time my wife was fifteen years old. I did not know anything about sex before her arrival in my house. I never went to her mother's place after our marriage. When she came to my place, I was happy to find her very sweet-natured. However, I did not indulge very much in sexual activities for I feared this might affect my achievements in wrestling and physical exercise. I was also discouraged as I could not get any issue even after five years of marriage.

At the age of twenty-four, my wife was attacked with smallpox (*Bari Mai*). Three times she almost lost her breath, but somehow she recovered ; but it took her about a year to regain her health. After this illness, I became more attached to her and I began to spend more time with her. At the age of twenty-six I was blessed with a daughter. It marked the beginning of the birth of children. I was blessed with eight daughters and three sons ; one of the daughters died of tuberculosis last year. She was married. She died at Patna Medical College Hospital. It was a great shock to us all and my wife fell ill after this mishap.

12

In her marriage, I had to spend about ten thousand rupees which I had to take on loan. It is a great headache, and expenditures on marriages in the family have been the main cause of our downfall.

I also became very close to Viyogijee (Sri Mohan Lal Mahto Viyogi, a Gayawal poet and well-known author of Hindi) who took me in his fold. I was very much influenced by the emotion and thought-provoking poem of Ram Vilas Ojha on the earthquake of January 15, 1934; which was corrected by Viyogijee. I made up my mind to write poems and Viyogijee gave me all the possible education and training in this effort. Under his inspiration I began to study for 10 to 15 hours daily. I had been continuing to write poems specially on tragedies and pathos (*his 30 poems recorded by the investigators*). Later, through Viyogijee, I came in contact with a number of Hindi poets and writers. B. S., the editor of *Yogi,* H. T. and many others have given me further encouragement to compose poems. I have published about sixty poems and I hope to bring out a collection of them.

Owing to this achievement in literature, some of the Gayawal look at me with jealousy. But some also appreciate my worth.

I am always alert to serve the cause of my own community. But for want of adequate cooperation I am unable to do anything for it. Now, for me, there is no way out but to pray god singly to improve our lot, the lot of the Gayawal.

General attitude—Ideal society: The society should be ideal-oriented and it should exercise adequate control to make its individual ideal-minded. A society, free from cruelty, jealousy, disunity, and inhuman behaviour, that aspires for the highest divine values and ethical practice is the best and exemplary human group.

In our community, in one word, we lack "humanism". Ram is no more our hero; Ravan is becoming our ideal. All the Gayawal, knowingly or unknowingly, are becoming devoid of reasoning and humanitarian feeling. I will give you my own example. Is it a human behaviour to forget the relationship of 40 or 50 years in a moment just for four pieces of copper?

Will you be surprised if I say that I have taken away the *jajman* of Viyogijee several times? Is it not all because of selfishness and greed that we have made our society so sick?

Our society suffers for want of the right type of education.

Narrowness, inferiority-complex, association with low caste people are all responsible for this degeneration. False pride has been another stumbling block for our society.

Religion and morality: The action that pleases my conscience is the religious activity. A group of such actions, then, would be religion. Religion should be also considered at a social level. Religion should occupy a very high position in a country. In our country, the traditional Brahmanic Hinduism is still continuing. But in the name of the improvement and secularization, we are forgetting our old ideals and practices.

'The Hindu Code Bill' is a great blow to the Hindu religion. Our ideal is Ram Rajya but we are heading towards something else.

In our own Gayawal society we find a peculiar situation. Actually only a few people practise religion sincerely; most of them are showy. They just pose to be religious-minded people. They imitate others and all are heading towards vicious goals. Everybody aspires to go to heaven but his actions conform to the achievement of hell.

Jajmani profession is being exploited in terms of money. In this profession they do not distinguish between the proper and the improper. If they observe prayer and worship, it is only to satisfy the public opinion. Nobody does them as part of his duty. Only a few people are left in our society who can be compared with the Gayawal of the past.*

Changes in the Society:

(*i*) The search for adequate means of livelihood.

(*ii*) The spread of education.

* They do not have the time to think of how to aspire to heaven. They are mad after earning their bread. To them prayer, worship, gift and merit, meditation and *shraddha*—all have become superfluous and showy affairs.

(*iii*) The changes in social organisation, e.g., feeling of cooperative spirit—a communal outlook, a professional unity, etc.

F

NAME: SRI P. B. N.
AGE: 37 ; Birth: Ashar (July), Krishna Shal 1975 (1918).
FATHER'S NAME: Sri P. K. L. ; age 63.

(Two sittings—each of two-and-a-half hours, covered in two days. At the first sitting informant's father was present. He gave me some useful information about his son during infancy and childhood. The informant was frank and truthful in his statements.)

At the time of my birth, my father and uncle lived together and it was a happy family. At the time of my birth I had two elder brothers. My uncle had no issue then. He used to love us all. Thoug my mother personally cared for me, there was a maid servant to look after my comforts. She used to massage me regularly twice or thrice in a day. She used to wash my clothes and used to suckle me. My mother also suckled me. I was fairly healthy. continued to live on the maid's and the mother's breast for four months. Thereafter I was given cow's milk and suckling was off and on.

During my infancy, I was in the habit of crying. I used to cry for hours and hours together. Owing to this my parents would get out of their room. I used to cry at the door for some time and, after some time, go to my aunt. At times she took me from the verandah to her room. She entertained me with all sorts of stories and songs. Generally she used to invite *Buia* (an imaginary fearful creature) to get hold of me if I would not sleep. In this way she used to make me sleep. (*From father of informant*) . . . . (*Father*). The maid servant used to shake my head for hours to make me sleep. Owing to this I formed the habit of shaking my head at the time of sleeping. This continued till my fifth year. (*Question.*)

After my birth, my mother was seriously ill for about six months. She was suffering from asthma and fever. She was under the influence of some evil star. She could survive only because the evil star (*Grah*) could be pacified with propitiation. During this period the maid servant was my constant companion and nurse ; and my aunt used to keep an eye on her. My father (as he said) was not very particular about my growing up. He was shy of his elder brother and always avoided me in his presence.

Five years and after: My father used to teach me from the age of five. It was his great desire that I should get educated. The headmaster of Gayawal Bigha Primary School used to come to teach me, and my two elder brothers. He was an old man and he also taught my grandfather and father. He used to receive Rs. 24 annually for this work.

I was not at all interested in studies. When the teacher came I deceived him. But I was very intelligent and my memory was very sharp, and as I used to complete the assigned tasks, the teacher was not very angry with me.

I was not allowed to go out of the house. Generally, I had to play with my brothers and the children of the servants in the courtyard or elsewhere in the house. But I did not like this confinement. R. B. H. was my best neighbour. He was very fond of me and I liked to stay for longer periods in his house for I used to escape to his house and usually spent the whole day there.

In the evening, my father used to take me out for a walk or in the carriage. This was my usual routine and I never liked to miss his company in the evening or the ride in the carriage.

At the age of seven, my Sacred Thread ceremony was observed. Now I began to go to *Math* to learn *Sandhya* (prayers and recitation, hymns) from the Guru. I was not at all interested in priestly activities. My elder brothers and father used to look after them and I had not to worry about them.

Spinning the top, flying the kite and Ha-du-du (Kabaddi) were my favourite games. Along with my brothers and children of the servants, I used to play these either in the courtyard or on the roof of the house. I was not at all inclined towards worship, etc., before the age of nine. However I had to observe *Sandhya* after my Sacred Thread ceremony.

At the age of seven, the Mother *Sitla* found expression on my body (I had an attack of smallpox). It was her violent attack on me. All types of cares and propitiations were made to please her (*Ethnographic*). I became alright within a fortnight but the weakness continued for two years. My eyesight was also affected and as you see, I have had to use spectacles. I did not keep good health after this attack. I used to get fever quite often. I was also growing lean and thin.

Ten years and after: When I was about ten years of age, a very unfortunate event took place. It was the death of my maternal grandfather who died at Calcutta. He was an Honorary Magistrate and was honoured with the title of Rai Bahadur. The moment the news of his death reached Gaya, his friend Sri B. L. who used to look after his property in his absence, began to remove the costly things to his own place. He took away huge amounts of gold, precious stones and also money in cash.

When we heard of his activities, we came to the house and established our right over the house and property. My maternal grandfather had no son and hence he made a legal declaration at the time of his death to distribute all his property equally among three of his daughters. My mother along with my father and children shifted to her father's place. We were owners of one-third of the whole property. Now we had to change our family title from Gayab to Dhokari.

The *Math* was very close from this house. I began to attend classes in the *Math*. The tutor also used to come to coach me at my house. Now I was free to move about. The *Math* and the Vishnupad temple were situated side by side. I used to abstain from the *Math* and go to secure money from the worshippers at the temple. My father was dead against it. He always warned me not to leave the *Math* to go to the temple for securing money. But it was not possible to check my temptation to go there and secure some personal money. During that time, we used to get a good amount of money in the shape of gifts. Within half an hour I used to be able to get Rs. 3, which is not possible today to get even in five days. I also used to get money from my parents and *jajman*. I used to spend all the money in buying sweets in the local market.

My father with the help of my elder brother used to look after the priestly activities (*Vriti*). I was still not interested in this work. I used to observe the morning prayer regularly. The rest of my time was spent in playing cards and flying kites. I used to take great interest in fooling my playmates and in getting into fights with them. It was a very active life for me. I used to play in a big crowd which I used to assemble every evening in my house. My sisters, who were young also, used to join us. For the children of the servants, it was an awful time. They used to get a heavy beating. I was not at all interested in religious activities before my marriage. Life was very easy. I used to spend money like anything on food from the market, and on decent clothes. It was all fun, joy and merry-making.

Marriage at sixteen. I was married at the age of sixteen. My wife was eleven years old at that time. The "second marriage ceremony" was held after five years and my wife came to my house for the first time. Before the "second marriage", I used to go to my father-in-law's place. But I was not in a position to stay there in the night owing to an old custom in my society. However, I used to get a chance to have sexual intercourse with my wife in the early night before leaving for my own house. Before marriage, I used to talk freely about sexual matters with my two sisters-in-law (brothers' wives). At times, I also used to enter into conversation about sexual matters with my friends. But it was done only in the strictest secrecy from the elders. However, on the whole, I was not very much interested in sexual matters. But I was very much pleased when the marriage was finalised and performed. The marriage was entirely finalised by my father and I had nothing to say to him in this connection. However, I was altogether willing to get married.

Marriage did not bring any change in me. I continued to wander about from pillar to post. It was the life of the vagabond engaged in gossip, play and in visiting the temples. My father did not like all these things. In order to make me steady, he initiated me to music. He, himself, is a good musician and is specially well-versed on the harmonium. He began to teach me to play on the harmonium. At first, I did not feel any interest in music and wanted to escape from it. But my father was adamant to see me concentrate on it. Later on, I also developed a taste for classical music and the harmonium. A well-known specialist in harmonium, Sri Hanuman Das, was appointed for me. He was an old and veteran musician. I found myself involved in music now. I also got a chance to be in the midst of his several pupils. This continued up to the age of twenty-seven and now I began to move in the company of Gayawal musicians.

I also became interested in riding. One by one, I bought three horses. Between the age of twenty and twenty-five, I was very active in riding. My father also taught me swimming. With my father I used to go to the foothills of Brahmyoni Hill. There is a big tank and there I learnt swimming. At that time I was about eighteen years old.

I also continued to go to the *Math* to learn Sanskrit. But it was not very effective. When I developed an interest in music and began to sing devotional songs, I also felt interested in reading the *Ramayana,* the *Bhagwat Gita, Kalayan,* etc. The interest further increased as now I began to listen to the religio-musical performances at the temple, like *Sankirtan, Bhajan, Ram Lila, Katha,* with a new perspective. I began to stay there for longer periods. I was now well-versed in playing *Bhajan* on the harmonium.

Regarding my domestic life, my wife came to live with me after five years of our marriage. I wanted her to obey me, to give me comfort and keep my things in an orderly manner. She proved up to my expectations. I look upon her with the eye of authority and she realises her subordinate position. This keeps us in order. We do not give each a chance to misunderstand the other. When she wants to go to her father's place, I allow her to go, and when I want her to come back, she does come. She may stay there from a few days to a month. This mutual adjustment does not give us a chance for the type of domestic quarrels which are prevalent in our society. In this way I began to combine my domestic activities and musical performances and "temple-begging".

Twenty-five years and after: By this age, I was perfectly devoted to religious performances. I started an organisation named Gayawal Sankirtan Samaj (the Gayawal Society of Religious Recitation), at the age of twenty-five. Since then I am engaged in activities concerning this organisation. I am solely responsible for musical recitations. Every evening I, along with other members, perform musical recitations before the temple for two hours. On the 25th day (Shukla Ekadeshi) of every month, I organise non-stop musical recitation for twenty-four hours. We celebrate the Chait Ram Naumi (birthday of Sri Ramchandra) with purity of mind, and much solemnity. On the occasion of Ramchandra's marriage anniversary, special musical recitations are organised. Our organisation is active in many other ways (*Ethnographic*).

We have composed about a thousand religious songs in Magadhi which we recite here. You can see the eight copies of such songs that we have with us. Besides, I have also collected a few books on Hindi *Sankirtan*. Yes, we always had such a socicty in ouur community (*Ethnographic*).

Our society also visits places out of Gaya. In the last two years, we have been to Daltongunj (100), Tekari (12), Deo (30), and Patna (57).

Two years after the organisation of the society, my eldest brother died. With his death, my responsibilities towards domestic affairs increased. I began to help my father and elder brother (Munni Babu) in looking after *jajmani,* and other priestly activities. Now, I began to feel the need of money. My eldest brother was very helpful in this matter. After one year of his death, I was blessed with a daughter. She is eleven years old now. After six years of her birth, another daughter was born. But she died on the ninth day of her birth. After the birth of the second daughter, my wife was attacked with several types of diseases. The main cause of her ill-health was the weakness that was caused after the premature delivery of our second daughter. The delivery was under the advice and treatment of the doctor. Asthma, pain in the chest, fits, etc., that started after the delivery, continued. Owing to all this my expenditure increased. My father was not in a position to meet all the expenditures from the *jajmani* income. The number of pilgrims were dwindling and, with this, the amount of gifts decreased. Big Zamindars and Rajas and such other wealthy persons coming to Gaya were few and far between. I continued to go to the temple to secure some money to supplement the income. But now, I used to feel great reluctance to go there for this purpose. In doing so, I had to speak lies, I had to pick up quarrels with other fellow Gayawal, I had to enter into dirty rivalry, which I began to hate. But what to do?

This question continued to haunt my mind for several months. In the end, I decided to buy a pasture-machine. I thought if I bought it, I would earn some money by selling pasture and it would also be a service to the cattle. But should I consult my father and brother in this connection and should I ask them for the money? I thought over it again and it did not take me much time to realise that it was a foolish idea to break my idea to them. They would never allow me to buy (such) a machine. But I was determined to translate my idea into action. I consulted my wife and persuaded her to give me her ornaments. Without disclosing anything to anybody, I went to Calcutta, bought the machine, procured the license from Patna and came to Gaya. On all these things, I spent about Rs. 3,000.

I installed the machine in my garden. This, to me, historic event took place about seven years ago. I was very vehemently criticised both in my family and in the Gayawal society. My brothers wanted to discourage me. They demanded rent for the house and the garden. The members of the Gayawal society used to jeer at me. When they passed near the garden and saw me working there, they rebuked me in bitter words. They began to hate me and said: "You claim to be a son of a Gayawal Panda, but work as a labourer. You are a big black spot on the face of the community."

At times, I was perplexed by all these criticisms. Anyhow, I continued this work. The labourer used to come every morning to cut the pasture out of straw and I used to sell it personally. For three years it continued as usual. Then, I installed an electric dynamo to propel the machine. It cost me about Rs. 1,500. Now, my income increased. I employed a full-time servant to sell the pasture. I pay him Rs. 30 per month. With this I began to get more leisure for religious activities. I am perfectly satisfied with my present economic situation. The machine is sufficient to satisfy the wants of my family. At times I also give money to my father. Some members of the Gayawal community have also begun to appreciate my enterprise now. Owing to deteriorating conditions of the priestly profession, they come to me with great distress and seek my advice to start such a business. But I know, only a few think sincerely of starting any business. They just know how to talk at length and do nothing.

I am also carrying on the activities of the Society for Musical Recitation but it is a great strain to maintain it. There are two types of membership in this society: Reciter membership, and Associate membership. The number of reciter-members is fast decreasing while that of the latter is almost constant. About four years back there were about 35 reciter-members but now its strength has reduced to 10. Several types of obstacles hamper its smooth functioning. Last year, a number of things were stolen from its office. Some of the people want that it should die out like other Gayawal organisations. But I have made up my mind to keep it alive till my death.

General attitude: I consider that society to be the best in which the gods and goddesses are worshipped and the people do social service. In any healthy society, education is very important.

In my society, religious activities are being neglected and devotion to god is dwindling. Especially, the young Gayawal neglect their daily Brahmanic duties. About 75 per cent of them do not observe prayers (*Sandhya*). It is a great sin. (*Question.*) Youths of my family, my uncle's family, and of the families of B. L., G., (R. B.), never observe prayers. I know it for certain else I would not have named them to you. My community also needs educational training. There has been tremendous downfall of my society owing to mutual jealousy, rivalry and lack of education. It is very shocking to inform you that there are persons who do not go to the temple for *Darshan*. They do not use *Chandan* paste on their foreheads and are not afraid of God.

How our community can improve: Our community can improve again only when all of them surrender themselves to Vishnu and implore Him to give them spiritual wisdom. In my meditation before the commencement of the musical recitation every day I pray the god earnestly to give light to my fellow Gayawal.

Religion in India: Religion occupies the highest place in the human society. Its practice distinguishes a man from an animal. Religion is on its decline in India. Temples do not attract so many devotees as they used to. Some persons go to the temple without taking their bath. Some want to take a Muslim friend to the temple. Some say: 'If he will not be allowed, I will also not go there.'

Our community—changes needed: Disunity is the great disease of our society. It can be accounted for in terms of the rise of rivalry in the profession, the exploitation of the poor Gayawal by the rich Gayawal, respect for the rich Gayawal and hatred for the poor. The lack of education both in secular and religious learning is an important cause of it. I would suggest the following to the Gayawal:

(1) They should maintain their religious activities and ritual performances. They should give up the path of irreligious activities and come to the right path of religion. They should not show injustice to the pilgrims who come from far off lands. They should not press them hard in matters of gifts, etc.
(2) It is not possible to 'digest' all that they get in the shape of gifts. They should give something out of their gifts to the poor and the needy.
(3) All should observe Brahmanic duties. They must observe the daily prayers.
(4) The spread of education must be arranged for.
(5) There should be an end of jealousy or rivalry.
(6) They should take up other kinds of jobs.

G

NAME: SRI R. L.
AGE: 23; Birth: 1, Aghan, Margshrish 1989 Sambat (November 14, 1932).
FATHER'S NAME: SRI K. L.

(Autobiography written by the informant himself. An outline (as appended) was provided by the author for his guidance. Originally the autobiography was written in Hindi in a very 'sentimental' tone. The informant told me that he had to shed tears many times as he wrote these lines. He also remarked, "I don't know why I wrote this for you and exposed my family and social life to you." Besides the biographical data, the choice of words, the style of expression and literary usages are also revealing. *I give here a literal translation of his autobiography.*)

My name is Sri (Mr.) R. (God) L. T. and the name of my respected father is Sriyut (Respected Mr.) K. (God) L. (another form to express respect) T.

I was born on November 14, 1932 (1, Aghan or Sansk, Margshrish 1989 Saṁbat) in a very respectable family of widely revered Panda (Pilgrimage Priest) society in my own paternal house (Krishna Dwarika). As I was the first son of my father, my birth brought immense joy in the family. But it was my misfortune that changed the happy atmosphere of the family into a fearful gloom after three months of my birth. It was the physical decay (death) of my affectionate mother. That is the most horrible day of my life as it marked the accidental and premature death of my mother that occurred owing to burning in fire. Though I was only three months old at the time of this unfortunte death and I cannot think of the event at all, I strongly feel the absence of my affectionate mother every moment.

The above event was a great stumbling block in my nursing and rearing (Pālan Poshān). But this obstacle was averted in some proportion owing to the cooperative efforts of my late respected grandfather (Sriyut M. L.), respected grandmother (no name) and revered father. Maids were also employed to look after me. During my infancy, in this way, I was reared anyhow by several relatives and maids.

At the age of three, my first hair-cutting ceremony was observed. I do not remember any important event of that time but as I could gather, my birth was not considered very auspicious for the family, as, very soon, it was followed by the death of my mother. It was discovered by the astrologer that the position of the stars in my horoscope was so placed that I was not destined to enjoy my mother's love. Anyway, it did not affect my position. However, the feeling continued that my stars were responsible for her death and I am a "mother-eater" (Ma-Khauka). The hair-cutting ceremony marked the beginning of a period of illness in my life which continued for three years. One or the other disease always kept me weak and unhealthy. The main cause of illness, as I understand, was my contact with several mothers. Though (why not) I accept their gratitude, it is bitter truth that their milk affected my blood badly and owing to this I fell prey to several types of disease during my childhood. This was also a great headache for my family and treatment of all types caused a heavy drain on the family money. After six years of age, my health improved and then my Sacred Thread ceremony was observed. This marked the beginning of my disciplined Brahmanic life. I was taught a number of do's and dont's. (*Ethnographic*) During this time, I was also initiated to Education (*Shiksha*) and Precept (*Diksha*). I was admitted in the local primary school. A teacher used to come regularly to teach me at my home and my revered late grandfather (respected) who was himself famous for knowing English, kept me under his supervision. How to describe the affection of my late grandmother (jee) ; had she not been alive, I would not have survived. I was provided with all comforts by her and I never felt the need of anything. In the morning I used to go to school, in the noon, after bath and lunch, I used to sit regularly at the feet of my grandfather to receive education in subjects like worship and prayer. The latter was my regular and special routine work. In the evening at 4 o'clock I used to go to the garden of my father's father's brother to play with his sons. Up to 7 o'clock, I used to play with them either Ha-du-du (Kabaddi) or football. After my return from my evening game, I used to eat my dinner and then used to read for an hour up to 8-30 p.m. with my tutor.

The tutor was not very harsh to me but still he used to chide me for all my failings.

Regarding the attachment of my relatives, firstly, my father with his affectionate behaviour was also very, very cruel to me. I even today remember the cruel expression of his face for my petty mistakes and the regular beatings for my faults. It was next to impossible for others except my grandfather and grandmother to relieve me from the clutches of his punishment. Some years after the death of my mother, father was repeatedly asked by many of our relatives to marry again. But my father always turned down their attempts and he made it clear to them: "When I have got a male child, I do not require to marry again." I also remember this event and it is the most important event of that time. (*Question*). My father beat me for a variety of things. When I returned home late, when I failed to get up early, when I abstained from school, when I failed to take my daily bath, especially during the winter, when I failed to observe *Sandhya* (Prayer), etc., he used to punish me in one way or another, varying from telling me harsh words to beating me. The strict discipline imposed by my father was very troublesome at that time, but it proved very helpful to me in the future. And owing to this, I always remained immune from bad habits, and actionlessness or laziness. To get up at the right time; to eat, to read and to play in the proper period, were all controlled and regulated. The daily activities, as structured and regulated in childhood, are still observed almost in the same way. Of course, I have had to make some alterations with my age. In this way I spent ten years of my life. I do not remember any other remarkable events except a series of punishments (*Ethnographic*) imposed on me by my father.

At the age of eleven, I was in the 5th class of the Upper Primary School. During that time, the teaching of English was introduced in the 4th class but, thanks to the coaching of my late lamented grandfather, I could achieve the standard of 7th class even then. Regarding the worship and ritual recitation, (Shōrshopehar, Prāt, Madhayan, Saiya Sandhyā, Sloke, Mantra, etc.), I also became well-versed. By the order of my grandfather, I had to repeat all the *mantras* (that I used to get by heart) several times before friends and relatives who used to visit us.

During this year Sri Pradhymnacharya, the main disciple of our Guru Sri 108, Mahamadhyuācharya (head of Dwaitbadi Uddupi, Madras). He stayed for a few months in the Madhwācharya Math and started to educate and conduct examination for Gayawal boys. My grandfather took advantage of this auspicious occasion and asked me to appear at the next examination. I appeared at the examination, and owing to his blessing, I came out successful in the First Division. For this success, I was rewarded by Sriyut Pradhymnacharyajee with a beautiful brass case (container) bedecked with all types of things required for worship. At the end of the year, I fell a prey to the clutches of a horrible disease, the remittent fever. After undergoing twenty-five days of fast and proper medical treatment, I was relieved of this deadly illness. But, physically, I was very weak and owing to this I was unfit for any work for six months after my recovery. In the meantime, I also suffered from dysentery, diarrhoea, etc., which further checked my attempts to regain my health rapidly. I was not strong enough even to move out of my house. All of my relatives were deeply concerned about my health. At this time, a class fellow of my grandfather was transferred to the local hospital as the civil surgeon. I went to him with my grandfather. I was under his treatment for one month and his treatment set me perfectly healthy.

It was the month of Ashar (July). At that time I was about 12 years old. Accidentally my revered (worth worshipping) grandmother began to become unhealthy. In the beginning, she had fever, but within 15 to 20 days her condition deteriorated very much. Blood began to come out of her mouth with phlegm. This was specially a matter of great anxiety. She was under the treatment of an assistant surgeon. But it was too late. At the beginning she refused to take 'English' medicine but under great persuasion, she took this type of medicine and her condition improved. She gained some strength and in spite of the direction of the doctor not to leave the bed, she began to move about. Our repeated persuasions for her to be in bed also bore no fruits. She thought everything was all right. But there was a relapse. Blood came out from her mouth and she was again confined to the bed. The treatment continued as usual but the number of medicines were increased. We were strictly forbidden by the doctor to go to her. It was very troublesome for me. I was not in a position to resist myself from going to her. Within 24 hours, I used to go to her at least once or twice. Relatives in the house used to keep a watchful eye upon me. However, I left no stone unturned to meet her by escaping their eyes. Now, my grandmother had also become conscious of her dreadful disease. Hence tears used to trickle down from her eyes. She used to fix her eyes on me for two to four minutes with restlessness and then she used to compel me by her gesture to go away. My soul used to groan, as it were, and I had to be away from her sight. I used to weep for hours—the love and affection, the care and the nursing of that revered grandmother that kept me alive since my mother died at 3 months, God was now not willing that I should enjoy her affection any more. However, this situation continued for about one-and-a-half year. All the best doctors of the city were consulted, money was spent liberally like water. But her condition was not to improve, it did not improve. My father and (his youngest sister) *Fufu* used to take special care about her medicine, treatment, rest, etc. They were most concerned and worried about her ailment. In the family, there were other members—uncle, aunt, two brothers (uncle's sons) and three sisters (uncle's daughters). But they were not on very good terms with my grandmother. Domestic quarrels between my grandmother, and my uncle and aunt were the usual features in my family. These quarrels usually revolved round any issue concerning me. They used to think —and it was perfectly true—that she loved me the most and neglected their children. Owing to this, these people were not at all particular to look after her. My grandmother was very old, so only my father, along with her youngest sister who came to live in our home during grandmother's illness, cared for her. A day seemed equivalent to an year. Yes, a very horrible period for me. No affection, instead, neglect and hatred ; no joy, instead, mental agony and fear.

Now, my grandmother felt a strong urge that she should see me married before her death. She would be more sorry for not being able to see my marriage than for her own death. She began to talk with my father in this connexion. For some time, no special attention was given to her persuasion. But the matter was not further suppressed owing to the frequent proposals for the marriage brought by the girls' parents. Negotiations proceeded with a few parties and it was finalized at one place according to the wishes of my grandmother. The horoscope was interchanged and after due consultation, my father gave his word for my marriage. My grandmother's joy knew no bounds. To her it was not only that the negotiations were finalized, but as if I was married . . . .

During this time, only two months were left for my annual Middle School Examination. I was busy preparing for it. I was not only hopeful but quite sure of my success in the examination. I appeared at the examination and waited for the result. In one sense it was disappointing. I passed in all the subjects except in English and got the certificate for vernacular middle examination. Now I had to seek admission in some high school. At that very time, the disease of my grandmother returned violently and all of us were worried and busy around her. However, it did not last long and she came back to her usual condition within a fortnight. Then I, along with my father, went from school to school but I could not get a seat in any school. All the seats were filled in all the local high schools. Being disappointed, there was no other alternative but wait for the next year. My grandfather was also not in a position to teach me any further. He was very much worried about the illness and domestic disagreements in the family. A tutor used to come at my home to teach me. He was specially interested in Hindi and was himself preparing for the *Visharad* examination of Hindi Sahitya Sammellan, Allahabad. He also advised me to prepare for such an examination on lower level. I brought the books recommended for *Prathma* examination, and was busy in preparing for the same. However, I was not free from anxiety. Conditions in the family were going from bad to worse. All were in the ocean of anxieties and worries and being a part of the family, I had to share their sorrow and anxieties. I was, however, especially worried about the ensuing separation from my grandmother. I was at a loss to decide what would happen to me after her death. Anyway, the examination was held in *Shrawan* (Aug.-Sept.). The famous local library, the Mannulal Pustakalaga was the centre for the examination. There were four papers in Hindi literature. The first three papers were answered well. On the fourth day, the paper dealt with literary biographies and essays. It was a lengthy paper. I thought it better to procure a fountain pen to write with a good speed. In my home, my father had a fountain pen (I was always in the habit of writing with a plain pen). I asked him for it. I got it but as it was out of use for the last seven to eight months, it was practically out of order. But I was bent upon finding out a fountain pen as I was a slow writer. I was, perhaps, a slow writer, mainly because I used to write a fair and neat hand. I was famous among my class-fellows for my beautiful handwriting. My teachers were also very appreciative of this. Anyway, I was at a loss to decide what to do. Accidently, it came to my mind to ask for the fountain pen from my father's father's brother's son (*Dhachera Chacha*) who bought it only the other day. I got it from him and then went to the examination. But I do not know why, the pen was not working well. In spite of my best efforts, I could write only three pages in half an hour. Most of the questions were untouched. I brought out my plain pen and began to write. But in spite of my best efforts, I could not succeed. The scheduled hours left came to an end, and I had still two questions to attempt. I was allotted 10 minutes of extra time but it was not possible to finish these in ten minutes. The copy was snatched away by the invigilator. He looked at my copy and with a deep breath, he remarked, "You have spoiled all things." I could not understand his bitter statement. He pointed to the two different colours of the inks that were used. It was not allowed in the examination to use different inks in any one paper. Now, I realized my blunder; yes, a horrible mistake. I was very much upset and disappointed. On the one hand, though I remembered the two answers, I could not write them for want of time and, in the second place, I committed this horrible mistake of using two types of ink. I did not think that these mistakes would result into the main causes of my failure. But as it happened I was unsuccessful. This type of repeated accidental failures brought a very depressing influence on my life.

One day, the condition of my grandmother deteriorated very much. We thought this was the final scene of her life's drama. All of us were extremely anxious and restless but my grandfather was very grave. The doctor came. He examined her and expressed his anxieties. But my grandfather said, "Doctor, she will continue to remain alive. I have to die before her. Then she will have her chance." The situation was very tense, however. The doctor laughed at his prediction. I was also very much surprised at his statement. However, her condition began to improve and after one week, she was satisfactorily well.

On the occasion of the full moon of *Kartika,* every year, there is a cattle fair on the opposite side of the river Phalgu. My father's father's brother's son bought a cow there. It was the 4th day after the full moon of *Kartika.* As usual, my grandfather got up at 4-30 A.M. in the morning. After completing his daily regular work (*Ethnographic*), he ate country tobacco and betel leaves, and he went down for a morning walk in the garden. When he was going to the garden, I was also awake. As usual, he wore a smiling look. Walking, he reached near the newly bought cow. For ten minutes he looked at her. Accidentally, he felt giddy and he was about to fall. Near by, there were two persons ; they gave him support. But the body was becoming lifeless, he could not remain standing. The two persons brought him to the nearest room and laid him down on the cot. We were informed, and all of us ran to him. But we found he was becoming completely unconscious. We were at a loss to decide as to what happened to him. He was all right just a few minutes before. My father began to enquire about the incident. But my grandfather was completely unconscious. I remember, he could just open his eyes and two drops of tears came out of his eyes. In spite of his efforts, he could not speak. The face had become slightly oblique. Seeing this my father said to me that he had been attacked by paralysis, and asked me to call the neighbouring doctor. Without delay I brought the doctor with me. He also suspected the same disease and advised my father to call a competent doctor. My father went to the civil surgeon but he was out on duty in the district jail. My father went there and the doctor was kind enough to come. However, he took about one hour to come. The doctor examined my grandfather who was now completely unconscious. He suggested operation on the head to relieve him of excessive high blood pressure. He also advised my father to call some other competent doctor for this purpose. Some person went to call him. But, before he reached the garden of my home, my grandfather was away from his perishable body. Not to speak of the home, the whole town was taken aback. In only one and a half hour, the deadly disease took away the life of my revered grandfather. We were all very, very depressed. Some suspected the cow to be the cause of this disease. But what of that? The cow was removed from the house, but how can I associate her with this disease? Decades have passed, but this strange death is still fresh in my mind.

My grandfather (Dadajee) was famous for his peaceful nature and benevolent activities. He was always very kind to the poor. When the dead body was taken out in procession, it was difficult for some to believe that he was no more. Hundreds of persons joined the funeral procession. Thc body of such a pious man was burnt to ashes on the Gadhadhar Ghat of the river Phalgu. All were weeping for him, tears of blood were shed for him. But there was nothing left but a heap of ashes.

This mishap gave a further shock to my grandmother. What effects all these were producing in me it would be impossible to describe. However, with all this burden, we headed towards the future. It was just the next day of the *Holi* festival after four months of my grandfather's death. The condition of my grandmother became very serious. Doctors were called, but I thought, it was the second cruel deed of God on me. At about 10 a.m. the cherished body of my grandmother was lifeless and I was looking at the lamp of affection out of light. I wanted to weep but I was completely confused and was at a loss to decide how to face the situation. And again, as stated above, the pyre of my grandmother was burnt to ashes, within a few hours.

After four months of her death, (Magh, 15 years old), I got an attack of the remittent fever. I ate food after one month. I was practically reduced to a skeleton. Even after six months I could not recover adequate weight. One day my father's sister's son (Fufera Bhai) came to my house to meet me. He was very much worried to see my pitiable health. He inspired me to do physical exercise regularly. He requested me to come to his place specially for this purpose. I went to him. He showed me his gymnasium and from next day, every morning I began to go to him for physical exercise. In a fortnight I began to find some change in my health and within one and a half months I was completely healthy. I continued the physical exercise for about four years. Wrestling, *Dand, Baithki, Johri, Gadhe, Damble* etc., were the special exercises. These four years of physical exercise brought a radical change in my health. My muscles became well developed. This was the first success of its type. Now I was counted as one of the healthiest youths of our community.

I was married at the age of 18. The marriage was not in the family that was fixed up by my grandmother. The negotiations broke with the first family. (*Question*). The bride's party refused to have me. The reasons were not explained to us. The breaking of promise had a very critical effect on me. I took a vow not to marry. But several parties came to my father and one day I heard that the preparation for the marriage had started. One day I asked my cousin to tell my father that I did not like to marry in this life, and that I should not be given the trouble. He became suspicious about my opposition and disclosed the matter to some of his close relations and especially, to my Fufa (Father's sister's husband) i.e., Respected Sri S. L. They came to me. They tried to persuade me in all ways. When all their attempts failed, P. (Fufa) made a very sentimental appeal: "If not for you, you should think of your father, who has made such a sacrifice in his life for you. (He did not remarry on your account.) Can you not do something for him? Except your father, who is your sincere well-wisher? Let his dream be fulfilled. Don't resist."

These strong words of my Fufajee had a great sentimental appeal. On the other side I saw the sad face of my father. I could not refuse the marriage now. I had to express my agreement. The marriage ceremony was performed. About 2,000 rupees were spent. It was a marriage of simple type and some of the Gayawal did not like it. On this sacred occasion some of my nearest relatives showed such unmanly behaviour with me that I will always remember. (*Question*). Some of the relatives that co-operated in the marriage also deserve to be remembered. Anyhow, I was married with such unhappy experiences. This new relationship did not bring for me any real and internal happiness.

Regarding my profession, the Partition of India and then also the communal riots have very adversely affected my family. Due to communal riots, the Hindu inhabitants of West Pakistan migrated to India as refugees. The millionaires of yesterday were converted to beggars and they took refuge on footpaths. The inhuman activities of the Muslim also brought a good deal of change in our destinny. I had my (Vriti) professional attachments in the eight districts of West Punjab and North-Western Frontier Provinces. The chief means of our livelihood were brutally destroyed. From this area we used to get, on an average, Rs. 15 to Rs. 20, in addition to gold, silver, copper, pots, costly clothes, dry fruits and other things daily. We used to enjoy the company of healthy and beautiful Hindus of that area. But now, it is difficult for us to expect some of them even after an interval of three months or so.

We were not prepared to face such a drastic change and the economic status of the family began to fall very rapidly. On the whole my family, though educated and highly respectable, was never considered as one of the richest families. About 25 years before my birth, my family was proud having persons like Sri B. L. (my great grandfather's brother) who was honoured with the title of Rai Bahadur. During that time we had a large property like motor, horses, sky-kissing buildings, hundreds of servants and maidservants (which are owned by none of the present Gayawal families). But there were many others who had much more than we had. At the time of my birth and after, the property was divided into four to five divisions and our economic conndition was not good. Anyway, we were happy. But the communal riots and political up-heavels completely destroyed us.

My economic conditions were so bad that we were on the verge of starvation. The situation was such that I thought I should do something. But what should I do? Though somewhat educated, it was beyond my prestige to take up a job (or service). We depended on the pilgrims that we had in Jammu and Kashmir, and Udhan Pur and Kathara, Simla, in the districts of East Punjab, in some of the districts like Murshidabad, Birbhum, Burdwan, Bankura, (Manbhum), Maldah, etc., of West Bengal and in the districts of Banda, Farrukhabad, Mirjapur, Banaras in Utter Pradesh. These areas were not affected and we expected pilgrims from these districts. But it was not at all sufficient to feed and maintain our family. We never did have any experience in any business and secondly, we had no capital to invest in anything. We were so much chained and absorbed in the traditional profession of priesthood, that we could not see any other way out.

Vishnupad is one of the biggest pilgrimage centres for the followers of Sanatan Dharma. A large number of persons, both religious visitors and Shraddha functionaries, come to the temple. All the Pandas have equal rights on the gifts that are offered at the altar of the God, Vishnu. But this right can be enjoyed only when one attends the temple and entertains visitors. The attendance in the temple for securing gifts is considered to be a job of socially and economically inferior families of the Gayawal. Though we used to go to the temple for worship, we never went there with a view to enjoy the right to secure gifts from the visitors. But now there was no way out. The dying man will do anything to survive. This was the only way out to supplement the income of my family. Under compulsion, then, I, along with my two cousins (father's brother's son) began to attend the temple. Every morning we used to go there at 7 a.m. and come back at noon. Economically, it was useful to attend the temple but I had to give up wrestling which I thought essential to maintain my health. However, I continued some physical exercise which I used to do at my own place. But it was not up to my satisfaction. Now, I began to visit (C.L.) in the evening. We used to listen to the radio or play on musical instruments. His elder brother used to practise harmonium while he himself was interested in *tabla*. His youngest brother had also picked up harmonium-playing. Two of our other relatives used to come there. They were also interested in music. A music master (Sri Gabardan Singh, the son of the famous musician, the late Sri Sonujee Ustad) also used to come to teach us both the harmonium and *tabla*. But after some time the wife of (C.L.) died and this event brought a great shock to us all. The music assembly was dissolved for ever.

My attendance in the temple continued as usual. At times I used to think, "Most of the Gayawal youth and children come to the temple and stay there for five to six hours. Their time is almost uselessly spent there. If an organization of the youth is started, their time can be rightly planned and spent." I expressed this desire of mine to persons of my own age—L. L., R. L., N. L., K. L. All of them welcomed my proposal. So all of us directed our efforts collectively to organise the association. It took one year to convince and persuade all of the youths to join the organisation. We named it Gayawal Navyubak Samaj (The Gayawal Youth Society); all the Gayawal youths who used to attend the temple were the members. The office-bearers were elected, and I was elected Joint Secretary. (*Ethnographic*).

Under the auspices of the 'Samaj', we planned to make an attempt to resolve some of our problems. The Partition of India and many other factors had greatly and badly affected the whole community. The remaining 'Profession' (Vriti) was disorganised and exploited by the rich Gayawal [he calls them capitalists of the Gayawal society]. They had employed a number of agents who were posted at important railway junctions and whose job was to mislead the pilgrims to different priests. Their tactics were deceptively irreligious and unmanly. (*Ethnographic*). . . . These disruptive agencies were let loose about thirty years ago and a number of Gayawal burning with the zeal to reform their society had organised several types of association. (*Ethnographic*).

We started the Gayawal Youth Society in the year 1950. It worked only for a few months and then, like the other reformists' movements, it also broke down owing to internal disunity and differences of opinion. But, our enthusiasm was not damped and in order to amend some of the conventions associated with the temples we again organised Vishnupad Vriti

Sudhanini Sabha (The Conference for Reformation in Vishnu Temple Profession).

I wanted to see my community prosperous and happy. Our caste and profession were one. In spite of all these unifying forces, only a few differences were disorganizing the whole profession. I wanted to eliminate those differences, I desired to raise the sanctity and purity of my divine profession and thus aspired to bring our society on the level of unity, equality and purity, as it were. (*Ethnographic*).

Though I have been unsuccessful in my attempts, I still believe in my dreams and I am optimistic for the future.

Coming back to my family life, after four years of my marriage, my wife came to my home for the first time last year. Before this "second marriage ceremony" I traditionally was not allowed to meet her in the night even at her mother's place. So I used to go there once in a month or so, when invited by my mother-in-law. But I went in the daytime and was supposed to come back by the evening. But to be frank, both of us were so mature that we could not check the temptation of sexual intercourse. However, this was neither possible nor desirable in the daytime. So, I used to make excuses and stay there late in the evening. Several times, I was disappointed. However, I was never disturbed because of this.

I also spent the four years of time between the marriage and the "second marriage" in visiting distant places and cities. I had a strong desire for travelling and visiting cities from my very childhood. I have seen about 10 to 12 cities in the north and northeast India. I always feel a strong urge to visit north-western areas like Jammu, Kashmir, Simla, Kangra, Haridwar, Lachman Jula, Dehradun. Let me wait for that auspicious occasion when I will be able to see them. When the time comes, I will not have much difficulties. At all these places, I have my innumerable pupils (Shishya) who will welcome me with respect.

With the coming of my wife in my own home, life has become more enjoyable and I feel the life of man without woman is sure to be incomplete. Still the happiness that one receives in observing the religious Brahmacharya and doing physical exercise is unsurpassable. I keep my passion under control and never indulge excessively in all these matters. It is only because of this control that I have been able to maintain a good physique of which I am proud.

Last year we again organised the Gayawal Youth Society and I have been elected as the General Secretary. Again, we are attempting to attain our goal on the strength of the organisation. If the police and the administrative officers help us, there is no power that can deter us from achieving our objective of crushing the agency system. This is both my experience and the experience of others that they help the exploiters and owing to this our objectives are defeated.

Since my "second marriage ceremony", my father has almost retired from domestic and professional life. Most of his time is devoted to worship, visiting temples and observing prayers. My uncle looks after the affairs of pilgrims. I also co-operate with him in priestly activities. I look after all the pilgrims that come to us, and I arrange their accommodation, make provision for *Pinda*-gifts, foot-worship, *Suphal*-worship, etc.; but temperamentally I am more attached to pilgrims that come from West Pakistan—Rawalpindi, Peshawar, Hazara, Kohat, Jhelam, etc.—than those who come from any other place. I genuinely feel that they deserve all attention and merit as they come to Gaya in spite of so many difficulties. In the name of religion and in the name of their "poor" Purohit, they come to such a distant place. I do not find so much of truthfulness, beauty and cleanliness elsewhere as among them. In addition to them, I also give my special attention to the pilgrims from Simla and Kashmir.

GLOSSARY

Acharya (*āchārya*): A spiritual guide, a holy teacher; in Gaya, the secondary priests who guide and conduct the shraddha rituals performed by the pilgrims. Such priests are usually employed by the Gayawal and act under their supervision.

adharma (*adharma*): Irreligion.

Adi Gaya (*Ādi Gayā*): Literally, the original or the oldest part of Gaya; also, the name of a particular sacred centre at Gaya, now abandoned.

Aghan (*Āghan*, Skt. *Āgrahāyana*): November-December, a month of the Hindu calendar.

agni kund (*agni kūnda*): Fire-pit for fire worship.

Akshayavat (*Aksayavat*): The undying banyan tree; name of a sacred centre in Gaya represented by the banyan tree.

Alahabad (*Alāhābād*): "God's settlement," an Arabic term; name given to a locality in Gaya which is predominantly inhabited by Muslims.

Andar Gaya (*Andar Gayā*): The inner Gaya; name for the sacred part of Gaya.

Angiras (*Angiras*): Name of a famous Hindu sage (rishi).

Annapurna (*Annapūrnā*): The goddess of food and grains.

Arghya (*arghya*): A form of worship especially for the sun; act of pouring of water or milk in the name of the actual sun.

arti (*āratī*): Act of waving lights before an image.

Ashoka (*Ashoka*): A great Buddhist emperor of India in the fifth century B.C.

Asin (Skt. *Āshvin*): September-October, a month of the Hindu calendar.

astuti (*astuti* or *stuti*): Hymn of praise; appeal.

Atri (*Atri*): Name of a famous Hindu sage (rishi).

Bageshvari (*Vāgeshvarī*): The tigress manifestation of the goddess Kali; name of a sacred centre. Some also associate this goddess with learning.

Baisakh (*Vaisākh*, Skt. *Vaishākh*): April-May, a month of the Hindu calendar.

Baisakhi Prava (*Baisākhī Prava*): Name of a Buddhist festival.

Baitarani (Skt. *Vaitaranī*): Name of a sacred tank in Gaya which is named after the mythological river Vaitarani, the Hindu Styx.

baithaka (*baithakā*): Literally, a sitting place; name for a Gayawal club.

bali vedi (*bali vedi*): Sacrificial alter; the wooden frame in front of some Kali temples for sacrificing goats.

Banaras (Skt. *Varanasī*): A place of Hindu pilgrimage in the state of Uttar Pradesh in northern India.
bat vriksha (*vat vriksā*): A Sanskrit term for the banyan tree.
Bhado (*Bhādo*, Skt. *Bhādrapad*): August-September, a month of the Hindu calendar.
Bhagavat Purana (*Bhāgavat Purāna*): A religious book of the Hindus.
bhaivi (*bhaivī*): Brotherhood.
Bhaiya (*Bhaiyā*): "Brother" ; name of a Gayawal lineage.
bhakta (*bhakta*): Devotee.
bhakti (*bhakti*): Devotion to gods.
bhang (*bhāng*): A kind of marijuana which is usually eaten and drunk.
Bharati (*Bhāarati*): Name for one of the ten groups of Shaiva sadhus usually followers of Shankaracharya.
Bhim Gaya (*Bhīm Gayā*): Bhim's Gaya ; a sacred centre named after Bhim, one of the five pandavas of the Mahabharat who is said to have visited Gaya.
Bhuneshvar (*Bhuvaneshvar*): An ancient town noted for important temples in the state of Orissa in East Central India.
bhut (*bhūt*): A general name for ghosts and spirits.
bigha (*bighā*): A various unit of land measurement, often about half an acre.
Bihar (*Bihār*): A state of northern India.
Bishua (*Bisvā*): "Twentieth" ; name of an agricultural festival falling on the ninth day of the first half of Baisakh, usually after the rabi harvest.
Bodhi Drum (*Bodhī Druma*): The tree of knowledge ; a sacred centre represented by a pipal tree.
Brahma (*Brahmā*): One of the three important gods of the Hindu ; god of creation.
brahmacharya (*brahmāchārya*): One of the four stages of a man's life according to the ancient Hindu texts.
Brahma Kunda (*Brahmā Kunda*): A tank named after Brahma ; it is considered sacred for shraddha sacrifice.
Brahman varna (*Brāhman varna*): One of the four divisions of the Hindu caste hierarchy.
brahmabhoj (*brahma bhoja*): A meal given ceremonially to a Brahman.
Brahmyoni (*Brahmayoni*): Literally, a female energy of Brahma ; name of a hill having several shrines. Apparently this name has been derived from a natural fissure in the rocks at the top of the hill through which a person can just manage to crawl. This is looked upon as a symbol of the yoni (female organ) or womb, and it is believed that by crawling through it, one escapes rebirth from the human womb.

Buddha Gaya (*Buddha Gayā*): Literally, Buddha's Gaya. The locality around the temple of Buddha Gaya is called by this name.

Chadar (*chādar*): A sheet or woman's head cloth.

Chait (Skt. *Chaitra*): March-April, a month of the Hindu calendar.

Chalisa (*Chālisā*): "Forty couplets" ; the name of inexpensive sacred books for ritual reading.

Chandini (*Chāndinī*): Literally, the brillance of the moon ; a poetic name for the Gayawal's literary organization.

charan puja (*charan pujā*): Worship of the feet of priests by making offerings of flowers, coins, etc.

Chhatha Vrata (*Chhatha Vrata*): "Sixth vow": the name for a sacred performance dedicated to the sun and observed on the sixth day of the light half of the month of Kartik.

Chhota Nagpur (*Chhotā Nāgpur*): One of the administrative divisions of Bihar ; its districts are predominantly populated by aboriginals.

Chitragupta (*Chitragupta*): Accountant of Yama, the king of the dead. The Kayastha caste is said to have descended from Chitragupta.

Chukka (*chukkā*): A small earthen pot.

Dakhini (*Dakhinī*): Literally, southerner ; a term used to refer to the Gayawal guru who hails from South India.

Dakhinmanas (*Dakhinmānas*): "The southern tank" ; a name for a sacred centre which is now forgotten.

dakshina (*daksinā*): A gift to the Brahman priest for his religious service.

dan (*dān*): Alms to the beggars, sadhus, or to some institutions.

darshan (*darshan*): Literally, to see with eyes ; also means philosophy. In the ritual sense, it denotes the act of seeing and adoring the idols with all forms of worship.

darshaniya (*darshaniyā*): Those who come for the ritual acts of seeing and making offering to the deities are called by this name by the Gayawal.

darvani (*darvānī*): Literally, a place for watching ; name given to the raised platform located at the front gate of the Vishnupada temple. It is the place where the pujari wait and watch for the worshipers of darshaniya to come.

Dasnami (*Dasnāmī*): "Ten named" ; the ten orders of the Shaiva ascetics formed by Shankaracharya.

Deoghar (*Devghar*): A sacred town in the state of Bihar.

devata (*devataā*): Male god or godling.

devi (*devī*): Goddess.

Dhami (*Dhāmī*): A group of priests in Gaya usually considered by the local people as non-Brahmanical. They are also known as Dhamin or Pretiya Brahman.

Dhami Tola (*Dhāmī Tola*): "The colony of the Dhami"; name of a locality in Gaya.

Dhanuk (*Dhānuk*): A servant caste.

dharma patni (*dharma patnī*): An epithet for wife.

dharmashala (*dharmashālā*): "Religion house"; a house built by a rich devotee for the free sojourn of pilgrims and travellers. In some such places food is also served free.

dhoti (*dhotī*): Lower cloth, about five yards in length, especially the dress of Hindu men.

dhyan (*dhyān*): Meditation.

digvijay (*digvijaya*): "The great conquest", usually referring to the spiritual conquest by Shankaracharya over Buddhism in India.

durbar (*darbār*): Ceremony of homage to a ruler and rewards to subordinates.

Dvarka Troop (*Dvārkā Troop*): Name of a Gayawal scout troop, named after its founder, Dvarka Lal Sen.

Ekadashi (*ekādashī*): Eleventh day of each half of a Hindu month, a sacred day for ritual observances like fasts, special ritual baths, and temple worship—all of which if done on that day are said to bring great spiritual merits.

Fasal (*phasal*): "Harvest"; the Gayawal use it for indicating the largeness of pilgrimage during the three specific periods.

Gadadhar (*gadādhar*): Literally, the possessor of mace; an epithet of Lord Vishnu.

Gadalol (*Gadālol*): A sacred tank at Gaya named after a mythological demon (Asur) who was killed by Vishnu.

gaddi (*gaddī*): Throne.

gana (*gāna*): Singing.

Gandak (*Gandāk*): Name of a river in north Bihar.

Ganesh (*Ganesh*): The god of prosperity and learning.

ganja (*gānjā*): A kind of marijuana which is usually smoked.

Ganpatyas (*Ganpatyās*): The followers of Lord Ganesh; name of a sect.

Gautama (*Gautama*): Name of a famous Hindu saint.

Gaya (*Gayā*): The sacred city in the state of Bihar which derives its name after the demon (Asur) Gaya who was killed by Vishnu and other deities.

Gaya Asur (*Gayā Asur*): A mythological demon noted for his religious acts who was killed by the gods and goddesses, and on whose body reside all the gods and goddesses.

Gaya Kup (*Gayā Kūp*): "Gaya's well"; an ancient sacred well, now abandoned.

Gaya Mahatmya (*Gayā Māhātmya*): The text that embodies the sacredness of Gaya. It consists of the last eight chapters from the Vayu Purana (chaps. 105-112).
Gaya shraddha (*Gayā shrāddha*): The claborate ancestor worship observed by pilgrims at Gaya.
Gaya Shraddha Paddhati (*Gayā Shrāddha Paddhati*): Name of the book prescribing the process of ancestor worship at Gaya.
Gaya Sir (*Gayā Sir*): "Gaya's head", the head of Gaya Asur; a part of Old Gaya; also a particular sacred centre, now abandoned.
Gayatri (*Gāyatrī*): A verse from the Rigveda which is recited by pious Brahmans and other religious persons twice daily.
Gayawal (*Gayāvāla*): Literally, "people of Gaya"; the special caste of Brahmans controlling the Gaya shraddha.
Gayawali (*Gayāvalī*): The Magadhi dielect of the Gayawal Brahmans.
Gayeshvari (*Gayeshvarī*): "Goddess of Gaya", a local idol and shrine identified with the goddess Durga.
ghat (*ghāt*): Steps provided for bathing on the bank of a river or a pond.
ghee (*ghī*): Clarified butter.
Giddhkut (Skt. *Grīdhrakūta*): "Vulture's house"; name of a sacred centre at Gaya, now abandoned.
Giri (*Girī*): One of the ten orders of the Dasnami sadhu of the Shankaracharya Shaiva sect.
Gita (*Gītā*): The Bhagavad Gita, a famous philosophic portion of the Mahabharata epic.
goonda (*gūnda*): Ruffian or mischief-monger.
Go Prachar (*Go Prachār*): "Cow preaching"; name of a sacred centre at Gaya consisting of representations of the footprints of the cows of Lord Krishna.
gotra (*gotra*): A type of exogamous clan division among Hindus. The Gayawal, for example, are divided into fourteen gotras (clans), each gotra being named after a saint (rishi).
grahana (*grahana*): Literally, "capturing"; an eclipse of the sun or moon. The day of an eclipse is observed with a sacred bath and giving of alms.
guru (*gurū*): Spiritual teacher or philosopher.
Hanuman (*Hanumān*): The name for the "monkey" who was a great devotee and servant of the epic god Ram, he is worshiped as a giver of physical strength.
homa (*homa*): Offering oblaltions to gods by throwing ghee, barley, sesamum, etc., into the consecrated fire; a form of vedic worship.
homa agni (*homa agni*): The sacrificial fire.

homa kund (*homa kūnda*): The fire-pit for receiving the consecrated fire.
Jagir (*jāgir*): Free-lease land, usually granted to a chief retainer of a king.
jajman (*jajmān,* Skt. *yajamān*): "Sacrificer," patron; for the Gayawal, especially any pilgrim who is the hereditary employer of a particular Gayawal family for shraddha rituals observed at Gaya.
Jajmani (*jajmānī*): Pertaining to the sacrificer; especially, hereditary priestly employment.
jajmani vatra (*jajmāni vātrā*): Visit of a Gayawal priest to his patrons in the different parts of India.
Janardan (*Janārdan*): A name of Lord Vishnu.
Janmastami (*Janmāstamī*): "Birth eighth"; name for the sacred festival observed on the eighth day of the dark half of the month of Bhado as a mark of the birth anniversary of Lord Krishna, the epic god.
jap (*jāp*): Worship by repetition of sacred words.
jati (*jāti*): Caste.
Jeth (*Jeth,* Skt. *Jyestha*): May-June, a month of the Hindu calendar.
jhar (*jhār*): Magical sweeping with sacred leaves for curing disease.
jharphuk (*jhārphūk*): Magical sweeping and blowing for curing a disease.
Jhulan (*Jhulan*): "Swinging"; name of a religious festival observed with special worship, decoration, and dramatic and devotional performances in the thakurbadi.
ji (*jī*): A term of respect, usually added after the name of an invididual, god, or some sacred place as a mark of reverence.
Jitiya (*Jītīyā*): A sacred festival for observing ancestor worship especially prevallent in the village of Bihar.
jnana (*jnāna*): "Knowledge"; philosophical orientation.
Kachcha bhojan (*kachchā bhojan*): "Raw food": edibles prepared in water instead of ghee or oil; for the latter type of preparation, see pakka bhojan.
Kahar (*Kahār*): A caste of domestic servants; members of this caste also specialize in carrying palanquin.
kak bali (*kāk bali*): "Sacrifice to the crow," a common ritual of ancestor worship. At Gaya, the name of a sacred centre visited by pilgrims performing shraddha.
Kali (*Kālī*): The goddess of power; the mother goddess.
kanagat (*kanāghat*): A death ritual.
Kanauj (*Kanoj*): A caste of Brahman.

Kantaha (*Kantāhā*): A caste of lower Brahmans especially invited to accept gifts in the name of the dead on the eleventh day of the death sacrament.

karta (*kartā*): A term for the main functionary of any ritual.

Kartik (*Kārtik*): October-November, a month of the Hindu calendar.

Kartik Purnima (*Kārtik Purnimā*): The full-moon day of the month of Kartik.

katha (*kathā*): Recitation and/or reading of sacred mythological stories from the puranic and epic texts.

kesharbhat (*kesharbhāt*): An expensive dish of rice prepared with saffron. This dish has religious significance and is popular among the Gayawal.

khata (*khātā*): "Record book"; one of the large-sized books owned by each Gayawal family and maintained by the family clerk. These contain genealogies and other details about patron families.

Krishna (Skt. *Krisna*): An epic god, hero of the Mahabharat, and identified as the eighth incarnation of Vishnu.

kshetra (*ksetra*): "Ground"; especially, an extensive mythological holy area including numerous sacred centres. In one ancient text (Garuda Purana, Pt. i, chap. xvi, vs. 14), seven kshetras have been enumerated: Ayodhya; Mathura; Maya or Hardwar; Kashi or Banaras; Kanchi or Conjeeveram; Avanti or Ujjayini; and Dvaravat or Dwarka in Gujrat. According to other texts (Vayu Purana), two other sacred grounds—Gaya and Prayag or Allahabad—are recognized in norther India.

Kumhar (*Kumhār*): The caste of potters.

kusha (*kusha*): A kind of grass.

kusumvi kadhi (*kusumvi kadhī*): A delicious and expensive saffron curry used by the Gayawal.

Lakshmi (*Laksmī*): Name of the wife of Lord Vishnu.

lila (*lilā*): Dramatic performances from the lives of Ram and Krishna, adapted from the Ramayana and the Bhagavat Puran.

Madhava (*Madhava*), Madhavacharya (*Madhavācharya*): A great religious leader and philosopher of South India in the thirteenth century; advocate of dualism.

Magadha (*Magadha*): An ancient kingdom of Bihar that covered the present districts of Patna, Gaya, etc.

Magh (*Māgh*): January-February, a month of the Hindu calendar.

Mahabodhi society (*Mahābodhi* society): An international Buddhist organization.

mahalaya (*mahālalya*): The annual, general observance of ancestor worship which reaches its climax on the new moon day of Asin.
mahant (*mahanta*): Head of a temple or monastery.
Mahaprabhu (*Mahāprabhu*): The great lord; an epithet for Shiva and Vishnu; the followers of Chaitanya also call him by this name.
Maharashtra (*Mahārāstra*): A region of West-Central India included in the present Bombay State.
Mahavir (*Mahāvīr*): "Great hero," an epithet for the monkey-god Hanuman.
Maithil (*Maithil*): A caste of Brahmans.
Mali (*Mālī*): The caste of florists.
Manglagauri (*Mangalāgaurī*): The auspicious goddess Gauri, bride of Shiva, represented by a major shrine in Gaya.
mantra (*Mantra*): Sacred vedic words.
Manu Smriti (*Manu Smriti*): One of the famous law books of the Hindus.
Maratha (*Marāthā*): Loosely, any speaker of the Marathi language in Western India.
Marichi (*Mārīchi*): A famous Hindu saint.
math (*math*): A monastery; a house for monks and sannyasis.
Mithila (*Mithila*): An ancient kingdom in northern Bihar.
moksha (*moksa*): Salvation, release from transmigration, final spiritual emancipation.
mrityu sanskar (*mrityu sanskār*): The death sacrament.
munshiji (*munshījī*): Title for a clerk; in Gaya, especially a member of a Kayastha caste who usually does the work of accounting and writing for the Gayawal.
Murali (*Muralī*): "Flute" of Lord Krishna: name of a hill at Gaya.
Murarpur (*Murārpur*): Name of a locality at Gaya, named after an epithet of Krishna.
Nach (*nāch*): Dance.
Nai (*Nāi*): The caste of barbers.
namestin (*namestin*): A type of half-shirt popular with the Gayawal.
Narsinha (*Narsinha*): "The man-lion"; the fourth incarnation of Vishnu. Vishnu assumed the shape of a creature—half-man, half-lion—to deliver the world from the tyrant Hiranyakasipu.
natak (*nātak*): Dramatic performances.
Nava Yuvak Samaj (*Nava Yuvak Samāj*): The society for the youth; name of a Gayawal association organized by the youth.
Navratra (*Navrātra*): "Nine nights"; a festival in honour of the goddess Durga.

neg (*neg*): Customary presents usually given to lesser sacred specialists such as the barber, the florist, the potter, the domestic servant, etc., on the occasion of certain elaborate observances at the "master" house.
nitya yajna (*nitya yajna*): The daily sacrifice.
Ojha (*ojhā*): A magician, a shaman.
Pakka bhojan (*pakkā bhojan*): Edibles cooked in the ghee or oil.
pakvan (*pakvān*): Small cakes fried in deep ghee or oil.
palang (*palang*): Elaborate wooden bed.
pan (*pān*): Betel leaves chewed with areca nut, lime, and spices as a mild intoxicant.
panda (*pandā*): "Learned and wise man" ; the special type of priests who inhabit the places of pilgrimage and predominantly officiate as tirtha guru as, for example, Baranasi panda, Prayagwala, Gayawal.
panditji (*panditjī*): "Learned" ; title of address for a Brahman.
paranpuri (*pāranpūri*): Wheaten cakes with a sweet stuffing of split pulse, a dish which the Gayawal have probably borrowed from their Maharashtrian patrons.
parikrama (*parikramā*): Circumambulation of a temple or other sacred object as a ritual performance.
Parpitamaheshvar (*Parpitāmaheshvar*): "The great grandfather —great god," an epithet for Shiva ; name of a Shiva temple in Gaya.
Parvati (*Pārvati*): "Daughter of the mountain," a major Hindu goddess, wife of Shiva.
Pataliputra (*Pātalīputra*): Ancient name for Patna, a city in the State of Bihar.
path (*pāth*): Reading of a sacred text as a form of worship.
Pathar Devi (*Pāthar Devī*): The deity of stone ; name of a sacred centre.
pauniya (*pauniya*): Low caste specialists like the barber, potter, washerman, etc., who give services to other castes and receive small payments in return.
Phalgu (*Phalgu*): Name of the sacred river at Gaya.
Phalgun (*Phālgun*): February-March, a month of the Hindu calendar.
phuk (*phūk*): Magical blowing to cure a disease.
pinda (*pinda*): A ball of rice flour offered to the dead and to the manes at funeral rites or shraddha.
pindabechva (*pindabechvā*): A small group of caste specialists at Gaya who sell pinda or rice balls.
pindadan (*pindadān*): Offering of rice ball with all the elaborate rituals.
pindapujan (*pindapūjan*): Worship of the rice cake.

pipal (*pipal*): Name of a tree universally considered sacred.
pitamaheshvar (*pitāmaheshvar*): "The father of the great gods" ; an epithet for Shiva ; name of a Shiva temple at Gaya.
pitambar (*pītāmbar*): Yellow silken garment ; a sacred garment for the purpose of worship, etc.
pitri (*pitri*): "Dead fathers and forefathers" ; manes.
pitribhojan (*pitribhojan*): Food offered to the manes.
pitrijan (*pitrijan*): The whole body of ancestors taken collectively.
pitrikarya (*pitrikārya*): Oblations or sacrifice offered to the deseased ancestors.
pitripaksha (*pitripaksha*): "The manes' fortnight" ; the dark half of the month of Asin is called by this name.
Pitripati (*Pitripati*): An epithet for Yama, the lord of the manes.
Pitripujan (*Pitripujan*): Worship of the manes.
Pitritirtha (*Pitri Tirtha*): "Manes' pilgrimage" ; especially, pilgrimage to Gaya.
Pitritithi (*Pitri Tithi*): The day of the new moon, especially in the month of Asin.
pitriyoni (*pitriyoni*): The stage of being manes ; a phase in the after-life after the pretayoni or the stage of ghost.
prarthana (*prārthanā*): Prayer.
prasad (*prasād*): "Blessings" ; the remains of food offered to idols, distributed to the worshipers.
pratahkali (*prātahkāli*): Morning recitation.
preta (*preta*): A ghost or evil spirit ; the spirit of the dead before his funeral rites are performed.
Pretabhavani (*Pretabhavāni*): "Ghost-goddess" ; at Gaya, a shrine which is visited by shraddha sacrificers.
Pretaparvat (*Pretaparvat*): "Ghost-hill" ; a sacred hill at Gaya which is visited by the shraddha sacrificers. Now the name of the hill has been changed to Ramshila.
Pretashila (*Pretashilā*): "Ghost-rock" ; at Gaya, a hill noted for its many shrines worshiped by the shraddha sacrificers.
pretayoni (*pretayoni*): "Ghost-womb" ; the stage of ghost through which dead souls have to pass before attaining the manes-stage and ultimately heaven.
Pretiya Brahman (*Pretiya Brāhman*): An epithet for a group of priests who officiate over the shrines dedicated to ghosts ; at Gaya, the Dhami.
puja (*pūjā*): Worship, reverence, especially worship with flowers.
pujari (*pujārī*): Worshiper, usually this name is used only for an official priestly worshipper ; the shrine priest.
Pulaha (*Pulaha*): Name of a famous Hindu saint.

Pulastya (*Pulastya*): Name of a famous Hindu saint.
pund (*pund*): A system of worship.
punya (*punya*): Spiritual merit.
Purana Gaya (*Purānā Gayā*): "Old Gaya," especially the sacred zone of Gaya.
purdah (*purdā*): Seclusion of women by confinement to a certain part of the house, or by veiling the head and face.
Puri (*Puri*): One of the ten orders of the Dasnami sannyasis of Shankara's Shiva sect ; also the name of a place of pilgrimage in Orissa.
purnima (*purnimā*): The full moon.
purohit (*purohit*): A priest ; especially the domestic priest.
Pus (*Pus,* Skt. *Paus*): December-January, a month of the Hindu calendar.
pushkara (*puskara*): "A sacred bathing place" ; a shraddha performed at places of pilgrimage (Vishnu Sutra, Chap. LXXXV, vs. 1).
Rabi (*rabī*): Spring harvest consisting of wheat, barley, gram, etc., in March and April.
Rahu (*Rāhu*): A harmful mythical planet of Hindu astrology.
Rai Bahadur (*Rāy Bāhādur*): An honorary title given to eminent Hindus during the British rule in India.
Rai Saheb (*Rāy Sāheb*): An honorary title given to eminent Hindus during the British rule in India.
Ram (*Rāma*): The seventh incarnation of Vishnu, an epic god and the hero of the Ramayana. He is believed to have come to Gaya to perform shraddha of his father, Dashratha.
Ramayana (*Rāmāyana*): A religious book of the Hindus.
Ram Gaya (*Rāma Gayā*): "Ram-Gaya" ; a number of shrines at a particular area are said to have been visited by Ram and the area is named after him.
Ram Kund (*Rāma Kunda*): Name of a sacred tank dedicated to Ram, the epic god.
Ram Naumi (*Rāma Naumī*): Ram's Ninth ; name of the sacred festival observed in honour of the birth anniversary of Ram on the ninth day of the second half of the month of Chait.
Ramshila (*Rāma Shilā*): "Ram-rock" ; name of a hill at Gaya.
Rath Yatra (*Rath Yātra*): "Chariot travel" ; a religious fair consisting of bringing out the deities for a short procession in the respective cities. This sacred celebration is especially famous at Puri. At Gaya, also, it has been imitated.
Ratu (*Rātu*): Name of a famous Hindu saint.
rishi (*risi*): A sage.
riyasat (*riyāsat*): Estate, state.
rozgariya (*rozgāriya*): One who works for his daily earnings, hence a trader or wage-worker ; in Gaya, one who deals in

pilgrim contacts commercially on a commission basis, independent of traditional ties with certain Gayawal; a "pilgrim hunter."

Rumna (*Rumanāh*): Name of a locality in Gaya.

Sadhu (*Sādhu*): An ascetic, a holy man.

sagotra (*sagotra*): Being of the same clan or gotra, the members tracing their origin to the same common mythical ancestor.

Saheb Ganj (*Sāheb Ganj*): "Administrators or masters colony"; name for the area where the British administrators lived and where courts, jails, etc., were located. Later, it began to be used for the entire area except that of the Old Gaya.

Sakadvip (*Sakadvip*): A caste within the Brahman varna whose origin is sometimes traced from the Magian priests of Persia.

sakshi shravana (*sākṣī Shrāvana*): "Witness invocation"; one of the rituals observed by shraddha sacrificers at Gaya.

Saloni Mangala (*Salonī Mangala*): "Pleasant Tuesday"; one of the four Tuesdays of the month of Shravan.

Sanatan dharma (*Sanātan dharma*): "Eternal religion"; a popular name for the orthodox form of religion.

sandhya mantra (*sandhyā mantra*): Brahmans' ritual utterances for morning and evening.

Sangit Samiti (*Sangīt Samiti*): "Music society"; name of a musical organisation of the Gayawal.

sankalpa (*sankalpa*): Dedication; one of the preliminary rituals before commencing actual worship or sacrifice.

sankirtana (*sankirtana*): Group recitation of devotional songs.

sannyasi (*sannyāsī*): Ascetics; a name for those who have ceased to be householders.

saphal (*saphal*): "Fruitful" or "productive"; the final ritual of the Gaya shraddha in which the priest says: "Let it (the pilgrimage) be fruitful."

sapindikarana (*sapindīkarana*): The ritual act of combining the pinda dedicated to the deceased (preta) with that of the dead ancestors or manes (pitri).

sardar (*sardār*): Leader or head of an organisation, locality, or caste group.

Sati (*Satī*): A goddess, the first wife of Lord Shiva.

satsang (*satsang*): "True company"; name for sacred gatherings or meetings in which some holy persons speak about spiritual topics.

sattu (*sattū*): A mixture of the flour of several grains, gram, barley, etc., parched and sweetened.

Saura (*Saura*): The sect that believes in the worship of the sun.

Saurashtra (*Saurāstra*): A region in West India, Gujrat.

Shaiva (*Shaiva*): Sect devoted to the worship of Shiva.

Shakta (*Shākta*): A sect devoted to the worship of the goddess of power, Durga or Kali.
Shakti (*Shakti*): The goddess of power.
shastra (*shāstra*): All types of sacred texts.
Shiva (*Shiva*): One of the three major gods of the Hindus.
Shivalaya (*Shivālaya*): Shiva's house; some of the temples that enshrine the mystic idol of Shiva are called by this name
Shiva Ratri (*Shiva Rātrī*): Shiva's night; sacred celebration in honour of Shiva and his consort Parvati. In Bihar, this day is identified with Shiva's marriage.
shraddha (*shrāddha*): The common name for ritual performed in honour of the departed spirits of the dead ancestors.
shraddha divas (*shrāddha divas*): The anniversary of the death of a relative in whose honour the shraddha is performed.
shraddha puja (*shrāddha pūjā*): Ancestor's worship.
Shravan (*Shrāvan*): July-August, a month of the Hindu calendar.
Shrotriya (*Shrotriya*): "One who has studied the vedas"; in Gaya, a caste of Brahmans.
shukla ekadashi (*shukla ekādashī*): The eleventh lunar day of the bright half (in Gaya, the second half) of a month in the Hindu calendar.
sikha (*sikhā*): A system of worship.
Sita Kund (*Sitā Kunda*): Name of a sacred centre devoted to Sita, wife of Ram.
Sitla (*Shītalā*): Name of a sacred centre devoted to the goddess of small pox.
Sonpur (*Sonpur*): A town in North Bihar noted for having the biggest cattle fair in India.
sthapitkarana (*sthāpitkarana*): The ritual for temporary enshrinement of deities.
surya (*sūrya*): The sun.
Surya Kund (*Sūrya Kund*): A sacred tank in Gaya dedicated to the sun and associated with a sun temple.
Surya Mandir (*Sūrya Mandir*): A temple which enshrines the idol of the sun god.
sutra (*sūtra*): Name of religious texts.
svarga (*svārga*): Heaven.
Tarpana (*tarpana*): Ritual of offering water to sacred beings. performed by pouring water over the hand or hands.
thakurbadi (*thākurbādī*): "God's house"; part of the residential building or the whole of the building where usually epic gods are enshrined.
thakurji (*thākurjī*): A common name for deities, usually epic gods.
tirtha (*tīrtha*): Pilgrimage; place of pilgrimage.

thirthasthan (*tīrthasthān*): Place of pilgrimage; usually an established, organized, mythologically-famed sacred centre that attracts large numbers of worshipers on a regional and universal scale.

Tirtha Vriti Sudharani Sabha (*Tīrtha Vritti Sudhāranī Sabhā*): Pilgrimage Professional Improvement Association, a Gayawal organization.

tirtha yatri (*tīrtha yātrī*): A pilgrim.

tulsi (*tulsī*): A small sweet basil plant noted and worshiped for its sacredness. The Gayawal believe that Vishnu resides on it and some say that Vishnu infused his essence into it. A few regard the plant as a metamorphosis of Sita, wife of Ram, while some other few hold it to be an embodiment of all the deities together. The tulsi is a woman's divinity par excellence, and it is also thought useful as a medicine for several diseases.

Upanayan (*upanāyana*): The sacred thread investiture ceremony.

Urdhava-bahu (*Urdhava-bāhu*): An order to Shaiva ascetics.

Uttarmanas (*Uttarmānas*): "Northern tank"; a sacred tank visited by shraddha sacrificers at Gaya.

Vairagi (*Vairāgī*): Vaishnava ascetics.

Vaishnava (*Vaisnava*): Sect devoted to the worship of Vishnu.

vansh (*vansh*): Lineage or joint family group.

vanshnam (*vanshnām*): Name of a lineage or joint family.

varna vyavastha (*varna vyavasthā*): "Colour system"; system of four-fold division of the Hindu caste hierarchy and professional specialization: Brahman, Kshatriya, Vaishya, Shudra.

varshik shraddha (*vārshik shrāddha*): Anniversary ancestor worship.

Vasishtha (*Vāsistha*): Name of a famous Hindu sage.

Vayu Purana (*Vāyu Purāna*): One of the important sacred texts (Purana) of the Hindu which is dated to be between 350 B.C. and 500 A.D.

Veda (*Veda*): Name of religious texts.

Vikramaditya (*Vikramāditya*): A great emperor of India.

Vishnu (*Visnu*): One of the three major deities of the Hindu, usually noted as protector of the universe.

Vishnu Ashram (*Vishnu Āshram*): Vishnu Retreat, a Gayawal association.

Vishnupada (*Visnupada*): "Vishnu's foot"; a temple enshrining the foot-point of Vishnu; the most famous sacred centre at Gaya at the present time.

Vishnupada Vriti Sudharani Sabha (*Vishnupada Vṛitti Sudhāranī Sabhā*): Vishnupada Professional Improvement Association (for the temple), a Gayawal organization.

Vishnu Sutra (*Visnu Sūtra*): One of the ancient law books of the Hindus.

Vishva Deva (*Vishva Deva*): The god of the universe.
Vishvamitra (*Vishvāmitra*): Name of a famous Hindu saint.
vivaha (*vivāha*): The marriage ceremony.
Yajna (*yajna*): Sacrifice; elaborate observance of ritual and worship.
yajna karta (*yajna kartā*): A functionary for a sacrifice.
Yama (*Yama*): The king of hell and heaven; the god of the dead.
Zamindari (*zamīndārī*): Landlordism.

BIBLIOGRAPHY

APTE, V. M.

Religion and Philosophy, In R. C. Majumdar (ed.) The Vedic Age. London, George Allen and Unwin, Ltd., 1951

Social and religious life in the Grihya Sutra, Bombay, Popular Book Depot, 1954

BARUA, BENI MADHAB

Gaya and Buddha Gaya, Vol. I, Calcutta, Chuckervertty Chatterjee and Co. Ltd.

BHANDARKAR, R. G.

Vaiśhnavism, Śaivism, and minor religious systems, Grundriss-der Indo-Arish Philologie und Altertumskunde, III Band, 6 Heft. Strassburg, 1913

BHATTACHARYA, J. H.

Hindu castes and sects, Calcutta, 1896

BOSE, NIRMAL K.

Cultural Anthropology and other essays, Calcutta, Indian Associated Publishing Co., Ltd., 1953

BUCHANAN, HAMILTON

Patna-Gaya Report, Vol. 1, Patna, Bihar and Orissa research Society, 1811-12

CHATTERJEE, SUNITI K.

The Indian synthesis and racial and cultural intermixture in India, Poona, Bhandarkar Oriental Research Institute, 1953

COUSENS, HENRY

Mediaeval temples of the Dekhan, Madras, Government of Western Circle, India Publication, 1931

CROOKE, WILLIAM

The popular religion and folklore of northern India, London, A. Constable Co., 1896

Natives of northern India, London, A. Constable Co., 1907

CUNNINGHAM, A.

Report of the Archaeological survey of India, Vols. I and II., Simla, Government Printing Press, 1871

Report of a tour in Bihar and (northern) Bengal in 1879-80, Calcutta, Government Printing Press, 1882

CUNNINGHAM, A. and H. B. W. GARRICK

Report of the tours in north and south Bihar, Calcutta, Government Printing Press, 1883

DAVIDSON, EDWARD

Railways in India, London, 1868

DEHON, P.

The religion and customs of the Oraon, Memoirs of the Asiatic Society of Bengal, Vol. I., Calcutta, 1906

DIKSHITAR, V. R. RAMCHANDRA
The Purana Index, Vols. I, II, and III, Madras, University of Madras, 1951

DOWSON, J.
A classical dictionary of Hindu mythology and religion, geography, history, literature. 3rd edition, London, Kegan Paul, Trench, Trubner and Co., Ltd., 1891

DUBE, S. C.
Indian village, Ithaca, Cornell University Press, 1955

DURKHEIM, EMILE
The elementary forms of the religious life, London, George Allen and Unwin, Ltd., 1915

ELWIN, VERRIER
The religion of an Indian tribe, London, Oxford University Press, 1955

FA-HSIEN
Travels of Fa-hsien, Translated by H. A. Giles, Cambridge, The University Press, 1923

FICK, RICHARD
The social organization in north east India in Buddha's time, Translated by Shishir Kumar Maitra. Calcutta, University of Calcutta Press, 1920

FUCHS, STEPHEN
The children of Hari, Bombay, 1950

GHURYE, GOVIND S.
Indian Sadhus, Bombay, Popular Book Depot, 1953

GRIERSON, G. A.
Notes on district of Gaya, Calcutta, Government Printing Press, 1892.

GURDA, KANNUH LAL
Vrihat Gaya Mahatmya, Gaya (press not traceable)

HIUEN TSIANG
Travel of Hiuen Tsiang, Translated from Chinese by Samuel Beal, under the name Buddhist Records of the Western World. London, Kegan Paul, Trench, Trubner and Co. Ltd., 1906

INGHAM, KENNETH
Reforms in India, Cambridge University Press, 1956

KAPADIA, K. M.
Marriage and family in India, Bombay, Oxford Press, 1955

KASHYAPA, A. C.
History of Gaya, Unpublished work.

KAVIRAJA, KRISHNADAS
Chaitunya Charitamrita, Translated from Bengali by Jadunath Sarkar. Calcutta, M. C. Sarkar and Sons, 1913, 1922

KERN, H.
Manual of Indian Buddhism, Grundriss der Indo-Arischen Philologie und Altertumskunde, III Band, 8 Heft, Strassburg, 1913

KRAMRISCH, STELLA
The Hindu temple, Vols. I and II, Calcutta, University of Calcutta Press, 1946

LAL, R. B.
Gaya Ek Jankhi, Gaya, Gaya Printers, 1953

LEWIS, OSCAR
Peasant culture in India and Mexico, In McKim Marriott (ed) Village India. Chicago, University of Chicago Press, 1955
The festival cycle in a north India Jat Village, Proceedings of the American Philosophical Society, Vol. 100, No. 3, 1956

LEWIS, OSCAR with the assistance of VISTOR BARNOUM
Caste and the Jajmani system in a north Indian village, Scientific Monthly, Vol. 83, No. 2, 1956

MAJUMDAR, D. N.
Affairs of a tribe, Lucknow, Universal Publisher, 1950
Religious life of the Ho, Man in India, Vol. 34, No. 4, 1954

MANDELBAUM, DAVID G.
Form, variation, and meaning of a ceremony, In Robert Spencer (ed) Method and Perspective in Anthropology. Minneapolis, University of Minnesota Press, 1954

MARRIOTT, MCKIM
Little communities in an indigenous civilization, In McKim Marriott (ed) Village India. Chicago, University of Chicago Press, 1955
Social structure and change in a U. P. village, In M. N. Srinivas *et al.* India's village. Calcutta, Development Department, West Bengal, 1955

MITRA, RAJENDRALALA
Buddha Gaya, the hermitage of Sakya Muni, Calcutta, Bengal Secretariat Press, 1878

MITRA, R. C.
The decline of Buddhism, Vishva Bharati Annals, Vol. VI, 1955

MONIER-WILLIAMS, MONIER
Brahmanism and Hinduism, London, John Murry, 1891
Indian Wisdom, London, Luzac and Co., 1893

MOOKHERJEE, RADHAKUMUD
The fundamental unity of India, Calcutta, Longman, Green and Co., 1914

MOOR, EDWARD
Plates illustrating the Hindu pantheon, London, Williams and Norgate, 1861
MUKHERJEE, DHURJATI P.
Modern Indian culture, Bombay, Hind Kitab, Ltd., 1948
O'MALLEY, L. S. S.
Gaya and the Gayawal, Calcutta, Bengal Secretariat Press, 1901
Bengal District Gazetteer; Gaya, Calcutt, Bengal Secretariat Press, 1906
Indian caste customs, Cambridge University Press, 1932
India's social heritage, Oxford University Press, 1934
Popular Hinduism, Cambridge University Press, 1935
OPLER, MORRIS E.
The extensions of an Indian village, The Journal of Asian Studies (formerly Far Eastern Quarterly), Vol. XVI, No. 1, 1956
PANDEY, RAJ BALI
Hindu Sanskaras; a socio-religious study of Hindu sacraments, 1949
PATIL, D.
Cultural history from Vayu Purana, Poona, 1946.
PLANALP, JACK M.
Religious life and values in a north Indian village, Unpublished Ph.D. Thesis, Cornell University, 1956
PRASAD, BALDEO
Gaya ke Prachin tirthon ka nām, Gaya, The Society of Indian Culture, 1954
PRASAD, NARMODESHWAR
The Gayawal of Bihar, American Anthropologist, Vol. 54, No. 2, 1952
RAGHAVAN, V.
Variety and integration in the pattern of Indian civilization, Far Eastern Quarterly (now The Journal of Asian Studies), Vol. XV, No. 4, 1956
RAJAGOPALACHARIAR, T.
Vaishnavite Reformers of India, Madras, G. A. Natesan & Co., 1909
RAY, GAUTAM SHANKER, G. BANNERJEE, *et al.*
Religious beliefs of the Hos, Man in India, Vol. 34, No. 4, 1954
REDFIELD, ROBERT
The folk culture of Yucatan, Chicago, University of Chicago Press, 1941
The primitive world and its transformation, Ithaca, Cornell University Press, 1953

The little community, Chicago, University of Chicago Press, 1955

The social organization of traditions, Far Eastern Quarterly (now The Journal of Asian Studies), Vol. XV, No. 1, 1955

Peasant society and culture, Chicago, University of Chicago Press, 1956

Thinking about a civilization, In Milton Singer (ed.), Introducing India in liberal education, Chicago, University of Chicago Press, 1957

REDFIELD, ROBERT AND MILTON SINGER

The cultural role of cities, Man in India, Vol. 36, No. 3, 1956. Also published in Economic Development and Cultural Change, Vol. 3, 1954

RISLEY, H. H.

Tribes and castes of Bengal, Vols. I and II, Calcutta, Government of India Printing Office, 1891

ROY, S. C.

The Oraons of Chota Nagpur, Calcutta, The Brahmo Mission Press, 1915

Oraon religion and customs, Calcutta, Industry Press, 1928

ROYCHAUDHARY, P. C.

Gaya District Gazetteer, Patna, Govt. Printing Press, 1958

SANYAL, N.

Development of Indian railways, Calcutta, 1930

SINGER, MILTON

The cultural pattern of Indian civilization; a preliminary report of a methodological field study, The Far Eastern Quarterly (now The Journal of Asian Studies), Vol. XV, No. 1, 1955

The Indian village: a symposium, The Journal of Asian Studies (formerly the Far Eastern Quarterly), Vol. XVI, No. 1, 1956

SINHA, SURAJIT

Tribal culture of peninsular India as a dimension of little tradition in the study of Indian civilization: a preliminary statement, Man in India. Vol. 37, No. 2, 1957

SRINIVAS, M. N.

Relgiion and society among the Coorgs of south India, Oxford, Clarendon Press, 1952

A note on sanskritization and westernization, Far Eastern Quarterly (now the Journal of Asian Studies), Vol. XV, No. 4, 1956

STEED, GITAL P.

Notes on an approach to a study of personality formation in a Hindu village in Gujarat, In McKim Marriott (ed.) Village India, Chicago, University of Chicago Press, 1955

THOMAS, PAUL
Epics, myths and legends of India, 4th edition, Bombay, D. B. Tarporevalla Sons and Co.

THORNER, DANIEL
Investment in empire; British railway and steam shipping enterprise in India, Philadelphia, University of Pennsylvania Press, 1950

VIDYARTHI, LALITA P.
Gaya and its environs, Unpublished Field Report, Patna University, 1950
The Gayawal; A study in a dying community, Unpublished M. A. Dissertation, University of Lucknow, 1953
Origin and development of the Gayawal, The Journal of Bihar Research Society, Vol. XL, Pt. 3, 1954
Life-histories of sixteen Gayawal informants, Unpublished work
The Gayawal: a dying community, In A. Aiyappan and L. M. Bala Ratnam (eds.) Society in India, Madras, 1956

WHITEHEAD, HENRY
The village gods of south India, Madras, Oxford Press, 1916

WILSON, GODFREY AND MONICA WILSON
The analysis of social change, Cambridge University Press, 1945

WISER, WILLIAM H.
The Hindu Jajmani system, Lucknow, Lucknow Publishing Co., 1936

Dhammapada, Translated from Pali by S. Radhakrishanan, London, Oxford University Press, 1950
Census of India 1951, Vol. V (Bihar), Pt. IIA. Compiled by R. C. Prasad, Patna, Government Printing Press, 1953
The Life of Swami Vivekananda, a collection of writings, Calcutta, Advaita Ashrama, 1955
Manu Smriti, Translated by G. Buhler from the Sanskrit, The Sacred Book of the East series, Vol. XXV, Oxford, The Clarendon Press, 1886
Vayu Purana, Compiled by Hari Narayan Apte, Annandashrama Sanskrit Granthavali, 1905
Vishnu Sutra, Translated by Julius Jolly from the Sanskrit text with the title Institution of Vishnu. The Sacred Books of the East series, Vol. VII, Oxford, The Clarendon Press, 1880

INDEX